First Certificate Language Practice

MICHAEL VINCE

with Key

105

2005

8

Heinemann

Heinemann English Language Teaching
A division of Reed Educational and Professional Publishing Ltd
Halley Court, Jordan Hill, Oxford OX2 8EJ

OXFORD MADRID FLORENCE ATHENS PARIS PRAGUE
SÃO PAULO MEXICO CITY CHICAGO PORTSMOUTH (NH)
TOKYO SINGAPORE KUALA LUMPUR MELBOURNE
AUCKLAND JOHANNESBURG IBADAN GABORONE

ISBN 0 435 28167 4 without key
ISBN 0 435 28166 6 with key

Text © Michael Vince 1996
Design and illustration © Reed Educational and Professional
Publishing Ltd
First published 1996

The author would like to thank everyone who has made
comments on this book, and in particular the editors, Sue Jones,
Jill Florent and Xanthe Sturt Taylor.

The publishers would like to thank Dave Millican, Sara Katsonis
and James Roy.

Illustrations by:
Rowan Barnes-Murphy pp. 7, 8, 36, 37, 76
Ian Kellas pp. 86, 87, 121, 138, 150, 155, 175
Gillian Martin pp. 51, 108, 109, 126, 127, 207, 211, 234
David Parkins, pp. 15, 92, 93, 145, 165
Peter Richardson, pp. 2, 116, 137, 198
Bill Stott pp. 84, 89, 143, 154, 170, 173

Original design by Mike Brain
Layout and composition by Newton Harris

Printed and bound in Great Britain by The Bath Press

96 97 98 99 00 10 9 8 7 6 5 4 3 2 1

Contents

Introduction

Grammar

Vocabulary

Introduction

This book is designed to revise and consolidate grammar points at the level of First Certificate. It also provides practice in key lexical areas.

There are regular progress tests which include forms of testing commonly used in First Certificate examinations.

It can be used as a self-study reference grammar and practice book, or as supplementary material in classes preparing for examinations.
If used for classwork, activities can be done individually or co-operatively in pairs or small groups. The grammatical information provided can be used for reference when needed, or worked through systematically.

The grammar section includes recognition and concept-checking activities, as well as production activities.
Each vocabulary section includes focus on phrasal verbs, prepositions and particles, and collocations.

This new edition includes practice material which uses the forms of testing introduced in the revised examination in December 1996. The revised examination includes the following in Paper 3: a multiple choice 'modified close' text; 'key word' transformation sentences in which a gap is completed using a given word; a text containing errors, in which each line is either correct, or contains an extra or unnecessary word, which has to be identified; and a word formation activity in which the transformations based on a given 'stem' are part of a continuous text. The level of knowledge of the lexical and grammatical system required for the examination remains the same.

I am also grateful for comments and suggestions made by users of the book, and many activities have been revised accordingly.

Unit 1 Past time

Explanations

Narrative

1 Main events
The past simple is used to describe finished events in the past.
> Susan **went** into the station and **bought** a ticket.

2 Background description
The past continuous is used to describe actions still in progress, and is used for background description.
> There were a lot of people waiting in the station. Some **were sleeping** on the benches, and others **were walking** up and down. Susan **was looking for** Graham, so she didn't sit down.

3 Past before past
The past perfect is used to describe a past event which took place before another past event.
> By the time the train arrived, Susan **had managed** to push her way to the front of the crowd.

It is not always necessary if a time expression makes the order of events clear.
> **Before** the train arrived, Susan **managed** to push her way to the front of the crowd.

4 Interrupted past continuous
We often contrast an action still in progress with a sudden event which interrupts it.
> While Susan **was trying** to get onto the platform, a man **grabbed** her handbag.

5 Participle clauses
Participle clauses are introduced by the time expressions *before*, *after* and *while*. They have the same subject as the following clause.
> **After struggling** with him, **Susan pulled** the bag from his hands.

Habits in the past

1 Past simple
The past simple is used to describe past habits or states. A time expression is usually necessary.
> I always **got up** at six in those days.   (Habit)
> I **lived** in Austria for several years.   (State)

2 *Used to*
Used to is used to describe past habits, usually in contrast with the present. A time expression is not necessary.
> I **used to get up** at six, but now I get up at eight.

1

Used to can also describe past states.
> I **used to own** *a horse. (I owned a horse once.)*
Note these forms of *used to:*
> I **didn't use to** *like beer.*
> **Did you use to** *swim every day?*

3 *Would*
Would is used to describe a person's typical activities in the past.
It can only be used to describe repeated actions, and is mainly used in writing, and in personal reminiscences.
> *Every evening was the same. Jack* **would turn on** *the radio, light his pipe and fall asleep.*

4 Past continuous
The past continuous can be used to describe a repeated action in the past, often an annoying habit. A frequency adverb is necessary.
> *When Peter was younger, he* **was always getting** *into trouble.*

Politeness and uncertainty

The past continuous with the verb *wonder* has a polite meaning.
> *I was wondering if you could help me.*
With the verb *think* the past continuous suggests uncertainty.
> *I was thinking of having a party next week.*

Activities

1
Choose a suitable caption for each picture.

a) When he left, Peter forgot that he had put his passport and wallet in his other jacket.
b) After phoning the airport, Peter packed his suitcase.
c) Peter put his passport and wallet in his jacket pocket.
d) Before leaving, Peter phoned the airport to check his flight.
e) While Peter was packing his suitcase, he realised that he hadn't checked his flight.
f) While Peter was packing his suitcase, the phone rang.

2

Choose the most suitable tense. The first one is done for you.

a) I suddenly remembered that I forgot/had forgotten my keys.
b) While Diana watched/was watching her favourite television programme, there was a power-cut.
c) Tom used to live/would live in the house at the end of the street.
d) Who was driving/drove the car at the time of the accident?
e) By the time Sheila got back, Chris went/had gone.
f) David ate/had eaten Japanese food before, so he knew what to order.
g) I did/was doing some shopping yesterday, when I saw that Dutch friend of yours.
h) I used to like/was liking sweets much more than I do now.
i) What exactly were you doing/did you do when I came into your office yesterday?
j) Laura missed the party because no-one was telling/had told her about it.
k) Tanya would/used to be a doctor.

3

Put each verb in brackets into a suitable tense. All sentences refer to past time. Only use the past perfect where this is absolutely necessary.

a) While I (try) ..was trying. to get my car started, a passing car (stop) .... and the driver (offer) .... to help me.
b) The police (pay) .... no attention to Clare's complaint because she (phone) .... them so many times before.
c) Mary (not wear) .... her glasses at the time, so she (not notice) ..didn't notice.. what kind of car the man (drive) ....
d) Nick (lie) .... down on the grass for a while, next to some tourists who (feed) .... the ducks.
e) Tony (admit) .... that he (hit) .... the other car, but said that he (not damage) .... it.
f) Sorry, I (not listen) .... to you. I (think) .... about something else.
g) Helen (feel) .... very tired, and while she (finish) .... her studying, she (fall) .... asleep.
h) The police (get) .... to Clare's house as fast as they could, but the burglars (disappear) ....
i) I (phone) .... you last night but you (not answer) .... What (you do) .... ?
j) We (not go) .... out yesterday because it (rain) ....

4

Decide whether the tense underlined is suitable or not.

a) While I had a bath, someone knocked on the door. .unsuitable.
b) Sally didn't go to a boxing match before. ....
c) Harry tried to repair the car, but he didn't really know what he was doing. ....
d) What did you wear to the Ponsonbys' party? ....
e) Were you eating spaghetti every day when you lived in Italy? ....
f) I didn't know you had bought a new car. ....
g) They all wanted to believe her, but suspected she was lying. ....
h) As Peggy walked home, she tried to remember what happened. ....
i) 'What a terrible day!' thought Lucy. Everything had gone wrong! ....
j) Although it rained a lot, I was enjoying my holiday last year. ....

5
Put each verb in brackets into a suitable past tense.

When Professor Mallory, the famous archaeologist, (1) .invited... (invite) me to take part in his expedition to find the Lost City of the Himalayas, I (2) .... (not hesitate) to accept his invitation. Mallory (3) .... (discover) an ancient map showing the position of the city, although no European (4) .... (ever go) to the area before. In fact, most of Mallory's colleagues in Oxford either (5) .... (believe) that the city (6) .... (never exist) or (7) .... (feel) that it (8) .... (vanish) long ago and (9) .... (become) simply a legend. According to the Professor, the builders of the city (10) .... (hide) it among the mountains in order to protect its immense riches. He (11) .... (believe) that the descendants of these ancient people (12) .... (still keep) themselves apart from the rest of mankind for the very same reasons. So when we (13) .... (set off) on a cool May morning towards the distant mountains, each of us (14) .... (look forward) to exciting discoveries. For a week or more we (15) .... (climb) higher and higher, following the map, which Mallory (16) .... (study) from time to time. Then one afternoon, while we (17) .... (rest) at the top of a valley, we (18) .... (notice) that a rider on a horse (19) .... (wave) at us from the other side of the valley. A rider whose clothes (20) .... (shine) like gold!

6
Rewrite each sentence, beginning as shown, using a participle clause.

a) Norman collected the parcel, but then he realised it was the wrong one.
   After .collecting. the. parcel,. Norman. realised. it. was. the. wrong. one.............
b) Sue left the house, but first she checked that she had her keys.
   Before ....
c) Mark was parking his car when he noticed the wing-mirror was broken.
   While ....
d) Julia cleaned the house, but then she fell asleep on the sofa.
   After ....
e) Brian bought a new television, but first he checked all the prices.
   Before ....
f) Alan was skiing in Switzerland and met his old friend, Ken.
   While ....
g) Kate took two aspirins, and then she felt a lot better.
   After ....
h) Sheila went out for the evening, but first she washed her hair.
   Before ....
i) Michael was taking a bath when he heard someone at the door.
   While ....
j) First Trudy read the book, and then she decided that she didn't like it.
   After ....

7

Complete this table of irregular past tenses and their verb stems.

STEM	PAST TENSE	STEM	PAST TENSE	STEM	PAST TENSE
beat	....	feel	....	shoot	....
bend	....	fly	....	sink	....
....	bit	....	froze	....	sprang
....	bled	....	held	....	stole
blow	....	hurt	....	stick	....
build	....	lay	....	swing	....
....	caught	....	meant	....	tore
....	chose	....	paid	....	trod
cost	....	rise	....	wear	....
draw	....	send	....	win	....
....	drove	....	shook	....	wound
....	fell	....	shone	....	wrote

KEY POINTS

1 The past simple describes events in the past, such as the main events in a narrative. It can also describe habits and routines in the past.

2 The past continuous is used for:
a) Background description.
b) Actions in progress, often contrasted with a sudden event.
The past continuous cannot be used to describe past routines and habits.

3 Participle clauses can introduce a clause giving the main event.
The subjects of both clauses must be the same.

4 The past perfect describes a past event which took place before another past event. If *before* or *after* is used, the past perfect is optional.
The past perfect is not used to show that an event happened a long time ago in the past.

5 *Used* to only refers to past time, and has no present form.

6 *Would* can be used to describe habitual actions in the past, usually in writing, but not when these are contrasted with the present. Compare:
> *Jim **would always make** his mother a cup of tea after lunch.*
> *Jim **used to drink** tea, but now he prefers coffee.*

Would cannot be used to describe states:
> *Sally used to be a dancer.*

SEE ALSO

Unit 5
Progress test
Unit 2
Present perfect
Units 7 and 8
Unreal past tenses
Unit 14
Time expressions

5

Unit 2 Present Perfect

Explanations

Recent events

Present perfect simple
The present perfect simple is used to describe recent events without a definite time. The idea of time or place in the speaker's mind makes the event recent. A time expression may emphasise recentness.
> *I've left my shopping bag behind.*
> *I've just broken my watch.*

We can also describe events that have not happened.
> *I haven't found her phone number yet.*

The event may be connected with the present, because the result of the event is present. No definite time is given for the event.
> *I've broken my arm, as you can see.*

Indefinite events

1 Present perfect simple
No definite time is given for the event.
> *I've been to France three times.*

2 Compared with past simple
Events described using the past simple have definite times.
> *I went to France last year.*

The tense used can depend on the time expression.
> *This is the first time I have eaten Japanese food.*

3 Definite Places
If we think of a definite place for an event, this may suggest a definite time.
> *I left my shopping bag on the train.*

Extended or repeated events

1 Present perfect simple
With verbs that describe states, the present perfect simple describes a state which lasts up to the present.
> *I've lived in this house for five years.*

2 Present perfect continuous
The present perfect continuous can also describe a state which lasts up to the present moment.
> *I've been living in this house for five years.*

There is little difference of meaning between simple and continuous in this case, or with *How long* questions. The verbs *sit, lie, wait, stay* prefer the present perfect continuous.
> *How long have you been waiting?*

3 Present perfect simple
The present perfect simple can describe a habitual action in a period of time up to the present moment.
*I've **never worn** a tie to work, and I refuse to start now!*

For, since, ago   See Unit 14 for contrasts between these time expressions.

Contrasts
between simple
and continuous

1 Not completed
Use of the present perfect continuous can suggest that an action is not completed, or has recently finished.
*We've **been walking** for hours! Let's have a rest.*
*I've **been digging** the garden. That's why I'm so dirty!*

2 Completed
Use of the present perfect simple can show that an action is complete. Giving the number of actions suggests completion.
*I've **written** ten pages of my homework assignment!*

Activities

1
Choose a
suitable caption
for each picture.

a)

① Did you enjoy the match?
2) Have you enjoyed the match?

b)

1) What have you been doing?
2) What have you done?

c)

1) He was married six times.
2) He has been married six times.

d)

1) How long have you been here?
2) How long are you here for?

e)
1) I've been waiting for two hours.
2) I waited for two hours.

f)
1) Where did Wendy go?
2) Where has Wendy been?

2
Choose the most suitable tense.

a) <u>Did you see</u>/<u>Have you seen</u> my bag anywhere? I can't find it.

b) Larry <u>is writing</u>/<u>has been writing</u>/<u>has written</u> his novel for the last two years without getting further than Chapter One.

c) From the minute he got up this morning Gary <u>asked</u>/<u>has asked</u>/<u>has been asking</u> silly questions!

d) <u>Have you given</u>/<u>Did you give</u> Helen my message when you <u>have seen</u>/<u>saw</u> her?

e) Sorry, could you say that again? I <u>didn't listen</u>/<u>haven't listened</u>/<u>haven't been listening</u> to you.

f) The police think that they <u>found</u>/<u>have found</u> your missing wallet, so call this number.

g) I don't think we'll go swimming after all because the weather <u>changed</u>/<u>has changed</u>/<u>has been changing</u>.

h) How was your holiday in Italy? <u>Did you visit</u>/<u>Have you visited</u> lots of interesting places?

i) <u>Did you two meet</u>/<u>Have you two met</u> before? Eric, this is Amanda.

j) <u>Did you meet</u>/<u>Have you met</u> anyone interesting at the reception?

3
Put each verb in brackets into a suitable tense.

a) I'm sorry about not coming last week. I (have) ..*had*...... a cold and so I (stay) .... at home.

b) Wait a minute. I (have) .... an idea. Let's go and see Roger. We last (see) .... him a long time ago.

c) It's nice to be back here in London. This is the second time I (come) .... here.

d) I'm phoning about your advertisement for a bicycle for sale, which I (see) .... in the local paper. (you sell) .... it? Or is it still available?

e) This place is in a terrible mess! What on earth (you do) .... ?

f) And now for an item of local news. Hampshire police (find) .... the dangerous snake which (go) .... missing earlier in the week.

g) This tooth (kill) .... me lately! So I (make) .... an appointment with the dentist for Tuesday.

h) I can't give you the report I (promise) .... for today because I (not finish) ....

i) Harry (not look) .... well since he (go) .... on a diet.

j) It says in the paper that they (discover) .... oil in Wales. They (look for) .... it for ages.

4

Choose the most suitable time expression.

a) I haven't seen Gerry (for)/since a long time. How is he?
b) It's ages ago/since I last went to a football match.
c) I've written to Deborah last week/recently.
d) What have you been doing today/yesterday?
e) Have you eaten Italian food before/already?
f) I've been living here in/since the end of last year.
g) Actually I had dinner with Sue last night/lately.
h) I've been trying to get in touch with David for ages/for the last time.
i) Terry hasn't been to Edinburgh since/when we went there together.
j) I can't remember how long/when I've had this watch.

5

Complete the second sentence so that it has a similar meaning to the first sentence, using the word given. Do not change the word given. You must use between two and five words.

a) Steve started learning the violin a month ago.
   learning
   Steve ..has been learning.. the violin for a month.
b) I haven't been to an Indian restaurant for ages.
   since
   It's ages .... an Indian restaurant.
c) When she heard the results, Mary began to feel more confident.
   become
   Since hearing the results .... more confident.
d) The last time Nancy came here was in 1986.
   since
   Nancy hasn't .... 1986.
e) This is my first visit to Japan.
   time
   This is the first .... to Japan.
f) How long have Helen and Robert been married?
   get
   When .... married?
g) Jack bought those trousers last month, and has been wearing them ever since.
   for
   Jack has .... a month.
h) It's a long time since our last conversation.
   spoken
   We .... long time.
i) Thanks, but I had something to eat earlier.
   already
   Thanks, but I've .... eat.
j) This is my first game of water-polo.
   played
   I .... before.

9

6

Put each verb in brackets into either the present perfect simple or the present perfect continuous.

a) Someone (eat) ..has..eaten...... all the cakes. I'll have to buy some more.
b) What (you buy) .... your sister for her birthday?
c) My throat is really sore. I (sing) .... all evening.
d) Brenda (learn) .... Russian, but she finds it difficult.
e) How many people (you invite) .... to your party?
f) Those two cats (sit) .... on that branch for the last hour.
g) It (rain) .... all day! Why can't it stop!
h) Diana (wear) .... twelve different dresses in the past week!
i) I (do) .... everything you asked. What should I do now?
j) Graham and Pauline (try) .... to find a house for ages, but they can't find one they can afford.

7

Put each verb in brackets into either the past simple, the present perfect simple, or the present perfect continuous.

It was announced in London this morning that the British Oil Corporation (1) .... (discover) oil under the sea near the Welsh coast. The company, which (2) .... (drill) for oil in the area since 1990, (3) .... (find) small amounts of oil near Swansea last month, and since then (4) .... (discover) larger amounts under the seabed nearby. Last year the government (5) .... (lend) over £50,000,000 to BOC, and (6) .... (give) permission for the company to build an oil refinery and other facilities in South Wales.

The reaction of local people to today's news (7) .... (be) mixed so far. Local MPs (8) .... (already welcome) the news, pointing out that the oil industry will bring badly needed jobs to the area. But local residents are worried about the danger of pollution. 'Nobody (9).......... (ask) us yet what we want,' said Ann Griffiths, leader of the Keep Out The Oil Campaign. 'Look what (10) .... (happen) when they (11) .... (find) oil in Scotland in the 1960s. The oil companies (12) .... (get) rich, not the local people. BOC (13) .... (not tell) us the truth about what this is going to mean for our people.' A BOC spokesman later (14) .... (refuse) to comment. Meanwhile local campaigners (15) .... (ask) the government to hold an inquiry.

8

Complete this table of irregular past participles and their verb stems.

STEM	PARTICIPLE	STEM	PARTICIPLE	STEM	PARTICIPLE
beat	....	feel	....	shoot	....
bend	....	fly	....	sink	....
bite	....	freeze	....	spring	....
bleed	....	hold	....	steal	....
blow	....	hurt	....	stick	....
build	....	lay	....	swing	....
catch	....	mean	....	tear	....
choose	....	pay	....	tread	....
cost	....	rise	....	wear	....
draw	....	send	....	win	....
drive	....	shake	....	wind	....
fall	....	shine	....	write	....

9

Look carefully at each line. Some lines are correct, but some have a word which should not be there. Tick each correct line. If a line has a word which should not be there, write the word in the space.

A Letter from the Builders

Dear Mrs Sangster,

Just a quick note to explain what we have been done	.been...
so far this month. The work on the kitchen has gone	...✓........
well so far, although we haven't already finished	1) ...already
knocking down the outside wall yet. So I wrote	2) ...so....
to you last week and have explained that two of	3) ....
my workmen were ill. They have quite recovered	4) ...✓....
now, I am glad to say, and they have came back	5) ...have...
to work yesterday. As the weather has been bad	6) ....
we have been work inside most of the time, and	7) ....
all the painting is now been finished. We have	8) ...been..
also put in a new window in the kitchen, as you	9) ...✓....
have instructed in your last letter. As you	10) ...have.
have not been visiting here for two weeks	11) ....
we have not had the chance to discuss the walls.	12) ....
When we checked them we have discovered	13) ...ha...
that they are in a dangerous condition. I'll	14) ...✓....
let you know what we have do to them.	15) ...have.

Best wishes,

Andrew Turner, Builder

KEY POINTS

1   The present perfect simple describes indefinite events. These events take place in a period of time leading up to the present moment, or the result of the event is still present. No definite time is given.

The choice between the present perfect simple and the past simple can depend on how the speaker thinks. Compare:

   A: *'What's the matter?'*   *'I've had an accident.'*
   B: *'What's the matter?'*   *'I had an accident.'*

In the second example, the speaker thinks of the event as finished rather than still connected with the present.

2   Events described with the present perfect simple may be recent, or not.

3   The present perfect continuous emphasises the length of time of an action. It suggests that the action is unfinished, or recently finished. The present perfect continuous is not used where the completion of an action is emphasised. Compare:

   I've been reading.   (Completion is not emphasised)
   I've read this book.   (Completion is emphasised)

4   *For* refers to a finished or unfinished period of time.
   *He's been sitting there **for ages**.*
   *I waited **for three hours**.*

Since refers to the point at which an unfinished period of time began.

*He's been sitting there **since two o'clock**.*

Ago refers to the time of a finished event.

*Jill arrived **a week ago**.*

SEE ALSO

Unit 1
Past time
Unit 5
Progress test
Unit 14
Time expressions

Unit 3 Future time

Explanations

Prediction

1 *Will*

Will is used to make predictions. It is often preceded by *I think* or by opinion words like *perhaps*. A time expression is also necessary.

> *I think **it'll rain** tomorrow.*   *Perhaps **she'll be** late.*

In speech, both *will* and *shall* are contracted to *'ll*. Use of *shall* after *I* and *we* is more common in formal speech.

See also Units 18 and 19 for functional uses of will and shall.

2 *Going to*

If a predicted event is very near, and especially in impersonal statements, *going to* is also commonly used for predictions.

Will can also be used in these examples, with no change of meaning.

> *You're **going to fall**!*   (See Present cause)
> *Liverpool **are going to win** the Cup.*

3 Present cause

We often make a prediction because we can see the cause of the event.

> *Look out! There's a bus coming! **It's going to hit** us!*
> *I can see **you're going to have** a baby. When is it due?*

4 Future continuous

The future continuous is used to describe a situation in the future at a particular time.

> *This time next week **we'll be eating** lunch on the plane!*

It is also used to predict a future state or habit at a particular time in the future.

> *In ten years time I expect **I'll be living** in London. And **I'll** probably **be cycling** to work.*

5 Future perfect

The future perfect looks back from a point in the future and refers to indefinite time up to that point.

> *By the time we get there, the film **will have started**.*

This means that at the future time when we get there, we can say:

> *The film has started.*

Future time clauses

1 After time expressions *when*, *until* and *as soon as* a present tense form is used, although this refers to future time.

> *I'll wait for you here **until you get** back.*

2 The present perfect can be used to emphasise the completion of an event.

> *I'll wait here until **you have finished**.*

Intention	1	*Going to*
		Going to is used to describe a present intention.

I'm going to fix the television tomorrow.

2 *Will*

Will is also used for decisions made at the time of speaking.

I know, I'll get him a wallet for his birthday.

Plans and facts

1 Present continuous

The present continuous is used to describe plans and arrangements which are definite. Such arrangements may be written in a diary.

*Sorry, I can't help you, **I'm leaving** in the morning.*

2 Present simple

The present simple is used to describe future events which we cannot control. They may be facts, such as events in a timetable, or a law.

*The plane for Paris **leaves** at 9.45.*

Activities

1

Choose the most suitable tense.

a) Why are you going to buy/will you buy a new mountain bike?

b) Don't phone between 8.00 and 9.00. I'll study/I'll be studying then.

c) Look out! That tree will fall/is going to fall!

d) Let me know as soon as Louise will get/gets here.

e) Great news! Jean and Chris will come/are coming to stay with us.

f) According to this timetable, the bus is going to arrive/arrives at 6.00.

g) I have a feeling that something strange is going to happen/is happening in a minute.

h) The doctor says I will have/am going to have a baby!

i) Can you call me at 7.00, because I'll leave/I'm leaving tomorrow.

j) If you arrive late at the sale, the best things will go/will have gone.

2

Put each verb in brackets into the most appropriate future time form. More than one answer may be possible.

a) I can't see you on Thursday afternoon. I (visit) .am. visiting....... our Birmingham branch.

b) George (not be) .... back until six. Can I take a message?

c) What (you buy) .... with the money you won in the lottery?

d) I don't think you (have) .... any problems at the airport.

e) (you take) .... your dog with you to Scotland?

f) Can you answer the phone for me? I (lie down) .... for a while.

g) All the hotels are full. Where (we spend) .... the night?

h) You'd better not come in July. My mother (stay) .... with me then.

i) What time (your plane leave) .... ?

j) Leave the car here. Maybe the police (not notice) .... it.

3

Put each verb in brackets into a suitable future time form. More than one answer may be possible.

a) By the time we reach home, the rain (stop) ..*will have stopped.* .
b) This time next week I (lie) .... on the beach in Spain.
c) In ten years' time I (work) .... for a different company.
d) If we don't get there by 6, Jack (leave) ....
e) In July they (be married) .... for twenty years.
f) In the year 2500 a lot of people (live) .... on the moon.
g) When you get to the station, I (wait) .... for you outside.
h) Don't worry! The plane (land) .... in a moment.
i) By the time you come home, I (finish) .... the decorating.
j) Come round between eight and nine. We (watch) .... the match on television then.

4

Put each verb in brackets into a suitable tense.

Have you ever wondered what exactly (1) ..*you will be doing*.. (you do) in ten years time? Well, according to computer expert Tom Vincent, computers (2) .... (soon be able) to make accurate predictions about the future. Professor Vincent, from Cambridge University, (3) .... (hold) a press conference next week to describe the computer which he calls 'Computafuture'. 'This computer can tell us what life (4) .... (be) like, based on data describing past events,' explains Professor Vincent. For example, Computafuture can predict how many people (5) .... (live) in a particular area, or whether there (6) .... (be) a lot of rain during a particular period. Professor Vincent also believes that by the year 2050, computers (7) .... (replace) teachers, and (8) .... (also do) most of the jobs now being done by the police. 'Computers are becoming more intelligent all the time,' says Professor Vincent. 'Soon they (9) .... (direct) traffic and (10) .... (teach) our children. And telling us about the future.'

5

Put each verb in brackets into a suitable tense. All sentences refer to future time.

a) When I (see) ..see...... you tomorrow, I (tell) .... you my news.
b) As soon as we (get) .... there, we (phone) .... for a taxi.
c) I (go) .... to the library before I (do) .... the shopping.
d) We (wait) .... here until the rain (stop) ....
e) I (get) .... some money from the bank when it (open) ....
f) After you (take) .... the medicine, you (feel) .... better.
g) You have to stay until you (finish) .... your work.
h) I (let) .... you know the minute I (hear) .... the results.
i) Before we (paint) .... the wall, we (have) .... a cup of tea.
j) We (climb) .... over the wall as soon as it (get) .... dark.

6

Look carefully at each line. Some lines are correct, but some have a word which should not be there. Tick each correct line. If a line has a word which should not be there, write the word in the space.

Keeping a Diary

Are you one of those people who will know   .will.....
exactly what they will be doing every day next   ..✓........
week? When the different days will arrive,   1) ....
will you have get out your diary, or are   2) ....
you the kind of person who will just guess?   3) ....
Some people will write their appointments   4) ....
in a diary, but others just hope that they will   5) ....
remember. For example, tonight I'm be going   6) ....
to the cinema, but perhaps I'll not forget all   7) ....
about it. You see, I will never keep a diary.   8) ....
I try not to forget my appointments, but I know   9) ....
that I will usually do. I just don't like planning   10) ....
my future. I know that one day I'm going to   11) ....
make a serious mistake. I'll be miss an important   12) ....
examination, or by the time I remember it and   13) ....
get there, it will have been finished. Perhaps   14) ....
that will be when I have finally buy a diary.   15) ....

KEY POINTS

1   *Will* and *shall* have other meanings. See Units 18 and 19.

2   The present continuous is used to describe fixed arrangements, and to ask about social arrangements.
    Are you doing anything this evening?

3   The present simple and present perfect can also be used to refer to future time.
    *I'll tell you the news **when I see you**.*
    *Call me **when you have finished**.*

Going to can be used instead of *will* in predictions. For some speakers this seems more colloquial.
    *I'm sure **you're going to enjoy** the film.*
    *I'm sure **you'll enjoy** the film.*

> **SEE ALSO**
>
> **Units 18 and 19**
> for Functional uses of *will* and *shall*.
> **Unit 5**
> Progress Test.
> **Unit 14**
> Time expressions.

Unit 4 Present time

Explanations

Present simple

1 Facts which are always true
The present simple is used to describe facts in science, and geographical descriptions.
> *The light from the Sun **takes** 8 mins 20 secs to reach the Earth.*
> *The River Po **flows** into the Adriatic Sea.*

2 Habitual actions
The present simple is used to describe habitual actions. A frequency adverb is often used.
> *I usually **take** the bus to work.*

3 Plot summaries and historical tables
The present simple is used to describe the events in a narrative, when the events are summarised. It is used to describe what happens in a film or book, or in a table of events.
> *In Chapter 1, Susan **meets** David, and **agrees** to go to the school dance with him.*
> *1789. The French Revolution **begins**.*
> *George Washington **becomes** the first president of the USA.*

Present continuous

1 Actions which are still in progress
The present continuous is used to describe actions which are temporary and not yet finished.
> *I'm **doing** the washing-up.*

2 Habits over a period of time
The present continuous can describe a temporary habit. A time expression is necessary.
> *At the moment **we're sending** all the mail by courier, because the Post Office is on strike.*

3 A repeated temporary event
The present continuous can describe a repeated temporary action. A time expression is necessary.
> *Whenever I see Tom **he's smoking**.*
> *You're **making** the same mistake again!*

4 An annoying habit
The present continuous is used to describe an annoying habit. A frequency adverb is necessary.
> *You're always **borrowing** money from me!*

Problems with
simple and
continuous

1 Some verbs are not normally used in the continuous, because they describe
activities which already extend in time. These are sometimes called 'state'
verbs.

be, believe, cost, depend, have, hear, know, matter, smell, suppose, taste,
think, understand

2 Some of these verbs can be used in continuous forms with a change of
meaning.

Tim is being *rather difficult at the moment.*   (Behave)
I'm having *breakfast.*   (Eat)
I'm tasting *the soup, to check if it needs more salt.*   (Sample)
I'm thinking *of buying a new car.*   (Consider)

3 The difference between simple and continuous can be one of attitude.

Do you sleep a lot?   (Your general habit)
Are you sleeping enough?   (Your situation at the moment)

Both questions could be asked in the same situation.

Activities

1

Choose the most
suitable tense.

a) What sort of work do you do/are you doing?
b) I can't talk now. I cook/I'm cooking the dinner.
c) What shall we have? Do you like/Are you liking fish?
d) Can I borrow this typewriter? Or do you use/are you using it?
e) What do the people here do/are the people here doing in the evenings?
f) Follow that bus. Then you turn/you are turning left.
g) A lot of people think that the Sun goes/is going around the Earth.
h) Excuse me, do you read/are you reading your newspaper? Could I borrow
it?
i) Do you wait/Are you waiting for the bus to Newcastle?
j) Andy builds/is building his own house in the country.

2

Put each verb in
brackets into
either the present
simple or the
present
continuous.

a) There's nobody here, and the door's locked. What (we do) ..*do we do*.. now?
b) What (you look) .... at? (I wear) .... the wrong clothes again?
c) I (look after) .... Jack's dog this weekend. (you want) .... to
take it for a walk?
d) Who (drive) .... that Mercedes that's parked outside?
e) I (still have) .... a pain in my leg but it (get) .... better.
f) Who (Sue dance) .... with? That's not her brother, is it?
g) Harry (look) .... very untidy! He (wear) .... dirty jeans all the time.
h) I (write) .... in reply to your advertisement in the Daily News.
i) That plant I bought (not grow) .... very much. And I (water)
.... it every day.
j) Which hotel (you stay) .... in whenever you (come) .... here?

3

Decide whether the verb underlined refers to present or future time.

a) Where <u>are you staying</u> on Saturday night? ..f.u.t.u.r.e......
b) George <u>retires</u> at the end of next year. ....
c) What are we doing when the guests <u>arrive</u>? ....
d) <u>I'm trying</u> really hard to understand this book. ....
e) Wait for me here until I g<u>et</u> back. ....
f) Sue <u>is leaving</u> in the morning. ....
g) <u>I'm waiting</u> for the bus. ....
h) I'm off now, and <u>I'm taking</u> the car. ....
i) <u>They're showing</u> a Woody Allen film on Channel 4 tonight. ....
j) <u>I'm going</u> for a walk this evening. ....

4

Make *-ing* forms of each verb given, and then complete the spelling rules below.

| write ...... | swim ...... | get ...... | admit ...... | annoy ...... |
| begin ...... | study ...... | like ...... | try ...... | decide ...... |

a) If a word ends in vowel + consonant + 'e' (write) ....
....

b) If a word ends in vowel + consonant (swim) ....
....

c) Words which end in 'y' (try, annoy) ....
....

5

Rewrite each sentence, replacing the underlined words by using one of the verbs from the list.

| be cost feel have see smell taste have think of have |

a) This flower <u>has</u> a wonderful <u>perfume</u>.
   ..This.flower.smells.wonderful.

b) I think you <u>are behaving in a</u> very silly <u>way</u>.
   ....

c) She <u>is expecting</u> a baby in the summer.
   ....

d) Nancy <u>is considering</u> moving to Scotland.
   ....

e) Don't go in. They <u>are holding</u> a meeting.
   ....

f) <u>I am meeting</u> Janet this evening actually.
   ....

g) Good clothes <u>are becoming</u> more and more <u>expensive</u>.
   ....

h) <u>I am just trying</u> the soup to see if it needs more salt.
   ....

i) Helen <u>is taking</u> a bath at the moment.
   ....

j) I <u>think</u> that you would be happier in another job.
   ....

6

Put each verb in brackets into either the present simple or the present continuous.

Dear Aunt Jean,

I (1) .am just writing. (just write) to tell you how much I (2) .... (appreciate) the money you sent me, and to tell you how I (3) .... (get on) in my first term at university. Actually, I (4) .... (really enjoy) myself! I (5) .... (study) quite hard as well, but at the moment I (6) .... (spend) a lot of time just making friends. I (7) .... (still stay) with my friend Sue, and I (8) .... (look for) somewhere of my own to live. Only a few of the first-year students (9) .... (live) in college here, and I (10) .... (seem) to be spending a lot of time travelling backwards and forwards. I (11) .... (go) to lectures every morning, and most afternoons I (12) .... (study) in the library. In fact I (13) .... (write) this letter instead of an essay on 'Hamlet'! I (14) .... (think) I'll buy some new clothes with the money you sent. Everything (15) .... (cost) a lot here, and I (16) .... (save) to buy a winter coat. It (17) .... (get) really cold here in the evenings. I (18) .... (know) lots of other students and generally speaking we (19) .... (have) quite a good time socially! I (20) .... (also learn) to drive.

See you soon,

Katherine

KEY POINTS

1 The present simple in general describes facts and habitual actions. The present continuous describes actions which are still in progress at the time of speaking.

2 Many verbs which describe states rather than momentary events can only be used in the simple. Many verbs describing mental activities (*understand, know*) are of this kind.

3 Some verbs have both state and event meanings, but the meanings are not the same.

4 When describing a photograph, we usually describe the scene as if it is happening now, and use the present continuous.

5 Present tense forms are also used to refer to future time.

6 In situations where some languages use present tenses, English uses the present perfect.

SEE ALSO

Unit 3
Future time
Unit 5
Progress test

Unit 5 Progress test

(Units 1, 2, 3, 4)

1
Complete the second sentence so that it has a similar meaning to the first sentence, using the word given.

a) There's a party at Mary's house next week.
   having
   Next week .... party at her house.

b) When you phoned me, it was my lunch time.
   I
   When you phoned me .... lunch.

c) I started working here three years ago.
   for
   I've .... three years.

d) Our meeting is tomorrow.
   a
   We .... tomorrow.

e) I haven't had a Chinese meal for ages.
   since
   It's .... a Chinese meal.

f) David went home before we arrived.
   had
   When we .... home.

g) The arrival time of Helen's flight is 8.00.
   at
   Helen's flight .... 8.00.

h) Hurry up! We'll get to the theatre after the beginning of the play.
   will
   By the time we get to the theatre, the play .... begun.

i) Oh no! My wallet is missing.
   lost
   Oh no! I .... wallet.

j) I've only recently started wearing glasses.
   wear
   I .... recently.

2
Put each verb in brackets into a suitable tense.

Moving house

I come from a very large family, and recently my parents (1) .... (decide) that they (2) .... (spend) long enough living in an overcrowded house in Birmingham. 'We (3) .... (move) to the country,' my father (4) .... (announce) one evening. 'I (5) .... (sell) this house, and we (6) .... (live) on a farm.' So last week we (7) .... (load) all our possessions into two hired vans, and for the last few days we (8) .... (try) to organise ourselves in our new

22

home. Yesterday, for example, my three brothers and I (9) .... (start) painting the downstairs rooms. Unfortunately while I (10) .... (mix) the paint, one of my sisters (11) (open) .... the door. Nobody (12) .... (tell) her that we (13) .... (be) in the room, you see. So instead of painting the walls, we (14) .... (spend) all morning cleaning the paint off the floor. But worse things (15) .... (happen) since then. This morning when I (16) .... (wake up), water (17) .... (drip) through the ceiling next to my bed. We (18) .... (spend) today so far repairing the roof. It's not all bad news, though. The school in the village nearby (19) .... (close down) two years ago, and my parents (20) .... (not find) another school for us yet.

3

Complete the second sentence so that it has a similar meaning to the first sentence, using the word given. Do not change the word given. You must use between two and five words.

a) Jack left the office before I arrived there.
already
When I arrived at the office .... left.

b) Do you know how to drive this kind of car?
ever
Have .... this kind of car before?

c) This is my first visit to Scotland.
I
This is the first time .... Scotland.

d) During dinner, the phone rang.
I
While .... phone rang.

e) Do you have any plans for Saturday evening?
doing
What .... Saturday evening?

f) I started this job five years ago.
been
I have .... five years.

g) Is this car yours?
you
Do .... car?

h) Look at those black clouds! There's rain on the way!
to
Look at those black clouds! It's *going to* .... rain.

i) Our twenty-fifth wedding anniversary is at the end of next year.
for
By the end of next year we .... twenty five years.

j) I haven't been to the cinema for two months.
time
The *last time I went to* .... the cinema was two months ago.

4

Put each verb in brackets into a suitable tense.

At the dentist's

I was on time for my dentist's appointment, but the dentist was still busy with another patient, so I (1) .... (sit) in the waiting room and (2) .... (read) some of the old magazines lying there. While I (3) .... (wonder) whether to leave and come back another day, I (4) .... (notice) a magazine article about teeth. It (5) .... (begin): 'How long is it since you last (6) .... (go) to the dentist? (7) .... (you go) regularly every six months? Or (8) .... (you put off) your visit for the last six years?' Next to the article was a cartoon of a man in a dentist's chair. The dentist (9) .... (say): 'I'm afraid this (10) .... (hurt).' I (11) .... (suddenly realise) that my tooth (12) .... (stop) aching. But just as I (13) .... (open) the door to leave, the dentist's door (14) .... (open). 'Next please,' he (15) .... (call), as the previous patient (16) .... (push) past me. 'Actually I'm not here to see you, I (17) .... (wait) for my friend,' I (18) .... (shout), leaving as rapidly as I could. (19) .... (you ever do) this kind of thing? Surely I can't be the only person who (20) .... (hate) the dentist!

5

Look carefully at each line. Some lines are correct, but some have a word which should not be there. Tick each correct line. If a line has a word which should not be there, write the word in the space.

Meeting again

Dear Harry,

Do you remember me?   ....✓......

We have met last year when you were on holiday   ..have...

in Brighton. I'm sorry I haven't been written to you   1) ....

since by then. I have been working abroad and   2) ....

I have only just come back home to England.   3) ....

Next week I am planning is to be in Bristol, and   4) ....

I was thinking about that we could meet.   5) ....

Do you remember Shirley, the girl we have met   6) ....

in Brighton? We are getting married next month,   7) ....

and we are want you to come to the wedding.   8) ....

I have lost your phone number, but when   9) ....

I have get to Bristol I'll try to contact you.   10) ....

It will be great to see you again. Are you still   11) ....

studying, or I have you found a job?   12) ....

You won't recognise me when you will see me!   13) ....

I had my hair cut last week, and now I look at   14) ....

completely different. Shirley doesn't like men   15) ....

with long hair, you see!

Best wishes,

Graham Norris.

6

Decide which answer A, B, C or D best fits each space.

The latest news

Dear Linda,

I'm sorry I (1) .... to you for so long, but I (2) .... very busy lately. All last month I (3) .... exams, and I (4) .... anything else but study for ages. Anyway, I (5) .... studying now, and I (6) .... for my exam results.

As you can see from the letter, I (7) .... my address and (8) .... in Croydon now. I (9) .... that I wanted a change from central London because it (10) .... so expensive. A friend of mine (11) .... me about this flat, and I (12) .... here about two months ago. When you (13) .... to London this summer, please visit me. I (14) .... here until the middle of August. Then I (15) .... on holiday to Scotland.

Please write soon,
Margaret.

1) A) don't write   B) haven't written   C) am not writing D) wasn't writing
2) A) was being   B) had been   C) am   D) have been
3) A) had   B) was having   C) had had   D) have had
4) A) haven't done   B) don't do   C) wasn't doing   D) am not doing
5) A) stop   B) will have stopped C) have stopped   D) was stopping
6) A) wait   B) am waiting   C) have waited   D) was waiting
7) A) am changing   B) had changed   C) will change   D) have changed
8) A) will live   B) have been living C) live   D) have lived
9) A) decided   B) have decided   C) was deciding   D) decide
10) A) will become   B) becomes   C) has become   D) will have become
11) A) tells   B) told   C) was telling   D) will tell
12) A) have moved   B) had moved   C) was moving   D) moved
13) A) will come   B) came   C) come   D) were coming
14) A) am staying   B) stayed   C) stay   D) have stayed
15) A) have gone   B) went   C) am going   D) will have gone

Unit 6 Indirect speech

Explanations

With tense changes

1 Summary of tense changes
Tenses are moved into the past after a past tense reporting verb.
The past perfect remains the same.

> 'I'm leaving.'   Jane said **she was leaving**.
> 'No, I hadn't forgotten.'   Greg said that **he hadn't** forgotten.

For Modals (*can, may, must, shall, should*) see Unit 16.

2 Main verb changes only
In complex sentences, only the first verb is changed.

> 'I was walking home when I saw the accident.'
> James said he **had been walking** home when he saw the accident.

3 Reference words
Some words referring to persons, places and time change in indirect speech, because the point of reference changes.

> 'I'll see you here tomorrow, Jack,' said Mary.
> Mary told Jack she would see **him there the next day**.

> 'I gave you this yesterday.'
> John said he had given **it** to **her the day before**.

Other words of this kind are practised in the activity pages.

Without tense changes

1 Present tense reports
If the reporting verb is in the present tense, there is no change.

> Brenda **says** she's arriving at about 6.00.

2 Past tense reports
If the reported words are 'always true', there is no change.

> Harry told me that **he still likes you**.

If a message is being repeated immediately, there is no change.

> Mary said **she's too busy** to come.

Questions

1 Indirect questions
Yes/No questions are reported using *if*. The verb is not put into a question form, and there is no question mark.

> 'Do you like hamburgers?'
> Charles asked me **if I liked** hamburgers.

Wh- questions are reported with the question word. There is no question mark.

> 'Where are we going?'   I asked Sue **where we were going**.

2 Embedded questions
These are questions introduced by polite phrases. Note the word order.
   *'Could you tell me **where the station is**?'*
In indirect speech, the polite question becomes a reporting verb.
   I asked him where the station was.

Commands and requests

1 Commands are reported with *tell* and the infinitive.
   'Go away!'   *He told me **to go away**.*

2 Requests are reported with *ask* and the infinitive.
   'Please help me.'   *He asked her **to help him**.*

Reporting verbs

The activity pages include practice in common reporting verbs. The grammatical context for each verb should be learned.

Paraphrase

Often it is impossible or unnecessary to report every word spoken.
   'Excuse me, do you think you could tell me the time?'
   *He asked me **what the time was**.*

Activities

1

Choose the best verb underlined in the direct speech sentence.

a) Helen asked me if I liked visiting old buildings.
   'Do you like/Did you like visiting old buildings?' asked Helen.
b) Bill asked Mary if she had done anything the previous weekend.
   'Have you done anything/Did you do anything last weekend?'
c) The policeman asked me if the car belonged to me.
   'Does this car belong/Did this car belong to you?' asked the policeman.
d) Fiona asked me if I had seen her umbrella anywhere.
   'Did you see/Have you seen my umbrella anywhere?' asked Fiona.
e) Joe asked Tina when she would get back.
   'When will you get/have you got back?' asked Joe.
f) Eddie asked Steve who he had been to the cinema with.
   'Who did you go/had you been to the cinema with?' asked Eddie.
g) My parents asked me what time I had got home the night before.
   'What time did you get/have you got home last night?' my parents asked.
h) David asked a passer-by if it was the right road for Hastings.
   'Is this/Was this the right road for Hastings?' asked David.

2

Rewrite each sentence as direct speech.

a) Graham told Ian he would see him the following day.
   ..'I'll see you tomorrow, Ian,' said Graham..
b) Pauline told the children their swimming things were not there.
   ....
c) David told me my letter had arrived the day before.
   ....

d) Shirley told Larry she would see him that evening.

....

e) Bill told Stephen he hadn't been at home that morning.

....

f) Margaret told John to phone her on the following day.

....

g) Tim told Ron he was leaving that afternoon.

....

h) Christine told Michael she had lost her lighter the night before.

....

3

Rewrite each sentence as indirect speech, beginning as shown.

a) 'You can't park here.'
The police officer told Jack ..*that he couldn't park there*.....................

b) 'I'll see you in the morning, Helen.'
Peter told Helen ....

c) 'I'm taking the 5.30 train tomorrow evening.'
Janet said ....

d) 'The trousers have to be ready this afternoon.'
Paul told the dry-cleaners ....

e) 'I left my umbrella here two days ago.'
Susan told them ....

f) 'The parcel ought to be here by the end of next week.'
Brian said ....

g) 'I like this hotel very much.'
Diana told me ....

h) 'I think it's going to rain tonight.'
William said ....

4

Rewrite each question in indirect speech, beginning as shown.

a) 'What time does the film start, Peter?'
I asked ..*Peter what time the film started*..........................

b) 'Do you watch television every evening, Chris?'
The interviewer asked ....

c) 'Why did you apply for this job?' asked the sales manager.
The sales manager asked me ....

d) 'Are you taking much money with you to France?'
My bank manager wanted to know ....

e) 'When will I know the results of the examination?'
Maria asked the examiner ....

f) 'Are you enjoying your flight?'
The stewardess asked me ....

g) 'How does the photocopier work?'
I asked the salesman ....

h) 'Have you ever been to Japan, Paul?'
Sue asked Paul ....

5

Continue reporting each sentence, using only the number of words stated.

a) 'Do you think you could possibly tell me what the time is?'
David asked me ..*to..tell..him..the..time.*. (Five words)

b) 'Excuse me, but I wonder if you'd mind opening the window.'
The man sitting next to me asked me .... (Four words)

c) 'You go down this street, turn left, then take the second turning on the right. The cinema is just down the street on the left.'
A passer-by told me how .... (Five words)

d) 'I want to know how much this bike costs. Can you tell me?'
John asked how .... (Four words)

e) 'Look, don't worry, I'll help you if you like.'
Sue said she .... (Three words)

f) 'All right, I tell you what, the car's yours for, let's say £500.'
The salesman said I could .... (Five words)

g) 'I hope you don't mind my saying this, but you're being a bit silly, aren't you?'
Peter told me I .... (Five words)

h) 'It doesn't look as if I'll be arriving until after eight, I'm afraid.'
Jane said she probably .... (Six words)

6

Rewrite each sentence, beginning as shown, so that the meaning stays the same.

a) What time does the next boat leave?
Do you think you could tell me ..*what..time..the..next..boat..leaves*........?

b) Where can I change some money?
Can you tell me ....?

c) Where is the toilet?
Could you possibly tell me ....?

d) How much does this pullover cost?
I'd like to know ....?

e) How do I get to Victoria Station?
Can you explain ....?

f) Does this train go to Gatwick Airport?
Could you tell me ....?

g) Where do you come from?
Would you mind telling me ....?

h) What do you think of London?
Do you think you could tell me ....?

7

Put a form of either *say, tell* or *ask* in each space.

a) I ..*told*.. you that you had to be on time. Why are you late?
b) When you .... her if she'd work late, what did she .... ?
c) I think that Alan .... us a lie about his qualifications.
d) When I .... him what he was doing there, he .... me it was none of my business.
e) I .... I would help you, so here I am.
f) Did you hear what Sheila .... about her new job?
g) What did Carol .... you about her holiday?
h) There, you see! I .... you the bus would be on time.

8

Put a form of one of the verbs listed into the space in each sentence.

| accuse | agree | decide | insist | refuse | admit | apologise | deny |
| offer | remind | advise | confess | doubt | promise | suggest |

a) 'No, it's not true, I didn't steal the money!'
Jean ..*denied*.... stealing the money/that she had stolen the money.

b) 'Why don't we go to the cinema this evening?'
Peter .... going to the cinema/that they went to the cinema.

c) 'Yes, of course, I'll give you a lift, Helen.'
Liz .... to give Helen a lift/that she would give Helen a lift.

d) 'I've broken your pen. I'm awfully sorry, Jack.'
David .... for breaking Jack's pen.

e) 'Don't forget to post my letter, will you, Sue?'
Diana .... Sue to post her letter.

f) 'Let me carry your suitcase, John.'
Harry .... to carry John's suitcase.

g) 'All right, it's true, I was nervous.'
The leading actor .... to being nervous/that he had been nervous.

h) 'I don't think Liverpool will win.'
Vanessa .... whether Liverpool would win.

i) 'If I were you, Bill, I'd buy a mountain bike.'
Stephen .... Bill to buy a mountain bike.

j) 'Don't worry, Martin, I'll bring your book back.'
Leslie .... to bring Martin's book back/Martin he would bring his book back.

k) 'You murdered Lord Digby, didn't you, Colin!'
The inspector .... Colin of murdering Lord Digby.

l) 'No, no, you really must have another drink!'
Dick .... on my having another drink/that I should have another drink.

m) 'It was me who stole the money,' said Jim.
Jim .... to stealing the money.

n) 'Right. I'll take the brown pair.'
Andrew .... to take the brown pair.

o) 'No, sorry, I don't want to lend you my camera.'
Alex .... to lend me his camera.

9

Rewrite each sentence, beginning as shown, so that the meaning stays the same.

a) 'Sue, can you remember to buy some bread?'
Paul reminded ..*Sue to buy some bread*...................................

b) 'I don't really think it'll snow tomorrow.'
I doubt ....

c) 'I'm sorry I didn't phone you earlier.'
Jill apologised ....

d) 'I really think you should see a doctor, Chris.'
William advised ....

e) 'No, I'm sorry, I won't work on Saturday. Definitely not!'
   Catherine refused ....

f) 'Let's go out to the pub for lunch, shall we?'
   Wendy suggested ....

g) 'It's not true! I have never been arrested.'
   Larry denied ....

h) 'If you like, I'll help you do the decorating, Bob.'
   Ann offered ....

i) 'I'll definitely take you to the park on Sunday, children.'
   Tom promised the ....

j) 'Yes, all right, I'll share the bill with you, Dave.'
   Brenda agreed ....

10

Look carefully at each line. Some lines are correct, but some have a word which should not be there. Tick each correct line. If a line has a word which should not be there, write the word in the space.

Satellite Television

When my parents decided that to get a new	..that....
satellite television, I asked them why they	..✓........
thought this was a good idea. I doubted it	1) ....
whether it was really necessary, and told to them	2) ....
that I had thought they spent too much time	3) ....
watching television. They agreed they didn't	4) ....
go out very much, but were insisted that they	5) ....
had had thought about the matter very carefully.	6) ....
'We enjoy television,' they said me, 'and when we	7) ....
asked you, you said that you agreed with us.'	8) ....
I replied them that I didn't remember being asked,	9) ....
and that I would have tried to stop them. Then	10) ....
they were admitted that they had asked me while I was	11) ....
watching my favourite programme. I asked them	12) ....
what was I had been watching, and they said	13) ....
it was a football match. 'You told us that	14) ....
to keep quiet, so we thought that you agreed!'	15) ....

KEY POINTS

1 Tense changes are usually necessary after a past tense reporting verb.

2 Words referring to time and place also change in indirect speech.

3 Indirect questions are of two types. *Yes/No* questions are reported with *If*, and *Wh-* questions are reported with the question word. The verb is not put into a question form in an indirect question.

4 Indirect speech is often introduced by a reporting verb. These are followed by a variety of grammatical constructions. A good dictionary will include this information.

5 Indirect speech may also involve paraphrasing the main points of what was said.

> **SEE ALSO**
>
> **Unit 10**
> Progress test
> **Unit 17**
> Modals: Past

Unit 7 Conditionals

Explanations

Real situations: conditional 1

1 With *if* and *can*
This kind of sentence describes a real situation. Although a present tense is used after *If*, the time referred to is not present.
  *If you **fall**, I **won't be able** to catch you!*
This means that there is a real possibility this will happen as we are actually in the situation described. *Going to* can be used in place of *will*.
  *If it rains, **we're going to get** wet.*
Modal *can* is common in Conditional 1 sentences.
  *If the cases **are** too heavy, I **can help** you carry them.*

2 *Unless, provided, as long as*
Unless introduces a clause which tells us about an exception to the point made in the main clause.
  ***Unless** you **leave** at once, I'**ll call** the police.*
Provided and *as long as* can also introduce a condition:
  ***Provided** you leave now, you'll catch the train.*

3 With the imperative
It is common to use the imperative instead of *If*.
  ***Get** me some cigarettes, and **I'll pay** you later.*

4 With *should*
Should makes the action less likely. It is often stressed in speech.
  *If you **should** see John, can you give him a message?*

Unreal situations: conditional 2 (present/future)

1 With *if*
This kind of sentence describes an imaginary or unreal situation. Although the past simple tense is used after *if*, the time referred to is not past but imaginary.
  *If you **fell**, you **would hurt** yourself.*
This means that I am imagining a situation and its result. We could both be in a dangerous situation, or I could be imagining the whole situation. The past tense form does not refer to past time.

2 *Were, might, could*
Were is often used instead of *was* in formal language. Note that *were* is not stressed.
  *If I **were** taller, **I'd join** the basket-ball team.*
  *If I **were** you, **I'd leave** now. (I and you are stressed.)*
Modals *might* and *could* are common in this kind of sentence.
  *If you **became** a millionaire, you **might be** unhappy.*

3 *Were to*
    Were to is another way of expressing a Conditional 2 sentence.
        *If they **were to offer** me the job, **I'd turn** it down.*

Unreal situations: conditional 3 (past)

1 With *if* and *might*
    This kind of condition describes an imaginary or unreal situation. The time referred to is past time.
        *If you **had written** more, you **would have got** better marks.*
    Might is common in this kind of sentence.
        *If you **had tried** harder, you **might have succeeded.***

2 Mixed conditions
    For past events which have a result continuing in the present, it is possible to mix Conditionals 2 and 3.
        *If you **had saved** some money, you **wouldn't be** so hard up.*

If sentences

Not all *if* sentences are conditional sentences, and *if* can mean *whenever* or *if it is true that*.
    *If (whenever) it **rains**, we **play** football indoors instead.*
    *If (it is true that) you **have** a job like that, you **are** very lucky.*
    *If (it is true that) nothing **happened**, you **were** lucky.*

Activities

1
Choose the most suitable tense.

a) If the machine ~~stops~~/will stop, you ~~press~~/will press this button.
b) I can't understand what he sees in her! If anyone <u>treats/will treat/treated</u> me like that, I <u>am/will be/would be</u> extremely angry!
c) If you <u>help me/helped me</u> with this exercise, I <u>will do/would do</u> the same for you one day.
d) According to the timetable, if the train <u>leaves/left</u> on time we <u>will/would</u> arrive at 5.30.
e) If <u>it is/it will be</u> fine tomorrow, we <u>go/will go</u> to the coast.
f) If we <u>find/found</u> a taxi, we <u>will get/would get</u> there before the play starts.
g) It's quite simple really. If you <u>take/will take/took</u> these tablets every day, then you <u>lose/will lose/lost/would lose</u> weight.
h) I don't like this flat. I think <u>I am/I will be/I'd be</u> happier if I <u>live/will live/would live/lived</u> in a house in the country.
i) I don't know how to play baseball, but I'm sure that if I <u>will/do/did</u>, I <u>play/will play/would play</u> a lot better than anyone in this awful team!
j) If I <u>phone/will phone/phoned</u> you tonight, <u>are you/will you be/would you be</u> in?

2

Choose the most suitable tense.

a) Why didn't you tell me? If you told/had told me, I had/would have helped you.

b) If Bill didn't steal/hadn't stolen the car, he wasn't/wouldn't be/hadn't been in prison now.

c) If Ann wasn't driving/didn't drive/hadn't driven so fast, her car didn't crash/wouldn't crash/wouldn't have crashed into a tree.

d) Let me give you some advice. If you smoked/would smoke/had smoked less, you didn't feel/wouldn't feel/wouldn't have felt so tired.

e) What bad luck! If Alan didn't fall/hadn't fallen/wouldn't fall over, he won/would win/would have won the race.

f) If you invited/had invited me last week, I was able/had been able/would have been able to come.

g) I'm sure your letter hasn't arrived yet. If it came/had come I'm sure I noticed/had noticed/would have noticed it.

h) We have a suggestion to make. How do you feel/would you feel if we offered/would offer/had offered you the job of assistant manager?

i) If you lent/had lent us the money, we paid/would pay/had paid you back next week.

j) Terry never catches anything when he goes fishing. And if he catches/caught/had caught a fish, he throws/would throw it back!

3

Put each verb in brackets into a suitable tense.

a) Why didn't you phone? If I (know) ..*had known*.. you were coming, I (meet) .... you at the airport.

b) It's a pity you missed the party. If you (come) .... you (meet) .... my friends from Hungary.

c) If we (have) .... some tools, we (be able) .... to repair the car, but we haven't got any with us.

d) Thank you for your help. If you (not help) .... me, I (not pass) .... the examination.

e) It's a beautiful house, and I (buy) .... it if I (have) .... the money, but I can't afford it.

f) I can't imagine what I (do) .... with the money if I (win) .... the football pools or a lottery.

g) Mark isn't a serious athlete. If he (train) .... harder, he (be) .... quite a good runner.

h) If Claire (listen) .... to her mother, she (not marry) .... David in the first place.

i) It rained every day on our holiday. If we (not take) .... the television with us, we (not have) .... anything to do.

j) Jim is so untidy! If he (buy) .... some new clothes, he (not look) .... so bad!

4

Choose the most appropriate caption for each picture.

a)

1) If she falls, she'll land in the safety net.
2) If she fell, she'd land in the safety net.
3) If she had fallen, she would have landed in the safety net.

b)

1) It's worse if we order soup.
2) It would be worse if we ordered soup.
3) It would have been worse if we'd ordered soup.

c)

1) If I own a dog like that, I'll keep it on a lead.
2) If I owned a dog like that, I'd keep it on a lead.
3) If I had owned a dog like that, I'd have kept it on a lead.

d)

1) I like it more if it looks like someone I know.
2) I'd like it more if it looked like someone I knew.
3) I'd have liked it more if it had looked like someone I knew.

e)

1) If we hurry, we won't miss the train.
2) If we hurried we wouldn't miss the train.
3) If we had hurried, we wouldn't have missed the train.

5

Rewrite each sentence, beginning as shown, so that the meaning stays the same.

a) I didn't have an umbrella with me and so I got wet.
I wouldn't ..*have got wet if I had had an umbrella with me.*............

b) I'll call the police if you don't leave me alone!
Unless ....

c) In the snowy weather we don't go to school.
If ....

d) Without Jack's help, I wouldn't have been able to move the table.
If ....

e) You drink too much coffee, that's why you can't sleep.
If you ....

f) You press this button to stop the machine.
If ....

g) Make me some coffee, and I'll give you one of my biscuits.
If ....

h) If you hadn't told me about Sue's hair, I wouldn't have noticed.
Unless ....

i) If you see Peter, tell him he should be here at 8.00.
If you should ....

j) I wouldn't accept if you asked me to marry you!
If you were ....

6

Rewrite each sentence with all possible written contractions.

a) If I had known, I would have told you.
..If.I'd.known,.I'd.have.told.you...

b) Tony would not have crashed if he had been more careful.
..To...?.....

c) If you asked me, I would tell you.
....

d) If I had had my credit card with me, I would have bought the coat.
....

e) You would not have got lost if you had taken the map.
....

f) If you had asked me for a loan, I could have given you one.
....

g) If Graham had not lost his watch, he would not have missed his plane.
....

h) If you had not told me her name, I would have found out from someone.
....

i) If I were you, I would try getting up earlier.
....

j) No-one would have realised if Peter had not told them.
....

KEY POINTS

1 The present tense form in Conditional 1 sentences does not refer to present time.

2 The past tense form in Conditional 2 sentences does not refer to past time.

3 The difference between Conditional 1 and 2 sentences can depend on the attitude of the speaker.
    If she falls, she'll land in the safety net.
(This means that there is a real possibility that she will fall.)
    If she fell she would land in the safety net.
(I am commenting on an imaginary situation, and I probably do not think that she is likely to fall.)

4 Modal auxiliaries are common in conditional sentences when we may be uncertain about our predictions.
    *If you leave now, you **might catch** the train.*
    *If you asked him nicely, he **might agree**.*
    *If you'd gone through the red light, you **might have hit** another car.*

5 Mixed conditions are possible, especially where a past event has a present result.
    If Brenda hadn't stolen the money, she wouldn't be in prison.

6 *Unless, provided,* and *as long as* can introduce conditions.

7 Many sentences beginning *If...* are not true conditional sentences.
   If the police arrested him, they must suspect him.
   Here *if* means *since.*

> **SEE ALSO**
>
> **Unit 10**
> Progress test
> **Unit 17**
> Modals
> **Unit 18**
> Functions

Unit 8 Hypothetical and unreal tenses

Explanations

Wishes

1 Wishes about present states
These wishes use the past simple after the verb *wish*. The time referred to is an imaginary or 'unreal' present.
> *I wish I **knew** the answer to this question.*
(In this case, I do not know the answer.)
> *I wish I **didn't have** so much work to do.*

2 Wishes about past events
These wishes use the past perfect after the verb *wish*.
The time referred to is past time.
> *I wish I **had gone** to your party last week.*
(In this case, I did not go.)

3 Wishes about future events: *could* and *have to*
Wishes using *could* refer to ability or to future time.
> *I wish I **could drive**.*   (Ability)
> *I wish June **could meet** me next week.*   (Future time)
Wishes with *have to* can also refer to future time.
> *I wish I **didn't have to get up** early tomorrow.*

4 Wishes about future events: *would* (annoying habits)
These wishes use *would* after the verb *wish*. They often take the form of a complaint about a bad habit.
> *I wish Peter **wouldn't chew** gum all the time.*
There is very little difference in use between this kind of wish and the wishes in 1. This kind of wish may also refer to a specific action which you would like to happen.
> *I wish the police **would do** something about these people!*

If only

1 *If only* is used instead of *wish* to make emphatic wishes.
> ***If only** I knew the answer to this question!*
> ***If only** I had gone to your party last week!*

2 In speech, *only* is often heavily stressed.

It's time

1 *It's time* followed by a person is followed by an unreal past tense.
> *Sorry, but it's time **we went** home.*
This has a similar meaning to a Conditional 2 sentence:
> *If we went home, it would be better.*

2 *High* can be added for extra emphasis.
> It's **high time you learned** to look after yourself!

3 *It's time* can also be used with the infinitive + *to*.
> *It's time you started work!*   (You are being lazy)
> *It's time to start work.*   (A statement of fact)

I'd rather

1 *I'd rather* followed by a person is followed by an unreal past tense.
> *I'd rather **you didn't tell** John about this.*

This has a similar meaning to a Conditional 2 sentence:
> *If you didn't tell John about this, it would be better.*

2 *I'd sooner* can be used in the same way and has the same meaning.
> *Actually, I'd sooner **we left** now.*

Suppose and *imagine*

Both words can be used to introduce unreal situations.
> *Suppose **you lost** your keys. What would you do?*
> *Imagine **you were** rich. How would you feel?*

Activities

1

Choose the most suitable tense.

a) I wish Peter doesn't live/didn't live/wouldn't live so far away from the town centre. We'll have to take a taxi.

b) I feel rather cold. I wish I brought/had brought my pullover with me.

c) What a pity. I wish we don't have to/didn't have to/wouldn't have to leave. I've just started to enjoy myself.

d) I wish you tell/told/had told me about the test. I haven't done any revision.

e) I wish the people next door hadn't made/wouldn't make/couldn't make so much noise. I can't hear myself think!

f) Darling I love you so much! I wish we are/had been/would be/could be together always!

g) I'm sorry I missed your birthday party. I really wish I come/came/had come/would come.

h) I like my new boss but I wish she gave/would give/could give me some more responsibility.

i) Having a lovely time in Brighton. I wish you are/were/had been here. Love, Sheila.

j) This car was a complete waste of money. I wish I didn't buy it/hadn't bought it.

2

Put each verb in brackets into a suitable tense.

a) This train journey seems endless! I wish we (go) ..*had gone*.. by car.

b) I wish I (have) .... the money to buy some new clothes, but I can't afford it at the moment.

c) I wish the government (do) .... something about the pollution in this city.

d) I'm getting really soaked! I wish I (not forget) .... my umbrella.

e) I wish you (not do) .... that! It's a really annoying habit.

f) That was a lovely meal, but I wish I (not eat) .... so much.

g) I wish I (study) .... harder for my exams. I don't think I'm going to pass.

h) I wish you (not leave) .... your dirty shoes in your bedroom!

i) I'm afraid I have no idea where Diana has gone. I wish I (know) ....

j) I really enjoyed our trip to the theatre. I wish we (go) .... more often.

3

Choose the most suitable tense.

a) A cheque is all right, but I'd rather you pay/paid me cash.

b) Imagine you live/lived in New York. How would you feel?

c) If only I have/had/would have a screwdriver with me.

d) If you want to catch the last train, it's time you leave/left.

e) I'd rather you don't tell/didn't tell anyone about our conversation.

f) I've got a terrible hangover. If only I didn't drink/hadn't drunk that fourth bottle of wine.

g) If you don't mind, I'd sooner you practised/had practised/would practise your violin somewhere else.

h) It's high time you learn/learned to look after yourself.

i) Jean thinks that everyone likes her. If only she knows/knew what people say behind her back!

j) I'd rather we stay/stayed at home this Christmas for a change.

4

Put each verb in brackets into a suitable tense.

a) What can we do to get in touch with Robert? If only we (know) ..*knew*.. his phone number.

b) Come on children! It's time you (be) .... in bed.

c) Actually I'd rather you (not smoke) .... in here.

d) Suppose you (see) .... a ghost. What would you do?

e) I'm so annoyed about my car accident. If only I (be) .... more careful!

f) It's high time you (start) .... working more seriously.

g) I'd rather you (not put) .... your coffee on top of my book.

h) I've no idea where we are! If only we (have) .... a map.

i) Your hair is rather long. Don't you think it's time you (have) .... a haircut?

j) Visiting museums is interesting I suppose, but I'd sooner we (go) .... swimming.

5
Complete the second sentence so that it has a similar meaning to the first sentence, using the word given. Do not change the word given. You must use between two and five words.

a) It would be nice to be able to fly a plane.
 could
 I wish I ..*could fly*.. a plane.

b) Please don't eat in the classroom.
 you
 I'd rather .... classroom.

c) I think we should leave now.
 we
 I think it's .... left.

d) What a pity we ate all the food.
 only
 If .... all the food!

e) It's a shame we don't have a video.
 wish
 I .... a video.

f) Don't shout all the time, it's so annoying!
 wouldn't
 I .... shout all the time!

g) I don't want you to buy me a present.
 sooner
 I'd .... buy me a present.

h) I don't like being so tall.
 wish
 I .... so tall.

i) We ought to start work now.
 started
 It's .... work.

j) I regret not going to university.
 had
 I .... to university.

6

Look carefully at each line. Some lines are correct, but some have a word which should not be there. Tick each correct line. If a line has a word which should not be there, write the word in the space.

Losing Your Memory

Imagine it that one day you woke up and	..it......
discovered that you had completely lost your	..✓........
memory. How would you have feel exactly?	1) ....
I have thought about this recently after I was	2) ....
involved in a traffic accident. I woke up in	3) ....
hospital, and said to myself 'It's the time I	4) ....
got up and have went to school!' I soon realised	5) ....
my mistake. A nurse came in and asked to me	6) ....
what my name was. I thought about it for a	7) ....
moment and then said, 'I would wish I knew!'	8) ....
Then I tried to get up. 'I'd rather prefer	9) ....
you didn't do that,' said the nurse. 'Don't worry,	10) ....
you'll have it your memory back soon.'	11) ....
'I wish you hadn't have said that,' I replied.	12) ....
'Now I am really worried!' If I hadn't looked	13) ....
in my wallet, I wouldn't have been known my	14) ....
own name! Unfortunately my memory soon came	15) ....
back, and I realised I had a maths test the next day!	

KEY POINTS

1 Past tense forms are used in imaginary (hypothetical) situations after *It's time* and *I'd rather* when followed by a person.
   It's time we left.

2 Wishes about the present use a past tense form, and wishes about the past use a past perfect form.

3 Wishes with *would* refer either to annoying habits, or to possible future changes.

4 *Wish* and *hope* cannot be used in the same way. Wishes can be for impossible things, but hopes only for possible things.
   With a person: *I hope you have a good time.*
                        I hope you won't be late.
   Wish cannot be used in this way.

   With the infinitive: *I hope **to see** you next week.*
   Wish with the infinitive means *want* (a polite meaning).
        *I wish **to see** you next week.*
   Note also the formal expressions:
        We wish you a happy New Year/every happiness/luck.

> **SEE ALSO**
>
> **Unit 10**
> Progress test

Unit 9 Passive voice

Explanations

Uses

1 Transitive and intransitive
Only verbs with an object (transitive) can be made passive.
They sent the letter.   *The letter **was sent**.*
They arrived late.   (Cannot be made passive.)
Verbs with both direct and indirect objects can be made passive in two ways:
They sent me the letter.   ***I was sent** the letter.*
*The letter **was sent** to me.*

2 *Like* and *love*
Some verbs which are transitive cannot be made passive in some uses.
I like this place.   (A passive form of this sentence would not be
acceptable.)

3 Contexts
By placing the object at the beginning of the sentence, the passive can change
the focus of interest in a sentence.
United were beaten by Arsenal.   (We are more interested in United)
The passive is used in a variety of contexts.
Impersonal statements.   *Students **are asked** not to smoke.*
When the agent is unknown.   *My bike **has been stolen**!*
(This avoids using *someone* or *they*.)
When the agent is obvious.   *Mr Jones **will be arrested**.*
How something was done.   *The box **was opened with a knife**.*

Reporting verbs

1 The passive is often used with *say, believe, understand, know* and similar
verbs used in reporting to avoid an impersonal *they* or *people*.
People say that John Wilson lives in New York.
*John Wilson **is said to live** in New York.*

2 The past tense and continuous verbs can also be reported in this way.
*John Wilson is said **to be travelling** in Africa.*
*John Wilson is said **to have arrived** in Australia.*

To have or *get
something done*

1 Causative *have* describes services done for us by someone else.
*Last year I **had** new tiles **put** on the roof.*

2 The same construction can describe misfortunes which happen to us, caused
by an unspecified person.
*Peter **had** his car **stolen** last week.*
*And then he **had** his leg **broken** playing football.*

3   Using *get* instead of *have* can suggest managing to do something.
     It was difficult but we **got** *the painting* **done** *in the end.*

Needs doing

This is an idiomatic way of expressing some passive sentences, usually about things or people which need some kind of service.
     The floor is filthy. It **needs scrubbing**.

Verbs and
prepositions

If a verb is followed by a preposition and object, the preposition stays with the verb in a passive sentence.
     People shouted at the Prime Minister during his speech.
     The Prime Minister **was shouted at** *during his speech.*

Other problems

1   A passive form in one language is not necessarily translated by a passive form in another.
     I **was born** *near London.*

2   *Make* (when meaning *force*) is followed by *to* in the passive.
     They made David work hard.   *David* **was made to** *work hard.*

3   The agent is not always included for reasons given in Uses **3** above.

Activities

1
Underline the
verb forms
which are not
possible.

a) My car <u>has being</u> stolen.
b) Jack was borned on a Thursday.
c) Then I realised that none of the guests had been sent an invitation.
d) Mary's car is being serviced today.
e) Your order will been sent as soon as possible.
f) The hole in the road was being repaired when I came home.
g) This swimming pool is used by over a thousand people each week.
h) When was this church built?
i) An address is writing on the back of the envelope.
j) Customers are request to ask for a receipt.

2
Choose the most
suitable tense.

a) Their new house <u>hasn't been finished</u>/<u>wasn't finished</u> yet.
b) The robbers <u>were arrested/have been arrested</u> as soon as they left the bank.
c) Sue told us her baby <u>is born/had been born</u> two weeks earlier than expected.
d) If there is too much snow, the match <u>has been cancelled/will be cancelled</u>.
e) By the time we got there, the rain <u>had stopped/had been stopped</u>.
f) When <u>were you told/have you been told</u> about the new rules?
g) Most of the passengers <u>were swimming/were swum</u> easily to the shore.
h) The winning horse <u>was ridden/was riding</u> by Pat Murphy.
i) I looked again for the old man, but he <u>was vanished/had vanished</u>.
j) I don't think that you <u>will be asked/are being asked</u> to show your passport.

3
Put each verb in brackets into a suitable passive tense.

a) I'm sorry, madam, but this carpet (already sell) .has. already. been. sold.
b) The old house on the corner (knock down) .... last year.
c) When exactly (John give) .... his prize?
d) Most people agree that America (not discover) .... by Christopher Columbus.
e) All complaints about products (deal with) .... by our customer services department.
f) Police confirmed that the murder weapon (since discover) .... in a nearby lake.
g) It (announce) .... yesterday that the government has decided not to raise income tax.
h) Good news! I (ask) .... to take over as the new managing director.
i) I don't believe that this play (write) .... by Shakespeare.
j) Ann really likes (invite) .... to dinner parties.

4
Rewrite each sentence, putting the verb underlined in the passive where this is possible.

a) I really <u>like</u> this hotel.
..not. possible...
b) People <u>ate</u> most of the food at the party.
....
c) Jane <u>won</u> the poetry competition.
....
d) Peter's new car <u>cost</u> over £20,000.
....
e) Martin always <u>wears</u> casual clothes.
....
f) One of our visitors <u>lost</u> this cigarette lighter.
....
g) They <u>haven't decided</u> the exact time of the match yet.
....
h) Most of the guests <u>had left</u> the hotel by midday.
....
i) Some parents <u>read</u> to their children every night.
....
j) This bike <u>belongs</u> to my sister.
....

5
Complete the second sentence so that it has a similar meaning to the first, using the word given. (Two to five words)

a) Last Thursday we appointed a new marketing manager.
was
A new ..marketing. manager. was. appointed last Thursday.
b) Smith Ltd are supplying our company with furniture.
supplied
Our company .... by Smith Ltd.
c) William the Conqueror built the castle in the 11th century.
by
The castle .... William the Conqueror in the 11th century.

d) No decision has yet been made.
   decided
   Nothing .... yet.
e) People believe that someone murdered Jenkins.
   was
   It .... murdered.
f) Your hair needs cutting.
   get
   You ought .... cut.
g) The police were following the suspects.
   were
   The suspects .... police.
h) No-one has seen Peter since the day of the party.
   been
   Peter .... the day of the party.
i) We put up a notice about the trip on the notice board yesterday.
   was
   A notice .... up on the notice board yesterday.
j) People think that an apple a day is good for you.
   to
   An apple a day .... for you.

6

Rewrite each
sentence so that
it contains a form
of *have
something done.*
Do not include
the agent.

a) A painter painted our house last month.
   ...*We had our house painted last month.*....................................

b) The hairdresser is cutting my hair this afternoon.
   ....

c) Someone has stolen my motorbike.
   ....

d) The dentist has taken out all of Ricky's teeth.
   ....

e) I haven't been to the car-wash for a long time.
   ....

f) The men are coming to put in the new central heating on Saturday.
   ....

g) Someone broke Harry's nose in a fight.
   ....

h) Isn't it time someone fixed your television?
   ....

i) Helen's publishers have just published her book.
   ....

j) The police towed away Nigel's car.
   ....

7

Rewrite each sentence so that it contains a passive form, and does not contain the words underlined.

a) <u>Apparently</u>, Freddie has a wife in Scotland.
..*Freddie is said to have a wife in Scotland*..................

b) <u>Nobody</u> knows <u>anything</u> about Brenda's family.
....

c) <u>People</u> think that <u>someone</u> started the fire deliberately.
....

d) You should <u>ask</u> a doctor to see to that cut.
....

e) <u>People</u> say that Chris was in the army.
....

f) My trousers <u>need</u> to be pressed before I leave.
....

g) <u>No-one</u> has signed this letter.
....

h) Mary's hair still <u>needs</u> cutting.
....

i) <u>People</u> believe that Norma is living in Paris.
....

j) <u>The director of the school</u> has decided that smoking is no longer allowed.
....

8

Look carefully at each line. Some lines are correct, but some have a word which should not be there. Tick each correct line. If a line has a word which should not be there, write the word in the space.

Opening of New Fairdene Sports Centre

The Gulliver Sports Centre, which has been   ..✓........
completely rebuilt, was been reopened yesterday   .been...
by the Minister for Sport. The building it was   1) ....
originally used to as a market, but was sold   2) ....
to Fairdene Council in 1981, and it then converted   3) ....
into a sports hall. Local schools were played football   4) ....
and basketball indoors, and keep fit classes were held   5) ....
there. In 1990 the hall was damaged when by a fire   6) ....
which was broke out in the heating system. The hall   7) ....
could not be used, and remained empty while discussions   8) ....
continued about its future. It was then and decided that   9) ....
the hall would to be rebuilt, and an appeal for money   10) ....
was launched. Two years ago a local businessman offered   11) ....
to pay for the building work, and plans were drawn up.   12) ....
The new hall is includes a swimming pool, running track   13) ....
and other sports facilities which can be used by anyone   14) ....
in the Fairdene area. The Minister was made a speech   15) ....
in which she congratulated everyone involved.

KEY POINTS

1   Not all verbs can be made passive. You can check in a dictionary whether the verb is transitive or intransitive.

2   The agent is only included if this information is needed.

3   Passive forms are often used to give an impersonal view.

4   It is not usually possible to change from passive to active without changing the meaning. A passive form may be more suitable in some contexts but unsuitable in others.

5   Passive forms tend to be used more often in writing, especially in scientific and technical language.

6   In some languages, verbs can have passive forms but active meanings. This may mislead you into giving the verb a passive form in English.

> **SEE ALSO**
>
> **Unit 10**
> Progress test

Unit 10 Progress test

(Units 6, 7, 8, 9)

1
Choose the most suitable caption for each picture.

a)

1) He's had his hair cut.
2) He's going to have his hair cut.
3) He had his hair cut.

b)

1) I've been robbed!
2) I've been stolen!
3) I've had myself robbed!

c)

1) I'd rather your not smoking.
2) I'd rather you didn't smoke.
3) I'd rather you not smoke.

d)

1) My car has vanished!
2) My car has been vanished!
3) Someone has vanished my car!

2
Complete the second sentence so that it has a similar meaning to the first, using the word given. (Two to five words)

a) Please don't open the window.
   you
   I'd .... open the window.

b) Fiona wanted to know the time.
   what
   Fiona wanted to know .... was.

c) We won't go out if the weather is bad.
   won't
   We .... the weather is good.

d) I would like you to be here!
   wish
   I .... wish .... ve .... here.
e) Catherine refused to let me go.
   couldn't
   Catherine .... go.
f) If I were you I'd try to get some sleep.
   advise
   I ..... a .... to get some sleep.
g) What a pity we didn't see the match.
   wish
   I .... had .... the match.
h) The old man introduced himself.
   us
   The old man .... name.
i) David told me the time of the next train.
   what
   David told .... train left.
j) The police inspector said I had killed Mrs Burns.
   of
   The police inspector .... accuse .... m .... killing Mrs Burns.

3

Decide which answer A, B, C or D best fits each space.

The stolen bike

One morning last week I realised that my bike (1) .... stolen from my garden. I phoned the police and two officers called at my house the next day. They (2) .... me if I had seen or heard anything. I told (3) .... I had been out that evening, and hadn't noticed anything suspicious when I came home. 'If I had seen anything, I (4) .... you,' I replied. 'It was raining hard too. If the weather (5) .... so bad, I would have ridden my bike. 'The officers told me that lots of people (6) .... their bikes stolen lately. 'The thieves (7) .... to have put the bikes in a van,' said one of the officers. 'I (8) .... I had known about that,' I said. 'I saw a black van that evening. In fact, it (9) .... opposite my house.' The officers asked me what the van's number (10) .... , but I couldn't remember. '(11) .... you saw the van again, (12) .... you recognise it?' one of them asked. 'It (13) .... painting. I remember that,' I replied. However, there was a happy ending to this story. After the officers had left, I (14) .... by a friend of mine. 'By the way,' she said, '(15) .... you want your bike, I'll bring it back this afternoon. I borrowed it a couple of days ago.'

1) A) had   B) had been   C) had had itself   D) had not
2) A) reminded   B) questioned   C) told   D) asked
3) A) them   B) that   C) if   D) later
4) A) called   B) would   C) had called   D) would have called

5) A) wasn't   B) wouldn't be   C) hadn't been   D) wouldn't have been
6) A) had   B) had had   C) had to have   D) hadn't
7) A) think   B) are thought   C) have thought   D) are thinking
8) A) would   B) realise   C) wish   D) thought
9) A) was parked B) had parking   C) is parked   D) has parked
10) A) is   B) was   C) had   D) wrote
11) A) If   B) When   C) Remember   D) Suppose
12) A) do   B) can   C) would   D) if
13) A) needed   B) had been   C) looked like   D) seemed
14) A) called up B) was phoned   C) had a phone call D) heard some news
15) A) unless   B) if only   C) if   D) as long as

4

Put each verb in brackets into a suitable tense.

A friend in the rain

Last week I (1) .... (walk) home after playing tennis when it (2) ....
(start) raining very heavily. 'Oh no, I (3) .... (get) soaked before I (4)
.... (reach) home,' I thought. 'I wish I (5) .... (remember) to bring
my raincoat.' But unfortunately I (6) .... (leave) it at home. 'How stupid
of me! I (7) .... (always forget) to bring it with me.' Luckily just then a
friend of mine passed in her car and offered me a lift. '(8) .... (you go)
home?' she asked, 'or (9) .... (you want) to go for a drink?' 'I think I'd
rather you (10) .... (take) me home,' I said. 'If I (11) .... (not change)
my clothes, I know I (12) .... (fall) ill, and then I (13) .... (not be
able) to play in the tennis tournament next week. And I (14) .... (practise)
hard for the last month.' 'I (15) .... (wait) for you to change if you (16)
.... (like),' she told me. 'I think it's time you (17) .... (relax) for a
change. You (18) .... (worry) too much about things lately. And people
who (19) .... (worry) too much (20) .... (fall) ill more easily. It's got
nothing to do with the rain!'

5

Complete the second sentence so that it has a similar meaning to the first sentence, using the word given. Do not change the word given. You must use between two and five words.

a) Excuse me, is somebody serving you, sir?
   being
   Excuse me, ... , sir?
b) I think we should go home now.
   went
   It's .... home.
c) The painters painted our house last month.
   had
   We .... last month.
d) It's a pity that Charles is always complaining.
   wouldn't
   I .... so much.
e) Someone will meet you at the airport.
   be
   You .... at the airport.

f) People think that train-robber Dave Briggs has escaped.
   have
   Train-robber Dave Briggs .... escaped.

g) 'Don't forget to buy some bread, Mum,' said Pauline.
   reminded
   Pauline .... buy some bread.

h) Have you received your salary yet?
   been
   Have .... yet?

i) I think I'll manage to finish the letters by 4.00.
   get
   I think I'll .... by 4.00.

j) My parents made me study every night.
   was
   I .... every night by my parents.

6

Put each verb in brackets into a suitable tense.

The facts about sugar

Packet sugar from the supermarket (1) .... (extract) from either sugar cane or sugar beet. These products (2) .... (mix) with hot water, which (3) .... (dissolve) their natural sugar. Sugar (4) .... (also find) in fruit some of which, such as dates and grapes, (5) .... (contain) very high amounts of sugar. To be a little more scientific, sugar should (6) .... (call) sucrose. Sucrose (7) .... (make up) of two substances, glucose, which (8) .... (use) for instant energy, and fructose, which (9) .... (last) longer as a source of energy. The sugar in fruit is mainly fructose. So when we (10) .... (eat) fruit, we (11) .... (also eat) quite large amounts of natural sugar. Some scientists (12) .... (believe) that too much sugar (13) .... (eat) in sweets, cakes and biscuits. It (14) .... (say) to be generally bad for the health, although nothing (15) .... (definitely prove) so far. However, it (16) .... (know) that sugar (17) .... (cause) tooth decay. As one expert put it: 'If other foods (18) .... (damage) our body as much as sugar (19) .... (damage) our teeth, they (20) .... (ban) immediately.'

7
Look carefully at each line. Some lines are correct, but some have a word which should not be there. Tick each correct line. If a line has a word which should not be there, write the word in the space.

A holiday in Scotland

Some friends of mine decided to go on holiday ...✓......
to Scotland. They asked me if I was wanted to go ..was....
too, but I had already arranged to go to Italy. 1) ....
I told them so that I had been to Scotland before, 2) ....
so they asked me to give them some ideas. 3) ....
I advised them to take up warm clothes and 4) ....
raincoats. 'If I were like you, I'd always carry 5) ....
umbrellas!' I told them. 'I doubt that whether 6) ....
you'll have any sunny days.' I didn't see 7) ....
them again until was after their holiday. They 8) ....
were all very sun-tanned, and they told to me 9) ....
that they had had very hot weather. 10) ....
'If we had been taken your advice, we would 11) ....
have made a terrible mistake, ' they said me. 12) ....
'Luckily we were told us before we 13) ....
left that it was very hot in Scotland. 14) ....
It is said to they have been the hottest summer ever! 15) ....

Unit 11 Relative clauses

Explanations

Subject or object

1 Subject and Object
Relative clauses give extra information about a noun in the main clause.
They can refer to this as subject or object.

*That's the woman **who bought my car**.*   *The woman (Subject) bought my car.*

*That's the car **that I used to own**.*   *I used to own the car. (Object)*

2 Combining Sentences
Note how sentences are combined.
Subject: *This is Jean. She bought my car.*
     Jean is the person who bought my car.
(*She* is not repeated, as *the person* is the subject.)
Object: *That is Jean's car. I used to own it.*
     That's the car that I used to own.
(*It* is not repeated, as *the car* is the object.)

Defining or non-defining

1 Defining
Defining clauses give important information which tells us exactly what is being referred to.

*That book which you lent me **is really good**.*

2 Non-Defining
Non-defining clauses add extra information, separated by commas in writing, and intonation in speaking.

*The book, **which I hadn't read**, was still on the shelf.*

Omitting the relative pronoun

1 Object clauses
The relative pronoun can be left out in object clauses in both speaking and writing, provided these are defining.

*That's **the car I used to own**.*

2 Non-Defining clauses
The relative pronoun cannot be left out in a non-defining clause.

Which, who and *that*

1 *That* instead of *which*
That is often used instead of *which* in speech.

*Is this the house **that** you bought?*

2 *That* instead of *who*
   That can also refer to people in everyday speech.
      *Have you met the boy **that** Sue is going to marry?*

3 *Which* in non-defining clauses
   That cannot be used to introduce a non-defining clause.
      *The hotel, **which** was a hundred years old, was very comfortable.*

4 Prepositions
   That cannot be used after a preposition.
      This is the car (that/which) I paid £2000 for.   (Everyday Speech)
      *This is the car **for which** I paid £2000.*   (Formal)

Whose and *whom*

1 *Whose* means *of whom*, and usually refers to people.
      This is Jack. His sister is staying with us.
      *This is Jack, **whose** sister is staying with us.*

2 *Whom* is the object form of *who*, and has to be used after prepositions.
      This is the person I sold my car to.   (Everyday Speech)
      *This is the person **to whom** I sold my car.*   (Formal)

Activities

1
Underline any relative pronouns that can be left out in these sentences.

a) I think that my boss is the person <u>who</u> I admire most.
b) Harry, who was tired, went to bed very early.
c) We're taking the train that leaves at 6.00.
d) Have you seen the book that I left here on the desk?
e) The film which we liked most was the French one.
f) My radio, which isn't very old, has suddenly stopped working.
g) The clothes which you left behind are at the reception desk.
h) The couple who met me at the station took me out to dinner.
i) Last week I ran into an old friend who I hadn't seen for ages.
j) Don't cook the meat that I put in the freezer – it's for the dog.

2
Replace the relative pronoun underlined with *that*, where possible.

a) This is the magazine <u>which</u> I told you about.
   ...This is the magazine that I told you about..

b) John's flat, <u>which</u> is in the same block as mine, is much larger.
   ....

c) The girl <u>whose</u> bag I offered to carry turned out to be an old friend.
   ....

d) The policeman <u>who</u> arrested her had recognised her car.
   ....

e) I work with someone <u>who</u> knows you.
   ....

f) We don't sell goods <u>which</u> have been damaged.

....

g) Brighton, <u>which</u> is on the south coast, is a popular holiday resort.

....

h) I don't know anyone <u>whose</u> clothes would fit you.

....

i) There's a pub near here <u>which</u> serves very good meals.

....

j) People <u>who</u> park outside get given parking tickets.

....

3
Decide whether each sentence contains a defining or a non-defining relative clause.

a) Everyone who got to the sales early found excellent bargains.
....*Defining*....................

b) Leave the questions which you can't answer until the end.
....

c) Helen picked up the book, which had a green cover.
....

d) The guests who were late didn't have enough to eat.
....

e) Sue, who was extremely hungry, decided to cook some spaghetti.
....

f) The person I spoke to before said the repair would be free of charge.
....

g) My bedroom, which was rather small, looked out on a noisy street.
....

h) David's sister, who likes cats, offered to take one of the kittens.
....

i) The person who finishes first will be the winner, of course.
....

j) Smith, who had earlier missed a penalty, scored after twenty minutes.
....

4
Choose the most suitable word in each sentence.

a) My friend Jack, <u>that/who/whose</u> parents live in Glasgow, invited me to spend Christmas in Scotland.

b) Here's the computer program <u>that/whom/whose</u> I told you about.

c) I don't believe the story <u>that/who/whom</u> she told us.

d) Peter comes from Witney, <u>that/who/which</u> is near Oxford.

e) This is the gun with <u>that/whom/which</u> the murder was committed.

f) Have you received the parcel <u>whom/whose/which</u> we sent you?

g) Is this the person <u>who/which/whose</u> you asked me about?

h) That's the girl <u>that/who/whose</u> brother sits next to me at school.

i) The meal, <u>that/which/whose</u> wasn't very tasty, was quite expensive.

j) We didn't enjoy the play <u>that/who/whose</u> we went to see.

5

Put a suitable relative pronoun in each space, or leave the space blank wherever possible.

a) The person ..*whose*.. fingerprints are on the gun was the person .... killed Dr Martin.
b) My bike, ... I had left at the gate, had disappeared.
c) The shoes .... I finally bought were the ones .... I tried on first.
d) The bag in .... the robbers put the money was found outside the bank.
e) The medicine .... the doctor gave me had no effect at all.
f) Peter, ... couldn't see the screen, decided to change his seat.
g) The present .... you gave me was the one .... I gave you last year!
h) I really liked that tea .... you made me this morning.
i) What was the name of your friend .... tent we borrowed?
j) The flight ....Joe was leaving on was cancelled.

6

Make **one** new sentence from each pair of sentences, beginning as shown, and using the word given in capitals.

a) Brenda is a friend. I went on holiday with her.   WHO
Brenda is ..*the friend who I went on holiday with*..............
b) This is Mr Smith. His son Bill plays in our team.   WHOSE
This is Mr Smith ....
c) Her book was published last year. It became a best seller.   WHICH
Her book ....
d) This is the bank. We borrowed the money from it.   WHICH
This is the bank from ....
e) I told you about a person. She is at the door.   WHO
The person ....
f) Jack's car had broken down. He had to take a bus.   WHOSE
Jack, ...

7

Make **one** sentence from each group of sentences, beginning as shown.

a) The hotel was full of guests. The hotel was miles from anywhere. The guests had gone there to admire the scenery.
~~gone~~The hotel, which ..*was miles from anywhere, was full of guests who had*........ ..*gone there to admire the scenery*.
b) I lent you a book. It was written by a friend of mine. She lives in France.
The book I ....
c) A woman's jewels were stolen. A police officer was staying in the same hotel. The woman was interviewed by him.
The woman whose ....
d) A goal was scored by a teenager. He had come on as substitute. This goal won the match.
The goal which ....
e) I was sitting next to a boy in the exam. He told me the answers.
The boy I ....
f) My wallet contained over £100. It was found in the street by a schoolboy. He returned it.
My wallet, ...

g) My friend Albert has decided to buy a motorbike. His car was stolen last week.

My friend Albert, ...

h) Carol is a vegetarian. I cooked a meal for her last week. She enjoyed it.

Carol, ...

8

Put **one** suitable word in each space, or leave the space blank wherever possible.

Murder At The Station by Lorraine Small. Episode 5. *Trouble on the 6.15.* The story so far: Jane Platt, (1) .who. is travelling to London because of a mysterious letter, is the only person (2) .... witnesses a murder at Victoria Station. The detective to (3) .... she gives her statement then disappears. Jane goes to an office in Soho to answer the letter (4) .... she had received. There she discovers that her uncle Gordon, (5) .... lives in South America, has sent her a small box (6) .... she is only to open if in trouble. Jane, (7) .... parents have never mentioned an Uncle Gordon, is suspicious of the box, (8) .... she gives to her friend Tony. They go to Scotland Yard and see Inspector Groves, (9) .... has not heard of the Victoria Station murder, (10) .... was not reported to the police. Jane gives Inspector Groves the murdered man's ticket (11) .... she found beside his body. Then Jane and Tony decide to go to Redhill, (12) .... was the town (13) .... the murdered man had come from. On the train they meet a man, (14) .... face is somehow familiar to Jane, (15) .... says he knows her Uncle Gordon. Now read on.

9

These sentences are all grammatically possible, but not appropriate in speech. Rewrite each sentence so that it ends with the preposition underlined.

a) Margaret is the girl <u>with</u> whom I went on holiday.

..Margaret is the girl I went on holiday with...............................

b) The golf club is the only club <u>of</u> which I am a member.

....

c) That's the girl <u>about</u> whom we were talking.

....

d) It was a wonderful present, <u>for</u> which I was extremely grateful.

....

e) This is the school <u>to</u> which I used to go.

....

f) Is this the case <u>in</u> which we should put the wineglasses?

....

g) Can you move the chair <u>on</u> which you are sitting?

....

h) That's the shop <u>from</u> which I got my shoes.

....

i) Is that the person <u>next to</u> whom you usually sit?

....

j) This is Bill, <u>about</u> whom you have heard so much.

....

10
Make **one** sentence from each group of sentences, beginning as shown.

a) I got on a train. I wanted to go to a station. The train didn't stop there.
The train I ..*I.got.on.didn't.stop.at.the.station.I.wanted.to.go.to.*...................

b) I read a book. You recommended a book to me. This was the book.
The book I ....

c) The ship hit an iceberg and sank. Warning messages had been sent to it. The ship ignored these.
The ship, ...

d) The postman realised I was on holiday. You had sent me a parcel. The postman left it next door.
The postman, ...

e) I used to own a dog. People came to the door. The dog never barked at them.
The dog I ....

f) I bought my car from a woman. She lives in a house. You can see the house over there.
The woman I ....

g) We went to a beach on the first day of our holiday. It was covered in seaweed. This smelled a lot.
The beach we ....

h) My neighbours have three small children. The children make a lot of noise. My neighbours never apologise.
My neighbours, ...

i) I bought a new typewriter. It cost me a lot of money.
The new ....

j) I lost my wallet last week. It was found by a workman. He was digging a hole in the street outside our house.
The wallet ....

KEY POINTS

1 Long and complex sentences with relative clauses are not usual in speech. It is more usual in speech to join shorter clauses with conjunctions.

2 Relative pronouns are usually left out in object clauses in speech.
   This is the book I told you about.

3 In speech it is common to end relative clauses with a preposition.
   That's the girl I live next door to.

SEE ALSO
Unit 15
Progress test

Unit 12 Prepositions

Explanations

Movement
Prepositions used with verbs of motion (*come, go, run* etc.) show the direction of the movement.
> *Jack ran **out of** the room.   Sue moved **towards** the door.*
Other examples: *to, into, across, around, along, up, down, past.*

Position and place
Prepositions also show position.
> *Ted was sitting **next to** Janet.   The bank is **opposite** the cinema.*
Other examples: *before, below, beside, in front of, near, on top of, under*
Prepositions also show place.
> *I live **in** France.   Sue lives **on** an island.   John is **at** school.*
See below for problems of usage.

Other uses
1   Prepositions are also used in time expressions. (See Unit 14.)

2   Prepositions also cover a wide range of meanings.
> *This book is **about** Napoleon.   I can't drink tea **with/without** sugar.*

Problems of use
1   *At* and *to*
At is not used with verbs of motion.
> *We went **to** the cinema.   We arrived **at** the cinema.*

2   *Near* and *next to*
Next to means the same as *beside*. Near means *not far away from*, which can be a matter of opinion.
> *Peter always sits **next to** Mary.*
> *I live **near** the sea, it's only ten miles away.*

3   *Above* and *over*
Both mean 'higher than', but *over* suggests closeness or touching. There may be little difference in some contexts.
> *There was something written **above/over** the door.*
> *There was a plane high **above** them. Put this blanket **over** you.*

4   *In* and *at:* Places
In refers to towns, countries and the 'inside' of places.
> *She lives **in** Paris.   They arrived **in** Peru.   He's **in** the kitchen.*
At refers to points with a particular purpose rather than 'inside'.
> *She lives **at** home.*
> *They met **at the cinema**. (Place)   They met **in the cinema**. (Inside)*

5   Prepositions at the end of a sentence
Study these common examples:
*Who are you waiting **for**?*   (Question)
*You are very difficult to live **with**!*   (Infinitive)
*That's the company that I work **for**.*   (Relative clause)

Prepositions which are also adverbs

Some prepositions can be used as adverbs without an object.
*Ted was walking **along**, whistling.*
Examples: *around, along, behind, opposite*

Prepositions with more than one word

Examples: *according to, on behalf of, by means of*
Other examples are included in the activities.

Prepositional phrases

There are many fixed phrases containing prepositions.
Examples: *by mistake, on purpose, out of order*
Other examples are included in the activities.

Activities

1
Choose the most suitable preposition.

a)   I got at/<u>to</u> the station just in time to see Jack getting <u>from/off</u> the train.
b)   The pub is <u>among/between</u> the chemist's and the butcher's and <u>across/opposite</u> the library.
c)   Sue lives <u>at/in</u> Wales, which is a country <u>at/in</u> the west of Britain.
d)   I was brought up <u>in/on</u> an island <u>near/next to</u> the coast of Scotland.
e)   Travelling <u>by/in</u> your own car is better than going <u>by/on</u> foot.
f)   Jack was leaning <u>by/against</u> the wall with his hands <u>in/into</u> his pockets.
g)   Ann had a hat <u>on/over</u> her head and a veil <u>above/over</u> her face.
h)   We arrived <u>at/in</u> England <u>at/in</u> Gatwick Airport.
i)   I left my bags <u>at/from</u> the station <u>at/in</u> a left luggage locker.
j)   Peter came running <u>into/to</u> the room and threw his books <u>at/onto</u> the floor.

according to	because of	in common with	instead of	apart from
by means of	in favour of	on behalf of	as for	in case of	in front of
regardless of				

a)   I think I'd rather have coffee ...*instead of*........ tea.
b)   .... danger, Paul ran back into the burning house.
c)   .... fire, smash the glass and push the button.
d)   Personally, I am .... banning cigarette smoking completely!
e)   I would like to thank you, ... everyone who was rescued.
f)   .... you, no-one else knows that I have escaped.
g)   .... Steve, he believes that we should stay where we are.

h) Jim managed to climb into the house .... a ladder he found.
i) .... the rain the match was postponed.
j) .... the timetable, the next train isn't for two hours.
k) Julie has nothing .... Bill. They are quite different.
l) A large black car suddenly drew up .... the house.

3
Decide whether it is possible to leave out the words underlined, so that the remaining words make sense.

a) Most people were wandering around <u>the streets</u>, taking photos. ..*possible*...
b) I gave my bike to <u>my little sister</u>, when it became too small for me. ....
c) The people who live in the house opposite <u>our house</u> are Italian. ....
d) I left my coat <u>on the bed</u> in here but it seems to have disappeared. ....
e) I'll wait for you outside <u>the cinema</u>, on the pavement. ....
f) Peter took a deep breath, and then went under <u>the water</u> again. ....
g) Don't worry, the hotel's quite near <u>to where we are now</u>. ....
h) The children can sit behind <u>you in the back seats</u>. ....
i) We travelled all day and arrived at <u>our destination</u> in the evening. ....
j) I drove past <u>the house at the end of the street</u> but I didn't notice anything wrong. ....

4
Complete each sentence by using a word or phrase from the list. Use each word once only.

at	by	for	in	on	off	out of	to	under	without

a) Police officers don't have to wear uniform when they are ..*off*.... duty.
b) I feel very tired. .... times I consider giving up work.
c) The children were all upset, and some were .... tears.
d) This factory needs modernising. Everything here is .... date.
e) Don't worry, everything is .... control.
f) Sorry, I seem to have taken the wrong umbrella .... mistake.
g) Please hurry. We need these documents .... delay.
h) That wasn't an accident! You did it .... purpose.
i) We thought the two films were very similar .... a great extent.
j) We decided to take a holiday in Wales .... a change.

5
Choose the most suitable phrase.

a) I can't disturb John now. He's <u>at bed</u>/<u>in bed</u>.
b) Tony always arrives exactly <u>in time/on time</u> for his lesson.
c) Two pounds for each ticket, that makes £12 <u>in all/with all</u>.
d) I can't pick that last apple. It's <u>out of hand/out of reach</u>.
e) Joe and I met on the plane completely <u>by chance/by surprise</u>.
f) The children spend most of their time <u>out of doors/out of place</u>.
g) I'm sorry but Jane isn't here <u>at present/at a time</u>.
h) How can Sam love Lucy? They have nothing <u>in common/in general</u>.
i) They should be here soon. They are <u>in the way/on the way</u>.
j) Terry isn't here. He's away <u>in business/on business</u>.

6

Complete each sentence with a suitable word from the list. Use each word once only.

| breath | fail | impression | secret | strike |
| costs | hurry | return | stock | words |

a) This is important. You must catch the two men at all ..*costs*.......... .
b) He says he's ill. Or in other .... , he doesn't want to come.
c) I was under the .... that you enjoyed working here.
d) Sorry, I can't stop. I'm in a ....
e) Please hand your work in on Tuesday, without ....
f) We can't go by train. The train-drivers are on ....
g) Martin is supposed to have given up smoking, but he smokes in ....
h) I'm afraid we don't have your size, we are out of ....
i) If I give you the information, what will you give me in .... ?
j) I ran for the bus, and now I'm out of ....

7

Complete each sentence with a suitable word from the list. Use each word once only.

| average | force | particular | profit | sight |
| detail | himself | practice | public | whole |

a) Harry managed to sell his house at a ..*profit*.......... .
b) What was he doing here all by .... ?
c) Larry is so famous that he doesn't appear in .... very often.
d) That was a terrible shot! I'm rather out of ....
e) How many cars do you sell, on .... , every week?
f) The police are coming! Stay out of .... until they leave.
g) I might be able to help you. What do you want to know in .... ?
h) I suppose I enjoyed my holiday on the ....
i) Can you tell me about the plans in .... ?
j) The gun had to be taken away from David by ....

8

Complete each sentence with one of the phrases from the list. Use each phrase once only.

| by heart | in difficulties | in turn | on holiday | out of work |
| by sight | in pain | in two | on sale | without a doubt |

a) When I sat on the pencil, it broke ...*in two*........ .
b) Most of the people in the office are .... at the moment.
c) This is .... the best washing machine on the market.
d) Graham has been .... ever since he came to London.
e) I know her .... , but I don't know her name.
f) The lifeguard dived in to save a swimmer ....
g) John learned his first speech ....
h) Why don't you share the bike? You can ride it ....
i) You could tell he was .... by the way he kept groaning.
j) Cigarettes and ice-cream are .... in the foyer.

9

Complete each sentence with one of the phrases from the list. Use each phrase once only.

| at any rate | by surprise | in person | out of danger | out of tune |
| by all means | from now on | in private | out of order | under orders |

a) Jim's excuse was that he was acting ...*under orders*.... from his boss.

b) Things have changed. .... , no-one will leave before 5.00.

c) Thank goodness. All the passengers are now ....

d) The president would like to meet you and thank you ....

e) Your violin sounds awful! I think it's ....

f) It's a warm country. We won't need our pullovers, ...

g) Excuse me, but I'd like to have a word with you ....

h) You can't use the phone. It's ....

i) The news about Shirley took me completely ....

j) Yes, of course. Take the chairs, ...

10

Look carefully at each line. Some lines are correct, but some have a word which should not be there. Tick each correct line. If a line has a word which should not be there, write the word in the space.

The Psychology of Accidents

Most people are under the impression that ...✓......

doing something by a mistake is quite different ..a........

from doing something on purpose. In the fact, 1) ....

according to by some psychologists, many 2) ....

accidents do not, on the whole, really happen 3) ....

to by chance. There may be good reasons for 4) ....

actions which seem to be accidental. For an 5) ....

example, someone who fails to arrive on time 6) ....

as for a meeting at work may be worried about 7) ....

his or her job, or be in with difficulties at home. 8) ....

In other words, there are often good reasons for 9) ....

behaviour which seems at the first to be 10) ....

accidental. Of this course, some people are 11) ....

involved in more accidents than others. These 12) ....

people are called 'accident prone'. In the general 13) ....

they either suffer from stress, or could have in 14) ....

a physical illness without knowing about it. 15) ....

KEY POINTS

1 There is a group of prepositions used with verbs of motion.
   across, along, around, down, into, out of, past, to, towards, up

2 Some prepositions can be used without an object as adverbs.
   *Jean lives **opposite**.*

3 A sentence can end with a preposition.
   *Paul didn't have a chair to sit **on**.*

SEE ALSO
Unit 14
Time expressions
Unit 15
Progress test

Unit 13 Expressing purpose, result, and contrast

Explanations

Purpose

1 *So (that)*
So that is usually followed by *can, could, will* or *would*.
> *The police locked the door **so (that)** no-one could get in.*

2 Infinitive of purpose
The person in the main clause, and the person referred to by the infinitive, must be the same.
> *Jack went to England **to study** engineering.*

3 *In order to, so as to*
These are more formal ways of expressing purpose.
> *Scientists used only local materials, **in order to** save money.*
There are also negative forms: *in order not to, so as not to.*
> *The soldiers moved at night, **so as not to** alarm the villagers.*

4 *For*
This describes how something is used.
> *This button is **for starting** the engine. This is **for the lights**.*

Result

1 *So/such + (adjective) + (that)*
> *Jim was **so tall (that)** he hit his head on the ceiling.*
> *Helen is **such a busy person (that)** she never feels bored.*
Such is used with adjective and noun. Note also this formal use:
> *Helen is **so busy a person (that)** she never feels bored.*

2 *So much/many/few/little + (noun) + (that)*
> *There were **so many passengers (that)** we couldn't find a seat.*

3 *Too + (adjective) + to*
> *The table was far **too heavy to** lift.*
This can be explained as: The table was far too heavy (for me) to lift.

4 *Not (+ adjective) enough*
> *The table was **not light enough** to lift.*

Contrast

1 *Although, though, even though, while, whereas*
Although often becomes *though* in speech. *Though* can come at the end of a sentence, *although* cannot.
> ***Although** I asked her, she didn't come.*

In speech this might be:
> *I asked her, (but) she didn't come, **though**.*

Or ***Though** I asked her, she didn't come.*

Even though is a more emphatic form of *although*.
> ***Even though** I asked her, she didn't come.* (which was surprising).

While and *whereas* are more common in writing and formal speech. They contrast opposite ideas.
> ***While** United were fast and accurate, City were slow and careless.*

2 *However*

However is more common in formal speech or writing. It can go at the beginning or end of the sentence.
> *It's cheap. **However**, I don't like it./I don't like it, **however**.*

3 *Nevertheless*

This is a very formal way of expressing *however*.
> *Smith says he is poor. **Nevertheless**, he has bought a new car.*

4 *Despite and in spite of*

These are followed by nouns (or gerunds), and not by clauses.
> ***Despite losing, we celebrated**. In spite of **the rain, we went out**.*

Activities

1

Choose the most suitable word or phrase underlined in each sentence.

a) Janet went out <u>so that she bought/to buy</u> Harry a present.
b) This food is much too hot <u>to eat/to be eaten</u>.
c) <u>However/Though</u> it was late, I decided to phone Brian.
d) <u>Although/Despite</u> the car was cheap, it was in good condition.
e) Let's check once more, <u>for being/so as to be</u> sure.
f) We could go to the club. Is it worth it, <u>even though/though</u>?
g) It was <u>so windy/such a windy</u> that half the trees were blown down.
h) The batteries were <u>not enough small/too small</u> to fit the radio.
i) Despite <u>of the weather/the weather</u>, we went sailing.
j) Bill had <u>so much/so that</u> fun that he stayed another week.

2

Complete the second sentence so that it has a similar meaning to the first sentence, using the word given.

a) Sue went shopping so she could buy herself a new television.
to
Sue ..*went shopping to buy herself*.............................. a new television.
b) You use this to open wine bottles.
for
This .... wine bottles.
c) I put the food in the fridge because I wanted it to get cold.
would
I put the food in the fridge .... cold.

    d) Harry left early because he didn't want to miss the bus.
       as
       Harry .... to miss the bus.

    e) I saved up some money to buy a motorbike.
       could
       I saved up some money .... a motorbike.

    f) Jane gave up smoking because she wanted to save money.
       order
       Jane gave up smoking .... money.

    g) I came here so that I could see you.
       to
       I .... you.

    h) Use this money to buy the tickets.
       buying
       This .... tickets.

    i) I picked up the vase carefully, so as not to break it.
       that
       I picked up the vase carefully .... break.

    j) We put up a fence to prevent the rabbit escaping.
       couldn't
       We put up a fence .... escape.

3

Rewrite each sentence, beginning as shown, so that the meaning stays the same.

    a) Sam lost his job because he was lazy.
       Sam was ..*so lazy that he lost his job.*..

    b) I couldn't buy the house because it was expensive.
       The house was too ....

    c) The book was so interesting that I couldn't put it down.
       It was ....

    d) There was too much noise, so we couldn't hear the speech.
       There was so ....

    e) The house was too small to live in comfortably.
       The house wasn't ....

    f) William never makes mistakes because he is a careful reader.
       William is so ....

    g) We can't eat now because there isn't enough time.
       There is too ....

    h) I can't come to your party because I'm too busy.
       I'm too ....

    i) The class was cancelled because there weren't enough students.
       There were so ....

    j) It's such a lovely day today that I feel like taking a walk.
       It's so ....

4

Complete each sentence with one suitable word.

a) I couldn't run fast ..*enough*...... to catch the shoplifter.
b) There were .... good roads that we could drive at high speed.
c) It was .... dark that I couldn't see a thing.
d) The trousers were .... long enough to fit Jean.
e) We had .... a good time that we decided to go there again.
f) It was .... late that we couldn't get a bus home.
g) I took a taxi as it was .... far to walk.
h) There were .... many dishes that I couldn't make up my mind.
i) The ladder wasn't tall .... to reach the window.
j) There are .... lovely fish that you don't feel like eating meat.

5

Rewrite each sentence, beginning as shown, so that the meaning stays the same. Two sentences should be rewritten as one.

a) Despite the cold weather, we all went for a walk.
Although ..*it.was.cold,.we.all.went.for.a.walk.*...................
b) John has done well in French, but not so well in Maths.
While ....
c) I tried to persuade her. I didn't succeed, however.
Although ....
d) It was raining, but I went swimming anyway.
In spite of ....
e) I like fish, but I don't like catching them myself.
Although ....
f) Ann felt ill, but insisted on going to work.
Despite ....
g) I rang the doorbell. Nobody answered, though.
Although ....
h) In spite of his early lead, Hudson lost the race.
Although ....
i) I'm not going to pay, although I know that I should.
While ....
j) We expected Larry to accept the job, but he didn't.
Even though Larry ....

6

Explain what each object is for, using one of the verbs in the list. Use each verb once only.

boil cut lock paint stick clean keep open put wash

a) brush
..*It's.for.painting.things*...................
b) scissors
....
c) glue
....
d) kettle
....
e) fridge
....

f) sink

....

g) dustbin

....

h) toothbrush

....

i) corkscrew

....

j) key

....

7

Look carefully at each line. Some lines are correct, but some have a word which should not be there. Tick each correct line. If a line has a word which should not be there, write the word in the space.

Goodwriters...A Course for You!

Jane was one of those students who has problems   ..✓........
with writing. First, her handwriting it was so bad   ..it........
that most teachers couldn't to read it. The letters were   1) ....
so small, that the words were extremely difficult to   2) ....
read. Even although she tried to change her handwriting,   3) ....
she felt discouraged. Secondly, she made so the many   4) ....
mistakes in spelling and punctuation, so that her work   5) ....
always gave a bad impression. As well as this, she   6) ....
had problems with organising her writing, in despite   7) ....
making plans and writing notes. One day, though, she   8) ....
took a Goodwriter writing course, so to learn how to   9) ....
be an effective writer. At Goodwriters we taught her   10) ....
how to organise her ideas. Although however she found   11) ....
it difficult at first, so she soon made progress. She   12) ....
learned to revise her writing, so as to improve it.   13) ....
She started reading so too much that her spelling   14) ....
improved, so while her handwriting became clearer too.   15) ....
Goodwriters....send for details today!

KEY POINTS

1 The infinitive of purpose must refer to the same person as the main clause.
   I went to the shops. I wanted to buy some fruit.
   I went to the shops **to buy** *some fruit.*

2 *In order to* is more common in formal speech and writing.

3 Contrasts with *while, whereas* and *nevertheless* are used in formal speech and writing.

> **SEE ALSO**
>
> **Unit 15**
> Progress test
> **Unit 32**
> Text organisers

Unit 14 Time expressions

Explanations

This page focuses on problem areas. Other time expressions are included in the activities.

Present time

Nowadays and *These days*
Both contrast the present with the past.
  *What are you up to **these days**?*   ***Nowadays** more women have careers.*

Future time

1 *In*
   In can refer to future time.
     *I'll be there **in a moment**.*   *I'll be back **in a week**.*

2 Calendar references
   If today is Monday:
     *Wednesday is **the day after tomorrow** or **the day after next**.*
     *Wednesday is also **in two days' time**.*
     *Next Monday is **this time next week**.*

3 *Eventually* and *in the end*
   Both refer to what will happen after a long period.
     *I think that our side will win **in the end/eventually**.*

4 *Presently*
   This means 'in a few moments'.
     *Just a minute. I'll be with you **presently**.*

Past time

1 *Once*
   This can mean 'in the past'. It can also mean 'from the time when'.
     *I lived here **once**. (in the past)   **Once** she gets here, we can leave. (when)*

2 Periods of the day
   Last is not normally used with *morning, afternoon* or *evening*.
     *They left **yesterday morning** and came back **last night**.*

3 Calendar references
   If today is Monday: Saturday night was **the night before last**.

4 *In those days* and *at that time*
   Both refer to a past time already referred to.
     *I met Janet in 1980. **In those days** I was a keen dancer.*

5 *After,* later and *afterwards*
   After needs an object.
>   *I'll see you **after the holidays**.*
   Afterwards means 'after this or that'.
>   *The film is starting now. I'll tell you afterwards.*
   Later means 'at a later time'.
>   *I'm busy now. I'll call you back later.*

Other problems

1 *In:*   *In January, In 1968, In the morning/afternoon/evening*
   On: *On Thursday*
   At: *At six o'clock, At night, At midday/midnight*

2 *For:*   *I lived there for ten years.* (for a period of time)
   Since: *I have lived here since 1986.* (since a point in time)
   Ago: *Edward died two years ago.* (how long ago in the past)

3 *By:*   *I'll be home by 6.00.* (not later than 6.00)

4 *At last:*   *At last you have arrived!* (expressing relief)
   In the end: *We waited for ages, and in the end/finally we left.*
   At the end: *I left at the end of the film.*

5 *On time:* *Bill is never late, he's always on time.* (not late)
   In time: *Luckily the police arrived in time to help.* (early enough)

Activities

1
Choose the most suitable word or phrase underlined.

a) I haven't seen Jim before/since we worked together in London.
b) I'll finish the letter now and you can post it after/later.
c) What were you doing last evening/yesterday evening when I called?
d) Did you live here in/since 1987?
e) Diana hasn't finished her course already/yet.
f) What do you usually do in the afternoon/this afternoon?
g) Have you seen Jean and Chris nowadays/recently?
h) Helen arrived here at Thursday night/on Thursday night.
i) It's really ages since/when I saw you last.
j) Ann is going to be famous once/one day.

2
Put *one* word in each space.

a) Graham came to see us over a week ago, the Friday before ..last......
b) Is it very warm here .... the winter?
c) No thanks, I've had some tea ....
d) Don't worry, it won't hurt and I'll .... be finished.
e) I liked the book. I didn't know what was going to happen ....
f) I think that people had much more spare time in the ....
g) This is very urgent. Please send it at ....

75

h) Harry isn't here. He left about five minutes ....
i) The film doesn't start until 7.30. We're half an hour ....
j) Would you mind waiting for .... a moment, please?

3

Complete each
sentence with a
word or phrase
from the list. Use
each word or
phrase once only.

| afterwards | eventually | in the end | nowadays | soon |
| early | immediately | lately | once | yet |

a) There is far too much traffic on the roads ..*nowadays*..... .
b) Never mind. I'm sure we'll find what we are looking for ....
c) I haven't seen you for ages. What have you been doing .... ?
d) Jack hasn't left. He hasn't finished his work ....
e) Take some notes in the meeting, and we'll discuss them ....
f) If you don't mind waiting, Brenda will be back ....
g) I considered taking a new job, but decided against it ....
h) Norman and I worked for the same company ....
i) You didn't fool me! I recognised you ....
j) You can get more work done if you get up ....

4

Put **one** word in
each space.

a) You will receive your salary .*at/before*.. the end of the month.
b) I feel really tired. I think I'll go to bed early ....
c) The weather has been terrible so far .... month.
d) I'll see what David says, and .... I'll come back and tell you.
e) I'm a bit busy .... , but I can talk to you later.
f) If you haven't finished .... , don't worry.
g) Are you doing anything .... Friday evening?
h) Where's Brian? He should be here .... now.
i) We cannot accept applications sent .... the closing date.
j) .... upon a time, there were three bears.

5

Complete each
sentence with the
most suitable
word or phrase.

a) Jean bought an expensive watch, but regretted it ..*B*... .
    A at the end   B) later   C) then   D) after
b) Lunch will be ready .... the time you get back.
    A) at   B) during   C) in   D) by
c) I haven't been feeling well ...., doctor.
    A) recently   B) afterwards   C) suddenly   D) at last
d) Long ......, the valley you can see was actually a lake.
    A) past   B) ago   C) since   D) before

e) We ran into the station and caught the train .... in time.
   A) right   B) just   C) early   D) already

f) I haven't had a Chinese meal for ....
   A) long   B) it's ages   C) years   D) the summer

g) I've cleaned all the parts, but the motor .... doesn't work.
   A) at last   B) now   C) always   D) still

h) .... you get used to the job, it won't seem so bad.
   A) since   B) while   C) once   D) as

i) I haven't .... decided where to go on holiday.
   A) yet   B) already   C) still   D) just

j) The first time I noticed something wrong was ...... I got home.
   A) since   B) when   C) for   D) until

6

Complete each sentence with one of the words or phrases from the list. Use each phrase once only.

| all night long   from time to time   one at a time |
| all the time   in a few moments   over and over again |
| all the year round   in the nick of time   the other day |
| for hours on end   once and for all   this time next week |

a) Don't carry the boxes all together. We'll move them ..*one at a time*......... .

b) I've told you .... , don't leave your bag here!

c) It's time you stopped biting your nails ....

d) Sheila grabbed Bill .... before he could fall in the water.

e) Hurry up! The bomb will go off ....

f) We shouldn't have trusted Michael. He was lying ....

g) Gerry sits staring at the television ....

h) .... I'll be lying on the beach, not working in the office!

i) The swimming pool on the common is open ....

j) I met your friend Janet in the pub ....

k) Dave isn't a keen fisherman, but he goes fishing ....

l) The party finished at dawn after we had danced ....

7

Replace the word or phrase in italics with one of the words or phrases given, so that the meaning stays the same.

a) The weather was bad at first, but it cleared up *in the end*. ..B.....
   A) at last   B) eventually   C) lately

b) Jane was leading the race, but *all at once* she fell over. ....
   A) suddenly   B) one by one   C) after that

c) Have you been swimming *recently*? ....
   A) lately   B) already   C) yet

d) I enjoy going skiing *every now and again*. ....
   A) frequently   B) immediately   C) occasionally

e) I saw Terry in the street *the other day*. ....
   A) recently   B) yesterday   C) last night

f) I think we've solved this problem *once and for all*. ....
   A) in the end   B) for ever   C) temporarily

g) Kath told Martin that she was leaving *for good*. ....
   A) for ever   B) for a while   C) early

h) We arrived for the train *in good time*. ....
   A) on time   B) at the right moment   C) with time to spare

i) I believe we met *on a previous occasion*. ....
   A) once before   B) the last time   C) completely by chance

j) The political situation seems to be changing *minute by minute*. ....
   A) from time to time   B) time after time   C) very rapidly

KEY POINTS

1 Some time expressions are connected with particular tenses. (See Units 1 to 5.)

   *Claire **arrived** an hour ago.*
   *I've **been living** here **since 1977.***
   *John **worked** there **for two years.***
   *Sally **has been studying** French **for six months.***
   *I **haven't been** to the theatre **for ages.***
   *Terry **will have left** by then.*

2 *For* can sometimes be left out.
   *Sandra **waited three hours** in freezing weather.*

> **SEE ALSO**
>
> **Units 1 to 5**
> (Tenses)
> **Unit 15**
> Progress test

Unit 15 Progress test

(Units 11, 12, 13, 14)

1

Put **one** suitable word in each space.

An old school friend

When John saw the large crowd (1) .... had gathered (2) .... the street, he wasn't sure (3) .... first what had happened. There were (4) .... many people blocking the way into the hotel, that he had to push his way (5) .... them to get (6) .... the door. At the door he found two policemen (7) .... were trying to hold the crowd back. 'What (8) .... earth is going on?' he asked them. Then John noticed that some of the crowd were holding placards (9) .... read: 'We love you Sally.' (10).......... course, that was it. Sally Good was a footballer, the first woman to play for England. (11) .... John wasn't really interested in sport he decided to join the crowd and wait (12) .... she appeared. About ten minutes (13) .... , a smiling woman appeared and waved to the crowd. John was taken completely (14) .... surprise when she took his arm and said, 'Remember me? I'm the girl (15) .... used to sit next to you at school.'

2

Put **one** word in each space.

a) ...... the time you've done the shopping, I'll be ready.
b) I'm going home now, but I'll phone you ....
c) Harry has been working very hard ....
d) I'll write to you ...... the end of the week.
e) I waited for you .... 6.00, but then I left.
f) Peter sometimes goes walking .... hours.
g) I won't be long. I'll be ready .... a moment.
h) .... upon a time, there was a beautiful princess.
i) Guess who I saw the .... day? My old English teacher!
j) I'm not a regular swimmer but I go .... and again.

3

Put **one** suitable word in each space.

a) This is the book I told you ....
b) There's someone outside .... car has broken down.
c) Sue won the gold medal .... having a bad leg.
d) I suppose I agree with you .... a great extent.
e) The police, from .... I learned nothing, are being secretive.
f) Excuse me, but your bicycle is .... my way.
g) She bought me a present, ... I told her not to bother.
h) Tony knows most of Shakespeare .... heart.
i) The letter was addressed: 'To .... it may concern.'
j) There are no letters today. The post office is .... strike.

4

Rewrite each sentence so that it contains the word given in capitals, and so that the meaning stays the same.

a) I bought my car from that man.   WHOM
....

b) That boy's sister sits behind me at school.   WHOSE
....

c) Bill's typewriter had broken and he had to use a pencil.   WHOSE
....

d) The girls were hungry and decided to have a meal.   WHO
....

e) I live in Croydon – it's near London.   WHICH
....

f) Did you borrow this book?   THAT
....

g) This is Brenda – she lives upstairs.   WHO
....

h) You gave me a very useful present.   WHICH
....

i) The car was in good condition and wasn't expensive.   WHICH
....

j) Someone found the money and was given a reward.   WHO
....

5

Put **one** preposition in each space.

a) The plane landed .... Athens Airport, which is .... the sea.

b) He was cold .... bed so his mother put a blanket .... him.

c) I'm not ..... favour of nuclear power in ...... of accidents.

d) When Peter sheltered ...... a tree an apple fell ...... his head.

e) Sorry, I'm ...... a hurry. Come with me, we can talk ..... the way.

f) Quite .... chance I noticed that the house was ...... sale.

g) Can we discuss this ...... private? Alone, ... other words.

h) I went to Naples .... business, but not .... myself.

i) If you're .... difficulties with money, I'll help you ..... all means.

j) Hearing she was ...... of work took me .... surprise.

6

Complete the second sentence so that it has a similar meaning to the first sentence, using the word given. You must use between two and five words.

a) We were in Venice a week ago today.
   time
   We were in Venice .... week.

b) Joe had financial problems, but bought a new motorbike.
   despite
   Joe bought a new motorbike .... financial problems.

c) I couldn't drink the soup, as it was too hot.
   to
   The soup .... drink.

d) Susan was tired, so she decided to go to bed.
   that
   Susan was .... decided to go to bed.

e) We spoke in whispers as we didn't want to wake the baby.

not

We spoke in whispers .... to wake the baby.

f) I kept looking for my missing watch, but I knew it was no use.

even

I kept looking for my missing watch .... it was no use.

g) There were a lot of people, and I couldn't see the screen properly.

that

There were .... I couldn't see the screen properly.

h) The weather is fine, but my flowers haven't come out.

of

My flowers haven't come out .... weather.

i) It was a cold night, so we stayed indoors.

that

It was...we stayed indoors.

j) The swimming pool wasn't deep, so you couldn't dive into it.

to

The swimming pool .... dive into.

7

Decide which answer A, B, C or D best fits each space.

Arriving in Bluffville

Stephen arrived in Bluffville (1) .... the early evening, and walked (2) ....
the bus station through the town centre, looking for somewhere to stay. There
was a huge old-fashioned hotel, (3) .... it was obviously closed. The windows
(4) .... street level were covered (5) .... sheets of corrugated iron. (6) ....
there must have been many travellers passing (7) .... Bluffville, but now the
motorway (8) .... the south passed the town several miles (9) .... , and so
very few people stopped. Stephen found a telephone (10) .... a run-down bar,
and called the nearest motel (11) .... turned out to be seven miles away on the
motorway. He asked the barman, (12) .... was reading a comic book, how
(13) .... a taxi would cost to take him (14) .... the motel. The man stared
hard at Stephen (15) .... he said, 'No taxis here – haven't been any for more
than ten years.'

1) A) at   B) in   C) after   D) and
2) A) down   B) with   C) from   D) away
3) A) though   B) which   C) that   D) despite
4) A) at   B) the   C) under   D) across
5) A) and   B) with   C) from   D) up
6) A) over   B) so   C) soon   D) once
7) A) out   B) into   C) through   D) from
8) A) in   B) of   C) by   D) to
9) A) away   B) out   C) far   D) long
10) A) and   B) which   C) in   D) box
11) A) it   B) which   C) who   D) this

81

12) A) although   B) why   C) he   D) who
13) A) far   B) much   C) many   D) often
14) A) to   B) in   C) at   D) out
15) A) who   B) since   C) before   D) eventually

8

Look carefully at each line. Some lines are correct, but some have a word which should not be there. Tick each correct line. If a line has a word which should not be there, write the word in the space.

The Electronic Age

I recently learned how to use a computer, and	...✓.......
I have many friends who they play computer games	.they...
at home. However, although recently I have begun to worry	1) ....
that in nowadays we rely too much on electronic gadgets.	2) ....
Once before people managed to write and think using	3) ....
their brains, but now many people have become so	4) ....
accustomed to using machines, so that they can't do	5) ....
anything without them. There are many people who	6) ....
they depend on electronic gadgets completely. For	7) ....
an instance, many of my friends sit at home in the	8) ....
evening and watch television, and instead of going	9) ....
out so to meet people. I think that this makes everyone	10) ....
feel more lonely, even though they learn a lot about	11) ....
people all over in the world. Of course there are many	12) ....
electronic gadgets that save us time, though not all	13) ....
of them are really necessary. I am in favour of some	14) ....
gadgets, but I am against of having everything in life	15) ....
depending on pushing a button.	

Unit 16 Modal auxiliaries, present and future: ability, certainty, obligation

Explanations

Ability

Can and *be able to*
Be able to is used in situations where *can* does not have the necessary grammatical form.
> *I'd like **to be able to swim**. **Not being able to swim** is annoying.*

Certainty and uncertainty

1 *Must* and *can't*
These are used to make deductions, when we are more or less certain about something, especially with the verb *to be*.
> *You **must be** tired after your journey.*   (I suppose you are)
> *That **can't be** Sue. She's in Brazil.*   (I'm sure it's impossible)

2 *May, might* and *could*
These all express uncertainty or possibility. They are usually stressed in speech. *Might* is less likely than *may*. *Could* is not used with *not* in this context.
> *It **may** not rain. I **might** go out, I don't know. I **could** get wet!*

3 *Be bound to*
This refers to the future, whereas *must* refers to the present.
> *You're **bound to see** Paula if you go there.*   (I'm sure you will)
> *You **must see** Paula if you go there.*   (An obligation)

Obligation

1 *Must* and *have to*
Have to describes obligations made by someone else, while *must* is used to describe a personal obligation. There may be no difference.
> *You **must start** working harder!*   (I say so)
> *You **have to turn** left here.*   (It's the law)
> *Sorry, I **must leave/have to leave** now.*   (No difference)

2 *Mustn't* and *don't have to*
Mustn't describes something which is not allowed. *Don't have to* describes something which is not necessary.
> *You **mustn't leave** any bags here.*   (It's against the rules)
> *You **don't have to apply** yet.*   (It's not necessary)

3 *Should* and *ought to*
These have the same meaning. They describe 'what is a good idea' and can be used to give advice, or polite instructions.
> *I think you **should see** a doctor*   *You **ought not to continue**.*
> *You **should send in** your application by July 18th.*

4 *Should* as expectation
Should can also describe actions we expect to happen.
> *Brenda **should be** home by now.*   (She is expected to be)

5 *Had better*
This refers to present or future time, and gives advice about how to stop something going wrong.
> *I think you**'d better leave** now.*   (Before it is too late)
> *You**'d better not drive**.*   (It might be dangerous)

6 *Is/Are to*
This is used in formal instructions. *Not* is stressed.
> *No-one **is to leave** the room.*   *You **are not to leave** the room.*

Activities

1

Choose the most suitable word or phrase underlined.

a) There's someone at the door. It <u>can be/must be</u> the postman.
b) Don't worry, you <u>don't have to/mustn't</u> pay now.
c) I think you <u>had better/would better</u> take a pullover with you.
d) Jones <u>could be/must be</u> president if Smith has to resign.
e) Sorry, I can't stay any longer. I <u>have to go/might go</u>.
f) It was 5 o'clock an hour ago. Your watch <u>can't be/mustn't be</u> right.
g) It's a school rule, all the pupils <u>have to wear/must wear</u> a uniform.
h) I suppose that our team <u>must win/should win</u>, but I'm not sure.
i) Let's tell Diana. She <u>could not/might not</u> know.
j) In my opinion, the government <u>might do/should do</u> something about this.

2

Complete the second sentence so that it has a similar meaning to the first sentence, using the word given. Use between two and five words.

a) I think you should give up smoking immediately.
had
I think you ..*had better give up*............................... smoking immediately.

b) I expect we will get there by 5.00, if there isn't too much traffic.
   should
   We .... 5.00, if there isn't too much traffic.

c) Is it necessary for me to bring my passport?
   have
   Do .... my passport?

d) I am sure that the cat is in the house somewhere.
   be
   The cat .... in the house somewhere.

e) An aerial is not required with this radio.
   have
   You don't .... an aerial with this radio.

f) It is very inconvenient if you can't drive.
   to
   It's very inconvenient if .... drive.

g) I am sure that John is not the thief.
   be
   John .... the thief.

h) I am certain that Norman will be late.
   bound
   Norman .... late.

i) All students should report to the main hall at 9.00.
   are
   All students .... to the main hall at 9.00.

j) I thought that you would know better!
   ought
   You .... better!

3
Choose the most
suitable word or
phrase
underlined.

a) We can't be lost. It isn't allowed/I don't believe it.
b) Jane is bound to be late. She always is/She must be.
c) Late-comers are to report to the main office. It's a good idea/It's the rule.
d) You don't have to stay unless it's necessary/if you don't want to.
e) Astronauts must feel afraid sometimes. They're supposed to/It's only natural.
f) You can't come in here. It isn't allowed/I don't believe it.
g) All motorcyclists have to wear crash helmets. It's a good idea/It's the rule.
h) I ought not to tell Jack. It's not a good idea/It's the rule.
i) We should be there soon. I expect so/It's absolutely certain.
j) You'd better leave now. That's my advice/That's an order!

4
Complete each sentence so that it contains *might*, *might not*, *must*, *mustn't*, *can* or *can't*. More than one answer may be possible.

a) Don't stand up in the boat! You ..*might*....... fall in the river!
b) Sue says she's stuck in the traffic and she .... be late.
c) You really .... start spending more time on your work.
d) Tell Peter he .... stay the night here if he wants to.
e) That's a really stupid idea! You .... be serious, surely!
f) You .... realise it, but this is very important to me.
g) Don't be silly. You .... expect me to believe you!
h) We're not sure but we .... go to Prague for Christmas this year.
i) Me learn to fly! You .... be joking!
j) Bill cooked the lunch, so you .... expect anything special!

5
Rewrite each sentence so that it contains *can, could, must, have to* or *should* (including negative forms).

a) I'm sure that Helen feels really lonely.
...*Helen must feel really lonely.*...........................
b) You're not allowed to park here.
....
c) It would be a good idea if Harry took a holiday.
....
d) I'm sure that Brenda isn't over thirty.
....
e) Do I need a different driving licence for a motorbike?
....
f) What would you advise me to do?
....
g) Mary knows how to stand on her head.
....
h) You needn't come with me if you don't want to.
....
i) It's possible for anyone to break into this house!
....
j) The dentist will see you soon. I don't think he'll be long.
....

6
Choose the most suitable caption for each picture.

a)

b)

a)
1) He should be exhausted!
2) He must be exhausted!

b)
1) We mustn't pay to go in.
2) We don't have to pay to go in.

c)

1) I'm afraid we have to operate.
2) I'm afraid we should operate.

d)

1) Mind out, you could drop it!
2) Mind out! You can drop it!

e)

1) Thanks, but I'd better not!
2) I don't have to, thanks.

f)

1) We must be here for hours!
2) We're bound to be here for hours!

KEY POINTS

1 Most modal auxiliaries have more than one meaning. You may have to think carefully about the context, or tone of voice, to understand the meaning.

2 The negative forms *mustn't* and *don't have to* have different meanings.
   You **mustn't** go. (It is against the rules)
   You **don't have to** go. (It isn't necessary)

3 *Should* is a weaker obligation than *must* and *have to*, but is used as a polite way of expressing an obligation, in formal speech or in writing.
   *Passengers for Gatwick Airport **should** change at Reading.*

SEE ALSO
Unit 17 Modal auxiliaries: past **Unit 20** Progress test

Unit 17 Modal auxiliaries, past: ability, certainty, obligation

Explanations

Past ability

1 *Could*
   Could describes past ability.
   > *When I was young, I **could run** very fast.*

2 *Could* and *was able to*
   Was able to describes the ability to successfully complete an action.
   > *Mary **was able to help** us.*   (She actually helped us)
   > *Mary **could help** us.*   (But perhaps she didn't)

Certainty and uncertainty

1 *Must have* and *can't have*
   These are used to make deductions about past actions. The *have* form does not change.
   > *I **must have left** my wallet in the car.*   (I am sure I did)
   > *Jim **can't have noticed** you.*   (I am sure he didn't)

2 *May have*, *might have* and *could have*
   These express possibility or uncertainty about past actions. The *have* form does not change.
   > *Jean **might have missed** the train.*   (Perhaps she did)
   > *He **may not have received** the letter.*   (Perhaps he didn't)
   > *You **could have been killed**!*   (It was a possibility)

3 *Was/Were to have*
   This describes something which was supposed to happen, but didn't. It is formal in use. The *have* form does not change.
   > *He **was to have left** yesterday.*   (He was supposed to leave, but he didn't)

Obligation

1 *Had to*
   Had to is generally used as the past form of *must*.
   > *Sorry I'm late, I **had to take** the children to school.*
   The question form is *Did you have to?*
   > ***Did you have to work** late yesterday?*

2 *Should have* and *ought to have*

These express the speaker's feeling that a mistake was made. The *have* form does not change.

> *You **should have posted** the letter yesterday.* (You made a mistake)
>
> *You **shouldn't have told** me the answer.* (You were wrong)

3 *Needn't have* and *didn't need to*

Needn't have describes an action which happened, but was unnecessary. The *have* form does not change.

> *I **needn't have bought** more sugar.* (I did, but we had enough)
>
> *I **didn't need to buy** more sugar.* (I didn't, because we had enough)

Pronunciation and writing

Have is unstressed or weakly stressed in the past infinitive forms on this page, and cannot be abbreviated in writing.

Indirect speech

Must, shall and *should*

Must is reported as *had to* or *must. Shall* with future reference is reported as *would.* Other uses of *shall* are reported as *should.*

> *'You must go.'* *He told me I **had to go**. He told me **I must go.***
>
> *'I shall be there.'* *He told us he **would be** there.*
>
> *'Shall I help?'* *He asked if he **should help**.*

Activities

1

Choose the most suitable response to each comment or question.

a) A. What did I do wrong?
   B. ① You shouldn't have connected these two wires.
      2) You didn't have to connect these two wires.
b) A. Why is the dog barking?
   B. 1) It should have heard something.
      2) It must have heard something.
c) A. Why are you home so early?
   B. 1) I needn't have worked this afternoon.
      2) I didn't have to work this afternoon.

d) A. Why did you worry about me? I didn't take any risks.
   B. 1) You must have been injured.
      2) You could have been injured.
e) A. You forgot my birthday again!
   B. 1) Sorry, I should have looked in my diary.
      2) Sorry, I had to look in my diary.
f) A. We had a terrible crossing on the boat in a storm.
   B. 1) That didn't have to be very pleasant!
      2) That can't have been very pleasant!
g) A. Where were you yesterday? You didn't turn up!
   B. 1) I had to go to London.
      2) I must have gone to London.
h) A. What do you think about the election?
   B. 1) The Freedom Party had to win.
      2) The Freedom Party should have won.
i) A. There's a lot of food left over from the party, isn't there?
   B. 1) Yes, you couldn't have made so many sandwiches.
      2) Yes, you needn't have made so many sandwiches.
j) A. What do you think has happened to Tony?
   B. 1) I don't know, he should have got lost.
      2) I don't know, he might have got lost.

2

Complete the second sentence so that it has a similar meaning to the first sentence, using the word given. Do not change the word given. You must use between two and five words.

a) It wasn't necessary for me to go out after all.
   have
   I ...*needn't have gone out*... after all.
b) There was a plan for Jack to become manager, but he left.
   was
   Jack .... manager, but he left.
c) It was a mistake for you to buy that car.
   bought
   You .... that car.
d) I don't think that Sally enjoyed her holiday.
   have
   Sally .... enjoyed her holiday.
e) It's possible that Bill saw me.
   may
   Bill .... me.
f) I'm sure that Karen was a beautiful baby.
   been
   Karen .... a beautiful baby.
g) Perhaps Alan didn't mean what he said.
   meant
   Alan .... what he said.

h) It's possible that I left my wallet at home.
   could
   I .... my wallet at home.

i) I think you were wrong to sell your bike.
   shouldn't
   You .... bike.

j) The only thing I could do was run away!
   had
   I .... run away!

3
Choose the most suitable phrase underlined.

a) We should have turned left. (We've missed the turning)/We followed the instructions.

b) We didn't have to wear uniform at school. But I never did/That's why I liked it.

c) The butler must have stolen the jewels. He was ordered to/There is no other explanation.

d) You could have phoned from the station. I'm sure you did/Why didn't you?

e) You needn't have bought any dog food. There isn't any/There is plenty.

f) Ann might not have understood the message. I suppose it's possible/She wasn't supposed to.

g) You can't have spent all the money already! You weren't able to/I'm sure you haven't.

h) I shouldn't have used this kind of paint. It's the right kind/It's the wrong kind.

4
Rewrite each sentence so that it contains *can't, might, must, should* or *needn't*.

a) I'm sure that David took your books by mistake.
   ..David must have taken your books by mistake...............................

b) It was a mistake to park outside the police station.
   ....

c) It was unnecessary for you to clean the floor.
   ....

d) I'm sure that Liz hasn't met Harry before.
   ....

e) Ann possibly hasn't left yet.
   ....

f) I'm sure they haven't eaten all the food. It's not possible!
   ....

g) Jack is supposed to have arrived half an hour ago.
   ....

h) Perhaps Pam and Tim decided not to come.
   ....

i) I think it was the cat that took the fish from the table!
   ....

j) It was a waste of time worrying, after all!
   ....

5
Choose the most
suitable caption
for each
picture.

a)

1) You must have read the notice.
2) You should have read the notice.

b)

1) We can't have worn our raincoats.
2) We needn't have worn our raincoats.

c)

1) He must have hit him in the right spot!
2) He should have hit him in the right spot!

d)

1) You must have caused an accident!
2) You might have caused an accident!

e)

1) Sorry, I had to go to the dentist's.
2) Sorry, I should have gone to the dentist's.

f)

1) You shouldn't have stroked the lion!
2) You didn't have to stroke the lion!

6

Look carefully at each line. Some lines are correct, but some have a word which should not be there. Tick each correct line. If a line has a word which should not be there, write the word in the space.

Zoo Escape Shocks Residents

Residents in the Blackwood area complained last	...✓......
night that they should have had been warned about	..had.....
the escape of a dangerous snake. The snake, a python,	1) ....
is three metres long, and can to kill pets. 'I heard	2) ....
about it on the radio,' said Mrs Agnes Bird. 'I had gone	3) ....
to lock my dog in the kitchen this morning, because	4) ....
I thought the snake could easily have attack it. Now	5) ....
I am not sure what I ought to be do.' The snake, called	6) ....
Lulu, disappeared from Blackwood Zoo. 'It must be	7) ....
have found a hole in the wall, or it might have been	8) ....
slipped out while the door was open,' said zoo director	9) ....
Basil Hart. Mr Hart said that people didn't needn't have	10) ....
been alarmed. 'A local radio station must have had	11) ....
mixed up its reports,' he went on. 'We found Lulu a	12) ....
few minutes after we missed her. We have had to climb	13) ....
a tree and bring her down. So you see, you should have	14) ....
never believe silly stories you hear on the radio!	15) ....

KEY POINTS

1   There is a difference between *didn't have to do* and *needn't have done.*
      *I **didn't have to** pay.* (I didn't pay)
      *I **needn't have** paid.* (I paid but it was unnecessary)

2   *Have* is unstressed in past infinitive forms.
      You shouldn't have done it.

3   *Have* in past infinitive forms cannot be abbreviated in writing.

> **Unit 20**
> Progress test

Unit 18 Language functions 1

Explanations

1   What are functions?
Language is usually divided up into the parts of its grammatical system. It is also possible to describe language according to what it is used for.

If I were you, I'd leave now.   Conditional 2 (Grammatical)
If I were you, I'd leave now.   Giving Advice (Function)

2   How do we choose what to say?
What we say can be influenced by the situation we are in, by the person we are talking to, and by what we are talking about.
Asking Permission - from a friend:
Is it all right if I use the phone?
Asking Permission - from the same person, but a more serious topic:
Do you think I could possibly phone Australia?
Asking Permission - from a stranger:
Do you mind if I open the window?
What we say can depend on whether we want to be polite or not, or on how we feel. Although there are no exact rules about what we should say in any situation, there are *polite* ways of speaking which are generally used when we talk to strangers, to people who have higher status, and when we are talking about sensitive topics.

3   This unit practises the following functions. (Others are practised in Unit 19.)
The responses made are also included.
There may be other ways of expressing these functions which are not included in the activities.

Asking for and giving advice
Agreeing and disagreeing
Apologising
Complaining
Ending a conversation
Asking for and giving directions
Greeting
Asking how someone is
Asking for information
Introducing yourself and other people
Inviting
Accepting and declining invitations
Offering something
Offering to do something

Activities

1

Match each sentence a) to j) with a functional label from 1) to 10).

a) That's very kind of you, I'd love to.   ..4..

b) Well, it's been nice talking to you, but I'm afraid I have to go.   ....

c) Could you tell me how to get to the post office?   ....

d) You might have told me you were having a party!   ....

e) Shall I carry this bag for you?   ....

f) What do you think I should do?   ....

g) Actually, I don't think that's right.   ....

h) Would you like to come round for a drink later?   ....

i) Jack, this is my brother, Mark.   ....

j) Could you tell me what time the bank opens?   ....

1) Complaining.

2) Inviting.

3) Asking for information.

4) Accepting an invitation.

5) Asking for advice.

6) Asking for directions.

7) Introducing other people.

8) Offering to do something.

9) Disagreeing.

10) Ending a conversation.

2

Match each sentence a) to j) with a functional label from 1) to 10).

a) Would you like some more tea? ...6.....

b) I think you'd better phone the police. ....

c) I'd love to come, but I'm already going out that evening. ....

d) Good morning, I'm Brenda Watson, the Marketing Manager. ....

e) I'm sorry I'm late – it won't happen again. ....

f) Would you like me to do the washing up? ....

g) Excuse me, but is the bus station anywhere near here? ....

h) Hi, Sally, how are you? ....

i) I think that's the point exactly. ....

j) It's at the end of this street, opposite the church. ....

       1) Declining an invitation.
       2) Introducing yourself.
       3) Greeting a friend
       4) Offering to do something.
       5) Asking for directions.
       6) Offering something.
       7) Agreeing.
       8) Apologising.
       9) Giving directions.
     10) Giving advice.

3

Choose the most suitable response.

a) Do you feel like going to the cinema this evening?
   ① That would be great.
   2) Thank you very much for your kind invitation.

b) I'm awfully sorry about your carpet. You must let me pay to have it cleaned.
   1) Don't worry, it's all right.
   2) Forget it.

c) More coffee anybody?
   1) Would it be all right if I had some more?
   2) I'd love some.

d) Excuse me, but is it far from here to Anglesham?
   1) Just keep going along this road.
   2) Yes, it is.

e) I wish you wouldn't smoke in here!
   1) I don't agree, I'm afraid.
   2) Sorry, shall I open the window?

f) Well, it was nice talking to you, but I have to dash.
   1) Yes, I enjoyed talking to you too.
   2) OK, see you.

g) Could you tell me whether this train stops at Hatfield?
   1) I believe I could.
   2) I believe it does.

h) Shall I collect the tickets for you?
   1) That would be a real help.
   2) Yes, I think you shall.

i) What would you do in my situation?
   1) I think you should ask for a loan from the bank.
   2) I thought you would ask for a loan from the bank.

j) How do you do. I'm Bill Thompson.
   1) Very well thank you.
   2) How do you do.

4
Complete the
second sentence
so that it has a
similar meaning
to the first
sentence, using
the word given.
Do not change
the word given.
You must use
between two and
five words.

a) Can I offer you a lift home?
like
Would ..*you like a lift*... home?

b) What time does the next train leave?
tell
Could .... the next train leaves?

c) I think you should sell the car.
I'd
If I .... the car.

d) Shall I mow the lawn?
to
Would .... mow the lawn?

e) Am I going the right way for Downwood?
this
Is .... Downwood?

f) Do you have to make so much noise!
wouldn't
I .... so much noise!

g) What's your advice?
should
What do .... do?

h) Let's go for a pizza.
going
How .... a pizza?

i) I'm sorry, I'm to blame.
my
I'm sorry, ... fault.

j) I advise you not to go.
think
I don't .... go.

KEY POINTS

1 What we say depends on the situation, our relationship with the person we
are talking to, and what we are talking about.

2 Giving an appropriate response depends on judging how someone is talking
to us. People may not respond fully if we do not use polite forms.

SEE ALSO

Unit 20
Progress test

Unit 19 Language functions 2

Explanations

This unit practises the following functions. (Others are practised in Unit 18.)
The responses are also included.
There may be other ways of expressing these functions which are not included
in the activities.

    Things to say on special occasions or at special moments
    Asking for and giving an opinion
    Pausing to think
    Asking for permission
    Giving and refusing permission
    Expressing preferences
    Promising
    Reassuring
    Recommending
    Refusing to do something
    Making and responding to a request
    Suggesting
    Thanking

Activities

1

Match each
sentence a) to j)
with a functional
label from 1) to
10).

a) Wait a minute, let me see.   ..5....
b) What did you think of the film, then?   ....
c) I'll definitely bring your camera back tomorrow.   ....
d) Would it be all right if I left a bit early today?   ....
e) Sorry, no, I won't do it.   ....
f) Could you possibly turn on the air conditioning?   ....
g) I think I'd rather have fish, actually.   ....
h) Why don't we have a party next weekend?   ....
i) That's very kind of you, I appreciate it.   ....
j) Don't worry, everything will turn out all right.   ....

1) Promising.
2) Refusing.
3) Suggesting.
4) Expressing a preference.
5) Pausing to think.
6) Making a request.
7) Thanking.

8) Asking for an opinion.
9) Reassuring.
10) Asking permission.

2

Match each
sentence a) to j)
with an
explanation from
1) to 10).

a) Congratulations!   ...4...
b) Look out!   ....
c) Oh bother!   ....
d) Whoops!   ....
e) Well done!   ....
f) Excuse me!   ....
g) Pardon?   ....
h) Bless you!   ....
i) Cheers!   ....
j) You poor thing!   ....

1) Praising someone's performance.
2) Expressing annoyance.
3) Wishing someone good health when drinking.
4) Expressing happiness at someone's success.
5) Attracting attention or asking someone to move out of your way.
6) Expressing sympathy.
7) Expressing that something has/has nearly gone wrong.
8) Giving a warning.
9) Showing that you have misheard or misunderstood.
10) Said when another person sneezes.

3

Choose the most
suitable
response.

a) What do you think of my new car?
   ① It's all right I suppose.
   2) I think a lot.
b) Do you promise to pay me back at the end of the month?
   1) I'll pay.
   2) I promise.
c) Can I use your phone?
   1) You may not.
   2) Of course.
d) Where do you suggest I stay?
   1) I recommend the Hilton.
   2) Let's stay at the Hilton.

e) Do you want beer or wine?
   1) I'd prefer beer, please.
   2) I'd rather beer, please.

f) I can't stop worrying about my exam tomorrow.
   1) That's all right, never mind.
   2) I'm sure you'll do well.

g) Janet, make us some tea, will you?
   1) No I won't, I'm afraid.
   2) I can't, I'm afraid.

h) Would you mind moving your bag from the seat?
   1) Oh, sorry.
   2) No, I wouldn't.

i) How kind, you really shouldn't have bothered.
   1) It was nothing, really.
   2) Don't worry, I didn't bother.

j) Is it all right if I use your bike?
   1) Please accept it with my best wishes.
   2) Sure, go ahead.

4

Complete the second sentence so that it has a similar meaning to the first sentence, using the word given. Do not change the word given. You must use between two and five words.

a) What's your opinion of Roger's new book?
   think
   What do ..*you think of*.................................... Roger's new book?

b) Thank you very much for your help.
   am
   I .... for your help.

c) May I leave my bag here?
   if
   Is it .... leave my bag here?

d) Let's go to the beach tomorrow.
   we
   Why .... to the beach tomorrow?

e) I like going sailing more than going swimming.
   rather
   I'd .... swimming.

f) Could you open the window?
   think
   Do .... the window?

g) Is it all right if you take care of the children?
   mind
   Do .... care of the children?

h) I recommend going by train.
   go
   I think you .... by train.

i) Excuse me, I can't get past you!
in
Excuse me, you .... way.

j) 'You've passed your driving test, Ron! Well done!' said Carol.
on
Carol congratulated .... driving test.

5

Look carefully at each line. Some lines are correct, but some have a word which should not be there. Tick each correct line. If a line has a word which should not be there, write the word in the space.

Say One Thing, Mean Another

Do you ever get annoyed by people who say one	...✓.......
thing but mean another? For example, they say you,	..you......
'That's a very kind of you, I'd love to' when you	1) ....
are invite them to the cinema, but really they	2) ....
are thinking of an excuse so they can avoid you!	3) ....
People who ask for an advice also annoy me. They	4) ....
say things like 'What do you think I should do?'	5) ....
but then they don't listen to what you tell with them.	6) ....
Sometimes they don't even let you answer, but	7) ....
answer themselves! This really gets on to my nerves.	8) ....
Politeness is also a problem. When people ask to you	9) ....
to open a window, they say 'Excuse me, but it could	10) ....
you possibly open the window for me?' I prefer to	11) ....
be more direct. Why shouldn't we just ever say	12) ....
'Can you to open the window?' or something like that?	13) ....
I've tried this a few times, but people either look	14) ....
annoyed, or they don't do it what I ask them to. I	15) ....
wonder why?	

KEY POINTS

1 What we say depends on the situation, our relationship with the person we are talking to, and what we are talking about.

2 Giving an appropriate response depends on judging how someone is talking to us. People may not respond fully if we do not use polite forms.

SEE ALSO

Unit 20
Progress test

Unit 20 Progress test

(Units 16, 17, 18, 19)

1
Put **one** suitable word in each space.

Asking for directions

Have you ever tried asking people for directions? I (1) .... to go to London on business recently, and I soon realised that I (2) .... have bought a street map. Whenever I followed the directions of passers-by, I got lost. 'You can't (3) .... it,' they would say. 'Carry straight (4) ...., it's opposite the bank.' After walking for half an hour, I would realise that I (5) .... have gone wrong somewhere. '(6) .... you tell me where the bank (7) ...., please?' I would ask someone. I (8) .... to have known that this was a mistake. 'Which bank do you mean? I think you (9) .... go back to the station...' I now see that I (10) .... have taken a taxi. After all, London taxi drivers (11) .... to pass a test on their knowledge of its streets. But of course, whenever I thought of this, I (12) .... not find a taxi. In the end I found a solution. I went up to the first tourists I saw and asked if I (13) .... look at their tourist map. They turned out to be from Scotland, and they (14) .... me very detailed directions. The only problem was that I wasn't (15) .... to understand exactly what they said.

2
Complete the second sentence so that it has a similar meaning to the first sentence, using the word given. Do not change the word given. You must use between two and five words.

a) I'm sorry I broke your typewriter.
   apologise
   I do .... your typewriter.

b) Can you give me directions for the station?
   how
   Could you tell .... the station?

c) You must be thirsty, so can I offer you some tea?
   like
   You must be thirsty, so .... tea?

d) If I were you, I wouldn't buy a dog.
   should
   I don't .... dog.

e) I'm sure that Jack hasn't left home yet.
   have
   Jack .... home yet.

f) I suppose that this is Trafalgar Square.
   be
   This .... Trafalgar Square.

g) Perhaps Jean's plane was delayed.
   been
   Jean's plane .... delayed.

h) It was unnecessary for you to come early today.

have

You .... come early today.

i) Tony is supposed to be here by now.

been

Tony .... here by now.

j) Perhaps this is the answer.

be

This .... the answer.

3

Look carefully at each line. Some lines are correct, but some have a word which should not be there. Tick each correct line. If a line has a word which should not be there, write the word in the space.

Putting up a friend

Dear Brenda,

Thanks for replying so quickly to my last letter.	...✓.......
You must to have been surprised when you received	...to.......
a letter from me. I'm glad you will be able	1) ....
to have put me up when I come to London.	2) ....
Could you be possibly give me some directions	3) ....
for your flat? I'm bound to get lost. Do I	4) ....
have to take a taxi from the station, or is it	5) ....
near enough to walk? Perhaps if I should buy	6) ....
a street map of Birmingham when I am arrive. And	7) ....
is it all right if I can bring my little brother, Tim?	8) ....
By the way, congratulations on your new job.	9) ....
You must not be very happy. Do you think that	10) ....
you made the right decision, though? I think	11) ....
you should or have gone to university like me.	12) ....
I'm sure that you would have been enjoyed it. I	13) ....
have done to study a lot, but with any luck I should	14) ....
get a good job when I finish. I'd be better post	15) ....
this letter now.	

Best Wishes,
Sheila

4

Choose the most suitable expression for each situation.

a) You want to invite someone you have just met to go to the theatre with you.
1) May I go to the theatre?
2) Would you like to come to the theatre?
3) Do you think you should go to the theatre?

b) You are recommending a new restaurant to a friend.
1) You really must try the new Italian restaurant in Green Street.
2) You had better try the new Italian restaurant in Green Street.
3) You would try the new Italian restaurant in Green Street.

c) Your boss suggests that you work overtime on Saturday, but you don't want
    to.
    1) You must be joking!
    2) It's nice of you to ask, but I refuse.
    3) Sorry, but I have something already arranged.
d) You want to ask the waiter to bring you another drink.
    1) I'd like another beer, please.
    2) Excuse me, but do you think I could take another beer?
    3) You can bring me a beer if you like.
e) You want someone to move out of your way.
    1) Look out!
    2) Excuse me!
    3) Pardon!
f) You greet a friend you haven't seen for a few weeks.
    1) Hello Pauline, how do you do?
    2) Hello Pauline, what's going on?
    3) Hello Pauline, how are you?
g) You are sitting on a bus and want the person in front of you to shut the
    window.
    1) Could you shut the window, please?
    2) May I shut the window, please?
    3) Do you want to shut the window, please?
h) You want to know how to get to the station, and you ask a stranger.
    1) Tell me, where is the station?
    2) Do you mind telling me where the station is?
    3) Could you tell me the way to the station, please?
i) You want some advice from a friend.
    1) What do you think I should do?
    2) Tell me what I must do.
    3) What could you do if you were me?
j) You ask your boss for permission to leave work early.
    1) Do you mind leaving early?
    2) Is it all right if I go now?
    3) I'm off now, bye!

5

Decide which answer A, B, C or D best fits each space.

The Lost Property Office

Recently I read a magazine article about the things (1)..... people lose when they travel on the London Underground. I (2)..... believe it at first. (3)..... you are a violinist, and when you (4)..... off at your station, you leave your violin (5) ..... the train. It seems strange that nobody says, '(6) ..... me, but I think you have forgotten something.' I suppose the violinist (7) ..... have been thinking of something else, and there might (8) ..... have been any other (9) ..... on the train. Still, why didn't the violinist go (10) ..... the lost property office? All the lost property on the underground system (11) ..... to be sent to this office, so if you lose anything you (12) ..... easily get it back. In this case, the violinist must have (13) ..... very absent minded. Perhaps he or she didn't (14) ..... to play the violin ever again after this journey. Or perhaps they were just too embarrassed (15) ..... go to the office.

1)	A) who	B) whose	C) that	D) a
2)	A) wasn't	B) haven't	C) shouldn't	D) couldn't
3)	A) If	B) Suppose	C) Why	D) Sometimes
4)	A) get	B) go	C) fall	D) are
5)	A) at	B) for	C) on	D) by
6)	A) Help	B) It's	C) Excuse	D) Correct
7)	A) who	B) might	C) should	D) to
8)	A) not	B) then	C) often	D) so
9)	A) pedestrians	B) customers	C) audience	D) passengers
10)	A) in	B) at	C) to	D) for
11)	A) should	B) must	C) needs	D) has
12)	A) can	B) can't	C) don't	D) are
13)	A) been	B) or	C) had	D) because
14)	A) know	B) like	C) have	D) used
15)	A) and	B) to	C) must	D) so

Unit 21 Countables and uncountables. Problems with plurals

Explanations

1 Concept

Countable:	Singular	Plural
	a shoe	*(some) shoes*
Uncountable:	Singular	No Plural
	advice, some advice	

2 Change of meaning
Some words have different meanings in countable and uncountable forms.

Countable	*an iron*	(domestic appliance)
	a wood	(small area of trees)
	a paper	(newspaper)
Uncountable:	*some iron*	(a substance)
	some wood	(a substance)
	some paper	(a substance)

There is a similar contrast between:
Material: *coffee*   Item: *a coffee* (= a cup of coffee)

3 Uncountables and types
Some uncountables can be used as countables to describe a 'type' in a technical sense.
Uncountable: *fruit*   Technical type: *a fruit*

4 Food and portions
Uncountable: *chicken* (the meat) *some chicken* (a portion)
Countable: *a chicken* (the animal)

5 Others with change of meaning
business (in general)   *a business* (a company)
gossip (talking)   *a gossip* (a person)
hair (all together)   *a hair* (a single example)
help (in general)   *a help* (a helpful person/thing)
toast (grilled bread)   *a toast* (formal words before drinking)
work (in general)   *a work* (a work of art/engineering)

6 Typical uncountables

Substances: *plastic, iron, paper*

Liquids and Gases: *water, oxygen*

Abstract ideas: *happiness, anger*

Mass/Collection: *furniture, luggage*

Other words are practised in the activities.

7 Plural form, singular verb

Some words, ending in 's', have no singular form, but are used with a singular verb.

> *The news **is** very bad today.*   *Billiards **is** an interesting game.*

8 No singular form

Some words have no singular form.

> *My trousers **are** too tight.*   *The stairs **are** very steep.*

Other common examples are:

> *clothes, goods, jeans, means, outskirts, surroundings, thanks*

9 Groups of people

Some words which refer to groups of people can have a singular verb if we think of the group as a unit, and a plural if we think of the group as a number of people.

> *I think the government **is/are** wrong.*

Other common examples:

> *army, audience, class, company, crew, crowd, family, staff, team*

Some group words only take a plural verb: *cattle, police, people*

Activities

1

Choose the most suitable word underlined.

a) Different countries have different weather/weathers.

b) All areas of the skin are in fact covered in tiny hair/hairs.

c) We've looked at the menu and we'd all like chicken/chickens.

d) Jack is a millionaire and owns a lot of business/businesses.

e) Have you a copy of the complete work/works of Dante?

f) None of the passengers had insured their baggage/baggages.

g) During the afternoon there will be thunder and lightning/thunders and lightnings in many areas.

h) Students must pass their paper/papers to the front.

i) I'd like coffee, toast/toasts and marmalade please.

j) I'm afraid we can't find cheap accommodation/accommodations for all of you.

2

Complete each
sentence with
a/an, *some* or by
leaving the space
blank.

a) When the play ended, there was ..... lengthy applause.
b) I can't come out tonight. I have .... homework to do.
c) What shall we do tomorrow evening? How about .... dancing?
d) There is .... very beautiful countryside near here.
e) Sue received .... excellent education.

f) My trousers need pressing. Can you lend me .... iron?
g) My friends bought me .... coffee maker for my birthday.
h) David has just bought .... new furniture.
i) Let me give you .... advice.
j) The inside is strengthened with .... steel frame.

3

Choose the most
suitable word
underlined.

a) I would love to go on a long journey/travel by train.
b) What's the latest news? Can I look at your paper/journal?
c) I want to know about trains to Leeds. Can you give me a/an
   information/timetable?
d) Here's your ticket. Do you have any luggage/suitcase?
e) Don't forget to buy a sliced bread/loaf.
f) Why don't we leave the car in this car park/parking?
g) I can't come to work today. I have a bad cold/flu.
h) Excuse me sir, but do you have a licence/permission for this gun?
i) Brighton has quite a good beach/seaside.
j) I'm going out tonight with a few of my company/friends.

4

Put **one** suitable
word in each
space.

a) I'm looking for ..*accommodation*... Do you know anywhere I can stay?
b) Take my .... , don't go out alone after dark.
c) The government plans to improve .... by paying teachers
   more.
d) Can you lend me some .... ? I want to type a letter.
e) I need some .... about language schools. Can you help me?
f) Richard is unemployed, and he is looking for a ....
g) Could I have some .... ? Those apples and oranges look nice.
h) I used to have long .... , but I had it cut.
i) I can't do this on my own. Could you give me some .... ?
j) If you can't undo the knot, cut the string with some ....

5

Complete each sentence with the most suitable word or phrase.

a) I like your new trousers. Where did you buy ..B.. ?
   A) it   B) them   C) them both   D) them all

b) There is always a very large .... at the church I go to.
   A) congregation   B) audience   C) spectator   D) company

c) The local .... has agreed to repair the road outside our house.
   A) government   B) people   C) council   D) jury

d) When the police arrived, we were pleased to see ....
   A) him   B) him or her   C) it   D) them

e) The car turned over, but luckily it didn't suffer serious ....
   A) damage   B) injury   C) damages   D) injuries

f) Sorry, I'm late, but I had a lot of .... to do.
   A) job   B) work   C) task   D) labour

g) Julie bought herself a complete new .... for winter.
   A) outfit   B) cloth   C) clothing   D) wear

h) I feel like going out tonight. Let's go to a/an ....
   A) dancing   B) night   C) club   D) entertainment

i) Thanks for a great weekend! We really had a/an ....
   A) fun   B) enjoyment   C) hospitality   D) good time

j) In order to prove Smith is guilty, we must find some ....
   A) information   B) evidence   C) knowledge   D) means

6

Choose the most appropriate meaning for each sentence.

a) You mustn't lose heart.
   1) Don't have an operation.   ② Don't give up hope.

b) Where's my glass?
   1) I need a drink.   2) I can't see.

c) Jack has a new post.
   1) The postman has delivered a letter.   2) He has a different job.

d) All goods must be paid for in advance.
   1) Nothing enjoyable in life is free.   2) You have to pay for these things first.

e) I've joined a new company.
   1) I have a new job.   2) I have some new friends.

f) This hotel has class.
   1) You can study hotel management here.   2) It is a good quality hotel.

g) I don't have the means to help you.
   1) I'm not able to help.   2) I can't understand what help you need.

h) I'd like some china.
   1) I want to go abroad.   2) I need some cups and plates.

i) Do you have any cash?
   1) Do you only have a cheque?   2) Isn't there a place to pay in this shop?
j) They have a business in Leeds.
   1) They have to go there to do a job.   2) They own a company there.

7
Complete the second sentence so that it has a similar meaning to the first sentence, using the word given. Do not change the word given. You must use between two and five words.

a) This island has a large population.
   people
   There ..*are a lot of people*.. on this island.
b) Do you own these things?
   your
   Are .... belongings?
c) The weather was good on our holiday.
   had
   We .... on our holiday.
d) There were a lot of cars on the road to Manchester.
   traffic
   There .... on the road to Manchester.
e) Gerry is a very strong person, in my opinion.
   strength
   Gerry .... in my opinion.
f) There are pieces of paper all over the floor!
   litter
   There .... all over the floor.
g) There is definitely improvement in your work.
   made
   You .... progress in your work.
h) Can I park my car here?
   allowed
   Is .... here?
i) I know these machines are very expensive.
   machinery
   I know .... very expensive.
j) Could you get some bread from the supermarket?
   loaf
   Could you get .... from the supermarket?

8
Complete each sentence with **one** suitable word from the list. Use each word once only.

| blade | flight | item | piece | sheet | clap | head | lump | set | slice |

a) Let me give you a ..*piece*... of advice.
b) There is an interesting .... of news in the paper.
c) A .... of stairs takes you to the top of the house.
d) Could I have another .... of paper, please?
e) Put another .... of coal on the fire.
f) Helen has a lovely .... of hair.
g) Do you want another .... of toast?

h) We bought Mike and Lynn a .... of cutlery for a wedding present.
i) There was not a single .... of grass left standing.
j) The lightning was followed by a .... of thunder.

9

Complete each sentence with **one** suitable word from the list. Use each word once only.

accommodation bread cookery lightning spelling
advice cash information luggage parking

a) I can't cut this loaf. Do you have a proper ..*bread*.................. knife?
b) I'm afraid that 'neice' is a .... mistake
c) There's usually a/an .... space opposite the church.
d) We need a/an .... box to keep the money in.
e) The tourist board have built a/an .... centre near the castle.
f) We decided to put a/an .... conductor on the roof.
g) Marjorie used to write a/an .... column in a magazine.
h) These suitcases are heavy. We must find a/an .... trolley.
i) I must rush. I'm going to a/an .... lesson.
j) Julie found her flat through a/an .... agency.

10

Decide which answer A, B, C or D best fits each space.

Food Habits

Breakfast is one of those (1) ..... that varies from person to person, and country to country. For some (2) ..... it means a (3) ..... of toast and some coffee. In various places I've also been offered (4) ..... or fruit. (5) ..... executive might eat breakfast at the (6) ..... , while for many schoolchildren breakfast is a (7) ..... of milk at home, and then a long wait (8) ..... the first break of the morning, when they eat (9) ..... or (10) ..... chocolate bar. Some families sit down and eat together (11) ..... the morning, and listen to (12) ..... news on the radio or (13) ..... early morning television. For other people, the early morning is a rush (14) .....work or school, and there just simply isn't (15) ....

1) A) times	B) meals	C) foods	D) plates
2) A) people	B) persons	C) breakfasts	D) us
3) A) sheet	B) loaf	C) slice	D) sandwich
4) A) a cheese	B) the cheese	C) cheese	D) cheeses
5) A) Business	B) A business	C) Business's	D) Businessmen
6) A) train	B) street	C) morning	D) office
7) A) glass	B) piece	C) warm	D) box
8) A) to	B) is	C) until	D) which
9) A) sandwich	B) the sandwich	C) a sandwiches	D) sandwiches
10) A) a	B) some	C) a piece	D) a glass of
11) A) for	B) in	C) at	D) while
12) A) a	B) what	C) some	D) the
13) A) look	B) watch	C) see	D) regard
14) A) to	B) from	C) at	D) and
15) A) there	B) it	C) enough	D) time

KEY POINTS

1   Check in a dictionary to be sure whether a word is countable or uncountable.

2   The meaning of a word may change depending on whether it is used in a countable or uncountable sense.

3   Note that not all words ending in 's' have singular form, and that some words ending in 's' take a singular verb.

> **SEE ALSO**
>
> **Unit 22**
> Articles
> **Unit 25**
> Progress test

Unit 22 Articles

Explanations

Zero article

1 With uncountables and abstract or general ideas, and plurals (not previously mentioned and not post-modified: see below).
   I like orange juice.   Give peace a chance.   I hate wasps.

2 With most proper names (see below).
   We live in France.   I'll see you in January.

3 With names of meals when they refer to routine times.
   It's time for lunch.   What's for dinner?

4 With unique jobs or roles (definite article is also possible).
   Jim is (the) chairman of the company.

5 With prepositions of place, when the place plays a special role.
   Sally is in prison.   (She's a prisoner)
   Sally is in the prison.   (A visitor to the building)
   Similar are: *church, hospital, school, university*

6 With general means of transport.
   We went there by car.
   But if *in* or *on* is used: *We went there in a car/on a bus.*

Definite article

1 Previously mentioned items.
   *There is a bedroom and a living room. **The** bedroom is large.*

2 Single items, whose reference is clear.
   *Can you pass **the** marmalade? What happened after **the** war?*

3 Unique objects.
   ***The moon** is full tonight.*

4 Items which are followed by a descriptive phrase, which makes them definite (post-modification).
   *This is **the man I told you about**.*
   This category includes names:
   London Bridge but ***the** Tower of London* (post-modified)

5 National groups.
   ***The British** drink far too much tea.*

6 Classes of people.
   ***The rich** get richer and **the poor** get poorer.*

7 Individual items which represent a class.
  *The lion* is fast disappearing.

8 Names of musical instruments and ability to play.
  I can't play **the piano** but I can play **the guitar**.

9 Some geographical names.
  Plural countries, or where the name contains a noun.
  **The** Netherlands.   **The** People's Republic of China.
  Names of rivers and oceans, and regions.
  **The** Thames flows into **the** North Sea.   **The** Arctic.

10 Superlatives, ordinals, *the same*, *the only*.
  This is **the best**.   You are **the first**.   This is **the only one**.

11 Media.
  What's on **(the) television**?   I went to **the cinema**.

Indefinite article 1 Describing jobs.
  Peter is **a lorry driver**.

2 With singular fractions, group numbers and large numbers.
  One and **a half** kilos.   **A dozen** eggs.   **A hundred** envelopes.

3 Meaning *per*.
  He was doing ninety miles **an hour**.
  Julie earns £500 **a week**.

Activities

1

Put *a/an* or *the* in each space, or leave the space blank.

a) We went by ...—... train to .the. west of England.
b) .... people who live in .... Netherlands are called .... Dutch.
c) .... judge sent me to .... prison for .... ten years.
d) .... Columbus was one of .... first people to cross .... Atlantic.
e) As .... captain of .... ship, I have .... complete authority.
f) David learned to play .... violin when he was at .... university.
g) .... Trafalgar Square is near .... Charing Cross Station.
h) Did you read .... book I lent you .... last week?
i) We'll put up .... shelves and then go to .... pub for .... drink.
j) Is that .... present Bill gave you for .... Christmas?

2

Choose the most suitable phrase underlined.

a) Is this a person/the person you told me about?
b) This is the only cinema/an only cinema in the area.
c) Philip has just bought the Thames barge/a Thames barge.
d) Here is a thousand pounds/the thousand pounds I owe you.
e) Are you going to church/the church on Sunday?

114

f) Do you have <u>a milk jug/milk jug</u>?

g) <u>The Prime Minister/Prime Minister</u> will give a speech this afternoon.

h) <u>The computer/Computer</u> has already changed our lives dramatically.

i) I haven't been to <u>an open-air theatre/open-air theatre</u> before.

j) I'm going to <u>the British Museum/British Museum</u> this afternoon.

3

Complete each sentence with the most suitable word or phrase.

a) The butler was ..*C*.. I suspected.
   A) last person   B) a last person   C) the last person   D) some last person

b) Where .... you borrowed last week?
   A) is scissors   B) are the scissors   C) is some scissors   D) are scissors

c) Why don't we go to the park ......?
   A) in the car   B) with a car   C) with car   D) by the car

d) Too much rubbish is being dumped in ....
   A) sea   B) the sea   C) a sea   D) some sea

e) Let's go on holiday to ....
   A) Greek Islands   B) the Greece Islands   C) islands of Greece
   D) the Greek Islands

f) This is exactly .... I was looking for.
   A) job   B) a job   C) some job   D) the job

g) Of all these cars, I think I prefer ....
   A) a Japanese   B) some Japanese   C) the Japanese one
   D) a Japanese one

h) Interest on this account is only .... per cent.
   A) a four and a quarter   B) four and a quarter   C) four and quarter
   D) four quarter

i) I try to go jogging at least four times ....
   A) the week   B) of the week   C) a week   D) of a week

j) Sally spent six months out of ....
   A) work   B) a work   C) the work   D) some work

4

Complete each sentence a) to j) with one of the endings 1) to 10). More than one answer may be possible.

a) Some people say that the ..*9*...

b) Most people think that a/an ....

c) I don't agree that ....

d) I feel that a ....

e) I don't believe that a/an ....

f) I didn't realise that the ....

g) It's incredible to think that a/an ....

h) I didn't know that ....

i) I think it's quite unfair that the ....

j) Nobody nowadays thinks that ....

1) .... good job is an important part of life.

2) .... single injection can protect you from so many diseases.

3) .... hundred miles an hour is too fast even on a motorway.

4) .... the unemployed should receive more help from the state.
5) .... queen of England doesn't pay any income tax.
6) .... tiger may well become extinct very soon.
7) .... third of a person's income should be paid in tax.
8) .... women should just stay at home and look after the children.
9) .... English are difficult to get to know at first.
10) .... the Tower of London was built by William the Conqueror.

5

Put *a/an* or *the* in each space, or leave the space blank.

a) Neil Armstrong made .the. first footprint on .the. moon.
b) There was .... accident yesterday at .... corner of .... street.
c) I need .... time to think about .... offer you made me.
d) .... recipe for .... success is .... hard work.
e) .... people who live in .... glass houses shouldn't throw ...... stones.
f) .... worst part of .... living in a caravan is .... lack of space.
g) .... book you ordered .... last week is now in .... stock.
h) .... dancing is .... more interesting activity than .... reading.
i) .... people we met on .... holiday in .... north of England sent us .... postcard.
j) .... little knowledge is .... dangerous thing.

6

Complete the second sentence so that it has a similar meaning to the first sentence, using the word given. Do not change the word given. You must use between two and five words.

a) There is one problem here, and that's the weather.
only
The ..only.problem.here.is..the weather.

b) There are no good films on this week.
cinema
There is nothing .... this week.

c) Can't you swim faster than that?
fastest
Is .... can swim?

d) I haven't been here before.
time
This is .... been here.

e) A lot of wine is drunk in France.
French
The .... a lot of wine.

f) If you drive faster, it is more dangerous.
the
The .... dangerous it is.

g) It is difficult to discover what is true.
truth
The .... discover.

h) Are you a good pianist?
piano
Can you .... well?

i) Please do not enter the room all together.
one
Please enter the room .... time.

j) I saw a television film of Hamlet.
on
I saw a .... television.

7
Choose the most suitable phrase underlined.

a) I was under an impression/under the impression that you had left.
b) I have to go. I'm in a hurry/in hurry.
c) I managed to sell the old painting at a profit/at profit.
d) I think I prefer the other restaurant on the whole/on whole.
e) How many hours do you work, on average/on the average, every week?
f) I was in pain/in a pain after I twisted my ankle.
g) Jack recovered from his accident and is now out of danger/out of the danger.
h) Excuse me, but you're in the way/in a way.
i) Sue felt seasick on the cross-channel ferry/a cross the channel ferry.
j) The burglar hit me on my back of the neck/the back of my neck.

8
Put *a/an* or *the* in each space, or leave the space blank.

a) What's the use in taking ...—.. medicine for ..a... cold?
b) Is .... happiness of .... majority more important than .... rights of .... individual?
c) It's .... long way by .... train to .... north of .... Scotland.
d) .... philosophers seem to think that .... life is .... mystery.
e) .... most cars start badly on .... cold mornings.
f) There was .... time when I enjoyed .... skating.
g) Do you have .... reason for .... arriving late?
h) At .... time I arrive .... home I feel .... sense of .... relief.
i) .... end of .... book is .... by far .... best part.
j) .... friend always tells me .... answers to .... homework we have.

KEY POINTS

1 Meaning can change, depending on what kind of article is used.

   *Helen is **at the school**.*   (At the building, we don't know why.)

   *Helen is **at school**.*   (She is a student or a teacher.)

2 The context of meaning is also important, particularly where an item has been, or has not been, mentioned before.

   *The BBC reported that **the** two men have since been recaptured.* (The two men must have been mentioned before, and so this is an extract from a longer text.)

3 Many uses of the articles are idiomatic, and should be learned as part of a phrase.

   *Diana works as **a** graphic designer.*

SEE ALSO

Unit 21
Countables and uncountables
Unit 23
Determiners

Unit 23 All, no, each, every, either, neither, none

Explanations

All

1 As a quantity word, *all* can be followed by *of* before *the* and a noun.
   *Jim was there **all (of) the** time.*

2 It can also emphasise a plural personal pronoun or a noun or noun phrase. Note the position of *all* in these examples.
   *They **all** wore white shorts and shirts.*
   *Those stamps you bought me have **all** disappeared.*

3 It can also stand alone, when it tends to mean 'the only thing'.
   ***All** I want is some peace and quiet.*
   Compare the use of 'everything', meaning 'all the things':
   ***Everything** has gone wrong!*
   All would not be appropriate in this sentence.

No

1 As a quantity word, *no* can be used meaning *not any*.
   *There are **no** plates left.   **No** new students have joined the class.*

2 *No* can also be used as an adverb.
   *I suppose we are **no** worse off than before.*
   *There were **no** less than 500 applications for the job.*

3 *No* is not normally used alone before an adjective. Compare:
   *There are **no** interesting parts in this book.   It is **not** interesting.*
   There is an idiomatic use of *no* with *good:*
   *I tried hard but it was **no good**, I couldn't reach.* (useless)
   Another common idiomatic use is with *-ing* forms:
   *Remember, **no cheating**!   **No smoking**, please.*

Each, every, all

1 *Each* refers to single items in a group of items, one at a time.
   ***Each** member of the team received a medal.*
   *They were given £10 **each**.*
   All refers to the team as a whole.
   ***All** the team played well.*
   Each can refer to only two items, while *every* cannot.
   *She kissed him on **each** cheek.*

2 *Each* can be followed by *of* and a noun or pronoun.
   *When the team won the cup, **each of them** was given a medal.*

119

3 *Each* can also follow a noun or pronoun.
   *My two brothers were **each** chosen to act in the play.*
   *On the first night, they **each** forgot their lines.*

4 Repeated actions are generally described with *every*.
   *I practise the violin **every day**.*

Either, neither

1 *Either* and *neither* both refer to choices between two items.
   *I didn't like **either** of those films.*
   ***Neither** of the films was any good.*

2 *Either* can also mean *both*.
   *On **either** side of the house there are shops.*

None

1 *None* can mean *not one*.
   ***None** of us can ride a horse.*

2 *None* can also mean *not any*. It is followed by a singular verb, especially in formal speech or writing.
   ***None** of the members of the committee **has arrived** yet.*
   In everyday speech, a plural verb is often used.
   ***None** of these telephones **work**.*

Activities

1
Rewrite each sentence so that it contains the word given in capitals, and so that the meaning stays the same. Do not change the word in any way.

a) This is the only money I have left.   ALL
   ...This is all the money I have left...............

b) There wasn't anyone at the meeting.   NO
   ....

c) Both singers had bad voices.   NEITHER
   ....

d) All of the cups are dirty.   NONE
   ....

e) Everyone was cheering loudly.   ALL
   ....

f) You both deserve promotion.   EACH
   ....

g) I read both books, but I liked neither of them.   EITHER
   ....

h) Whenever I cross the Channel by boat I feel seasick.   EVERY
   ....

i) I only ate a sandwich for lunch.   ALL
   ....

j) Both sides of the street have parking meters.   EITHER
   ....

2

Rewrite each sentence, beginning as shown, so that the meaning stays the same.

a) Everyone in the office was given a personal parking space.
Each ..person in the office was given a personal parking space...

b) This town doesn't have any good hotels.
There are ....

c) Love is the only thing that you need.
All ....

d) These two pens don't write properly.
Neither ....

e) We are all responsible for our own actions.
Each ....

f) All of us feel lonely sometimes.
We ....

g) All of the shops are closed.
None ....

h) Both jobs were unsuitable for Helen.
Neither ....

i) All the cakes have been eaten.
The cakes ....

j) Unfortunately, the meal was the same as usual.
Unfortunately the meal was no ....

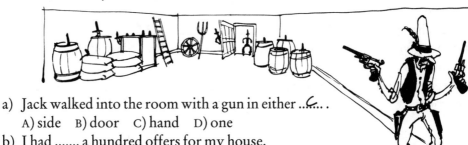

3

Complete each sentence with the most suitable word or phrase.

a) Jack walked into the room with a gun in either ..C...
A) side   B) door   C) hand   D) one

b) I had .... a hundred offers for my house.
A) neither   B) each   C) all   D) no less than

c) I feel so tired this evening. I've been working hard ....
A) all day   B) every day   C) each day   D) day by day

d) The two cars for sale were in poor condition, so I didn't buy ....
A) either of them   B) both of them   C) neither of them   D) each of them

e) I tried to lift the heavy trunk but it was ....
A) not good   B) no less than good   C) neither good   D) no good

f) The room was full of people and .... were speaking.
A) neither of them   B) all of them   C) none of them   D) each of them

g) .... spent more time walking a century ago.
A) People all   B) All persons   C) Each people   D) All

h) My friend Jonathan has a gold earring in ....
A) his two ears   B) each ear   C) every ear   D) the ears

i) I looked everywhere for my pen and it was here ....
A) none of the time   B) every time   C) all the time   D) each time

j) People say that there is .... like show business.
A) all business   B) no business   C) not business   D) all business

4

Put the most suitable word from the list into each space.

| all, each, either, every, neither, no, none |

a) Is ..either.... of you interested in working on Saturday this week?
b) I am afraid there are .... vacancies in the company at present.
c) I think we should be given at least £50 ....
d) .... other Saturday we watch our local hockey team.
e) Let's start now. There's .... time like the present!
f) .... you are interested in doing is going to the pub!
g) There are two beds. You can sleep in .... one, it doesn't matter.
h) Sally gave a present to .... and every one of us!
i) And the star of our show is .... other than Dorothy Rogers!
j) My company has treated me well, and given me .... chance to succeed.

5

Complete the second sentence so that it has a similar meaning to the first sentence, using the word given. Do not change the word given. You must use between two and five words.

a) I always go to the cinema on Thursdays in winter.
   Thursday
   I go to the cinema ...every Thursday... in winter.
b) This has nothing to do with you!
   none
   This is .... business!
c) I'm afraid there aren't any empty seats at the front.
   all
   I'm afraid .... at the front are taken.
d) From today, lorries are not allowed to go through the town centre.
   no
   From today .... to go through the town centre.
e) The days get colder and colder.
   it
   Each .... colder.
f) Both questions were impossible to understand.
   couldn't
   I .... question.
g) You only want to listen to rock music!
   is
   All you .... to rock music.
h) As many as 20,000 people are thought to have attended the concert.
   than
   No .... are thought to have attended the concert.
i) Each child was given £100.
   were
   The .... £100 each.
j) We cannot waste any time!
   no
   There .... waste.

6

Look carefully at each line. Some lines are correct, but some have a word which should not be there. Tick each correct line. If a line has a word which should not be there, write the word in the space.

Supermarkets

The every time I go to a supermarket I ask	..The.....
myself why I go shopping there so often.	..✓.......
Last time I ended up buying all the kinds of things	1) ....
when the all I really wanted was a packet of	2) ....
rice and a small loaf, but could find neither	3) ....
of them. I looked in every one corner of the shop	4) ....
but there was simply no a sign of these products.	5) ....
I looked carefully on either side of the aisles	6) ....
but it was no any good. I ought to confess here	7) ....
that I had forgotten my glasses! All of I could see	8) ....
was rows of colourful shapes of all sizes. I decided	9) ....
to ask an assistant. They were all a busy of course	10) ....
and none of them was anywhere nearby in any	11) ....
case. Meanwhile I had been filling my basket with	12) ....
all the kinds of things I thought I wanted. After I	13) ....
had paid, I had no money left for the weekend,	14) ....
but I hadn't bought the either of the things I wanted!	15) ....

KEY POINTS

1 If *all* is the subject of a sentence, it means 'the only thing'. Otherwise *everything* is used. Compare:
    All *we need now is a new car.*
    Everything *is missing, I'm afraid.*

2 Note these idiomatic uses of *no:*
    No *parking.*   **No** *smoking*
    It's **no** *use.*   *It's* **no** *good.*

3 *Each* refers to single items in a group one at a time. It is followed by a singular verb.
    Each *of these books has its interesting points.*

4 *Either* and *neither* refer to two items, separately, and are followed by a singular verb.
    Neither *of these hotels is very comfortable.*

5 *None* (not one) is followed by a singular verb in formal speech and writing.
    None *of these answers is correct.*

> **SEE ALSO**
>
> **Unit 25**
> Progress test

Unit 24 Making comparisons

Explanations

1 Comparatives with -*er*
One-syllable words, and two-syllable words ending in -*y*, generally add -*er* to make the comparative form (with -*y* changing to -*i*). Words ending in -*e* add only -*r*.
>   *late, later   early, earlier*

2 Comparatives with *more* or *less*
Other two-syllable words, and words of more than two syllables, use *more or less*.
>   *more modern   less interesting*

3 Two-syllable words
Some two-syllable words are used with either -*er* or *more*.
Examples are:
>   *clever   common   narrow   simple*

4 Irregular comparatives
Some irregular comparatives are:
>   *This is my **elder** sister.*   (This cannot be used to make a comparison.)
>   *How much **further/farther** do we have to go?*   (Meaning *more far*)
>   *I can't really advise you any **further**.*   (Meaning *more*)

5 Superlatives
Superlatives ending in -*est* or with *(the) most* follow the same rules outlined in **1** and **2**.
>   *the latest   the earliest   the most modern*

Comparatives of adverbs

1 These are normally made with *more* and *less*.
>   *more quickly   less carefully*

2 Some adverbs, which are not formed from adjectives, have a comparative formed with -*er*. Examples are:
>   *faster   harder*

Making comparisons

1 The simplest kind of comparison is with a comparative and *than*.
>   *You don't look **older than** your brother.*

2 Comparatives can be repeated to suggest continuing change.
>   *This lesson seems to be getting **longer and longer**.*
>   *Jim started feeling **more and more tired**.*

3   Comparatives can be made stronger by using these words:
    much   far   a lot   a little
    *This book is **much/far/a lot/a little** more expensive.*

4   Comparatives can be used in parallel constructions with *the*.
    ***The faster** you drive, **the more** petrol you use.*

5   Expressions with *best*.
    *Sorry, but this is **the best** I can do.   I tried **my best**.*
    *May the **best** man win.*   (This can refer to two people.)

Comparative   1   With *than*.
clauses   *Food here is more expensive **than I thought**.*

2   With *not as/so ... as*.
    *Being a nurse is **not as** interesting **as** being a doctor.*

3   With *(just) as ... as*.
    *Living in the country is **just as** expensive **as** living in London.*

4   With *such ... as*.
    *I've never been to **such** a good party **as** that one.*

5   Parts of the comparison that repeat the main verb can be left out, though
    auxiliaries (eg *can, be, have, will*) are repeated and the verb can be replaced
    by a form of *do*.
    *You paid more for your house **than I did**.*
    *Jack can swim a lot better **than I can**.*

Activities

1

Put **one** suitable
word in each
space.

a) My brother is two years older ...than.... me.
b) The train takes just .... long as the bus.
c) I've never tasted such delicious apples .... these.
d) I thought the second hotel we stayed in was .... more friendly.
e) Unfortunately we are .... well-off than we used to be.
f) Marion doesn't feel so happy there .... she did at first.
g) Do you think you could make a .... less noise?
h) These exercises seem to be getting harder and ....
i) Jean doesn't need as much help as Harry ....
j) David didn't enjoy the match as much as I ....

2
Rewrite each
sentence
beginning as
shown, so that
the meaning
stays the same.

a) Jill can run faster than Peter.
Peter ..*can't run as fast as Jill (can)*.....................................

b) I thought this journey would last longer than it did.
This journey didn't ....

c) I didn't arrive as early as I expected.
I arrived ....

d) You are working too slowly.
You'll have to ....

e) I have a brother who is older than me.
I have an ....

f) Martin thought the second part of the film was more interesting.
Martin didn't think the first ....

g) Paula's work is less careful than before.
Paula has been working ....

h) There aren't any trains earlier than this one.
This is ....

i) All other pubs are further away.
This pub ....

j) Is this the best price you can offer?
Can't you ....

3
Complete each
sentence by
choosing the
most suitable
word or phrase.

a) I really think that apologising is ..C... you can do.
A) not as much as   B) a little   C) the least   D) as far as

b) I can't stand this weather. It's getting ....
A) more and more   B) worse and worse   C) coldest and coldest
D) further and further

c) Although Brenda came last, everyone agreed she had .... her best.
A) done   B) made   C) had   D) got

d) I wish Charles worked as hard as Mary ....
A) did   B) can   C) will   D) does

e) The more you water this plant, the ...... it will grow.
A) best   B) tall   C) wetter   D) faster

f) From now on, we won't be able to go out as much as we ....
A) were   B) had   C) used to   D) will

g) I've never owned .... independent cat as this one!
A) a more than   B) such an   C) a so   D) as much an

h) Brian has been working .... since he was promoted.
A) much harder   B) as harder   C) just as hardly   D) more hardly

    i) I've been feeling .... tired lately, doctor.
        A) such a   B) the most   C) more and more   D) much

    j) This exercise will give you .... practice.
        A) farther   B) much more   C) as better   D) a lot

4

Put **one** suitable word in each space, beginning with the letter given.

a) Is William feeling any b*etter*..... today?

b) Everyone ate a lot, but Chris ate the m............. .

c) What's the l............. news about the situation in India?

d) I'd feel a lot h............. if you let me help.

e) Graham has been sinking d............. into debt lately.

f) It's 35 degrees today! It must be the h............. day so far this year.

g) Only £45? Is that all? Oh well, it's b............. than nothing.

h) He had to wait a f............. two months before he got his promotion.

i) Ruth wore her b............. dress to her sister's wedding.

j) Harry has got over the w............. of his cold.

5

Rewrite each sentence, beginning as shown, so that the meaning stays the same.

a) That's the best meal I've ever eaten.
     I've never eaten a .*better meal*...

b) Fish and meat are the same price in some countries.
     Fish costs just ....

c) I've never enjoyed myself so much.
     I've never had ....

d) If you run a lot, you will get fitter.
     The more ....

e) The doctor can't see you earlier than Wednesday I'm afraid.
     Wednesday is ....

f) I must have a rest. I can't walk any more.
     I must have a rest. I can't go ....

g) Home computers used to be much more expensive.
     Home computers aren't ....

h) I don't know as much Italian as Sue does.
     Sue knows ....

i) I thought that learning to drive would be difficult, but it isn't.
     Learning to drive is ....

j) Barbara can skate just as well as John can.
     John isn't ....

6

Complete the second sentence so that it has a similar meaning to the first sentence, using the word given. Do not change the word given. You must use between two and five words.

a) Your car was cheaper than mine.
   cost
   Your car ..*cost less than mine*.. did.

b) I'm not as good at maths as you are.
   better
   You .... I am.

c) Keith is slightly taller than Nigel.
   little
   Keith .... Nigel.

d) Bill was growing angrier all the time.
   and
   Bill .... angrier.

e) Sally tried as hard as she could.
   did
   Sally .... best.

f) I thought this film would be better.
   as
   This film .... I expected.

g) This is the bumpiest road I've ever driven along!
   such
   I've never .... road.

h) When you eat a lot, you get fat.
   more
   The .... you get.

i) George said he couldn't do any better.
   could
   George said it .... do.

j) This year's exam and last year's exam were equally difficult.
   just
   This year's exam .... last year's exam.

7

Look carefully at each line. Some lines are correct, but some have a word which should not be there. Tick each correct line. If a line has a word which should not be there, write the word in the space.

Transport Solutions

First of all, walking is obviously the cheapest   ...✓.......
means of travelling, and can be the quicker   ..the.....
in a city centre. Of course, the further you have   1) ....
to go, the more so tired you will become.   2) ....
In some ways walking is more healthier than   3) ....
travelling by bus or car, but it can be just as the   4) ....
unhealthy because cities are the much more   5) ....
polluted than they used to be. Cars are faster   6) ....
of course and more than convenient, but as cities   7) ....
become more of crowded, parking is getting   8) ....
harder. Sometimes public transport is better,   9) ....
even though buses don't go as fast as cars do it.   10) ....
Cars are a lot more and convenient but as they   11) ....
cause most pollution, it is the better to avoid   12) ....
using them if possible. In a city the fastest way   13) ....
of travelling is on a bike, which keeps you fitter   14) ....
and is not so that noisy as a motorbike or a car.   15) ....

KEY POINTS

1   Check spelling and formation rules for comparative and superlative adjectives.

2   Some adverbs have the same forms as adjectives, and form comparatives and superlatives like adjectives.

    fast   faster   fastest

3   In comparative clauses, auxiliaries are often used instead of repeating the verb a second time.

    *Wendy works twice as hard **as I do**.*

SEE ALSO

Unit 25
Progress test

Unit 25 Progress test

(Units 21, 22, 23, 24)

1

Put **one** suitable word in each space.

Holiday problems

Somehow I always have problems when I go away on holiday. (1) .... year my travel agent promises me that my holiday will be (2) ...... best I have ever had, but none of these promises has ever (3)..... true. This year I got food poisoning (4) .... day I arrived. It must have been the fish I ate at the hotel (5) .... evening. In (6) .... morning I felt terrible, and I was seen by two doctors. I tried to explain my problem to them, but (7) .... of them spoke English, (8) .... didn't help. It took me (9) .... of the first week to recover, and I spent three or four days sitting next to (10) .... hotel swimming pool reading newspapers. By the time I felt better, (11) .... weather had changed, but I was determined to go sight-seeing, and do (12) .... swimming. Unfortunately (13) .... of the museums was open, as there was (14) .... strike. I would have enjoyed myself (15) ...... if I had stayed at home.

2

Complete the second sentence so that it has a similar meaning to the first sentence, using the word given. Do not change the word given. You must use between two and five words.

a) That's the worst film I've ever seen.
    worse
    I've .... film.

b) There aren't any sandwiches left, I'm afraid.
    all
    I'm afraid .... eaten.

c) I thought that Martin's last novel was more interesting.
    latest
    Martin's .... interesting as his last one.

d) I talked to neither of Harry's sisters.
    either
    I didn't .... Harry's sisters.

e) Bob is a much better swimmer than George.
    swim
    George .... as Bob.

f) If you walk slowly, it takes longer to get there.
    longer
    The more .... it takes to get there.

g) Calling the police isn't any good.
    no
    It's .... the police.

h) I phoned Norman last of all.
    person
    Norman .... phoned.

130

i) This is the best party I've ever been to.
a
I've .... good party as this.

j) I thought this meal would cost more than it did.
much
This meal .... thought.

3

Complete each sentence with **one** suitable word. Do not use the word *piece*.

a) Would you like another ...... of cake?
b) There is another ...... of stairs after this one.
c) What a lovely ...... of hair you have.
d) Put up your hand if you need another ...... of paper.
e) There was an interesting ...... of news about Japan in the paper.
f) Could you put a few ...... of coal on the fire?
g) Pour me a ...... of water, would you?
h) They gave me a very large ...... of potatoes with my dinner.
i) There was a terrible flash of lightning and a ...... of thunder.
j) Oh bother, I've split my new ...... of shorts.

4

Rewrite each sentence so that it contains the word given in capitals, and so that the meaning stays the same. The word cannot be changed in any way.

a) You are not allowed to park here.   PARKING
....

b) There aren't any tables, chairs or beds in the house. FURNITURE
....

c) This city seems very crowded.   PEOPLE
....

d) Can you tell me about guided tours of the city?   INFORMATION
....

e) The people in the theatre were enthusiastic.   AUDIENCE
....

f) I like maths best.   SUBJECT
....

g) There are a lot of cars on this road today.   TRAFFIC
....

h) Sue has gone to see a play.   THEATRE
....

i) I'm looking for somewhere to stay.   ACCOMMODATION
....

j) Jim is out of work at the moment.   JOB
....

5

Complete the second sentence so that it has a similar meaning to the first sentence, using the word given. Do not change the word given. You must use between two and five words.

a) Jim teaches French.
   works
   Jim .... teacher.
b) Neil Armstrong stepped on the moon first.
   man
   Neil Armstrong .... to step on the moon.
c) Can't you do better than that?
   the
   Is .... do?
d) I haven't eaten lobster before.
   ever
   This is the .... eaten.
e) Is Julia a good violinist?
   play
   Can Julia .... well?
f) Actually, the only thing you need is a screwdriver.
   all
   Actually .... a screwdriver
g) Both of the lifts were out of order.
   of
   Neither .... working.
h) David told me that he always goes shopping on Fridays.
   every
   David told me .... shopping.
i) Both cases were too heavy to lift.
   couldn't
   I .... case.
j) George's annual salary is £15,000.
   earns
   George .... year.

6

Put **one** word in each space.

a) My trousers are creased. I must iron ....
b) Could you give me .... information about the Arts Festival?
c) I can't come out tonight. I have .... work to do.
d) Look at your hair! You must have .... cut!
e) I've decided to buy .... new furniture.
f) The news .... on at nine o'clock.
g) Thank you very much. You've been .... great help.
h) Is this .... pub you told me about?
i) Chris was .... last person to leave the room.
j) Don't .... English drink a lot of tea!

7

Look carefully at each line. Some lines are correct, but some have a word which should not be there. Tick each correct line. If a line has a word which should not be there, write the word in the space.

The house painters

Last week some painters came round to	...✓.......
paint my house. I usually do this kind of a job	...a.......
myself, but I've been here very busy for the last	1) ....
month. So I called a more local decorating firm,	2) ....
and they agreed to do it for a reasonable price.	3) ....
Three men arrived on Monday the morning to	4) ....
paint the outside walls. Of course, they were used	5) ....
the wrong colour and spilt paint all over the	6) ....
front door. Some one of the windows	7) ....
upstairs were open, and some of paint went	8) ....
inside the house and ruined both the carpet in	9) ....
the living-room. They also broke a window.	10) ....
I phoned their company, and the manager	11) ....
assured me that they would repaint than the	12) ....
walls. Then I went away on a business.	13) ....
I've just come back, and the walls are a different	14) ....
colour, but it is still such the wrong colour.	15) ....
If I had done the job myself, I would have	
finished it by now.	

Unit 26 Phrasal verbs 1

Explanations

1
Verbs with three parts

The object always follows these verbs, and cannot be put between any of the parts. Verbs marked * can be used intransitively without the final preposition.

*I've decided to **cut down on** smoking.*   *I've decided to **cut down.***

A selection of verbs is listed here with examples. Others, and other meanings of those listed here, are included in the activities.

Cut down on *
    *I've decided to **cut down on** smoking.*   (reduce the amount of)

Catch up with *
    *They are too far ahead for us to **catch***   (reach the same place as)
    ***up with** them.*

Come up against
    *I'm afraid we've **come up against** a*   (meet)
    problem we can't solve.

Come up with
    *Have you **come up with** an answer yet?*   (think of)

Drop in on *
    *I **dropped in on** Bill and Sheila on my way home.*   (visited)

Face up to
    *You must **face up to** reality!*   (accept, deal with)

Feel up to
    *You must **feel up to** going to work.*   (feel fit to do)

Get away with
    *Jack stole the money and **got away with** it.*   (avoid discovery)

Get along/on with *
    *Do you **get along with** your new boss?*   (have good relations with)

Get on with
    *Stop talking and **get on with** your work!*   (continue with)

Get out of
    *I managed to **get out of** working late.*   (avoid a responsibility)

Get round to
    *I haven't **got round to** decorating yet.*   (find time to do)

Get up to
    *What has young Bill been **getting up to**?*   (do, often something wrong)

Go in for
    *Do you **go in for** sailing?*   (have as a hobby)

Grow out of
    *Julie has **grown out of** playing with dolls.*   (become too old for)

Keep up with *
> *You're going too fast! I can't **keep up with** you!* (stay in the same place as)

Look down on
> *Our neighbours **look down on** anyone* (feel superior to)
> *without a car.*

Look up to
> *I really **look up to** my teacher.* (respect)

Look forward to
> *We are **looking forward to** our holiday.* (think we will enjoy)

Make up for
> *The wonderful dinner **made up for** the bad* (compensate for)
> *service.*

Put up with
> *I can't **put up with** these screaming children!* (bear)

Run out of *
> *Oh dear, we've **run out of** petrol!* (have no more of)

Stand up for
> *You must learn to **stand up for** yourself!* (defend)

2
Verbs with two parts: transitive and inseparable

These verbs take an object, but the object cannot be put between verb and preposition.
> *I can't **do without** coffee in the morning!*

Ask after
> *Jim **asked after** you yesterday.* (ask for news of)

Call for
> *I'll **call for** you at six.* (come and collect)

Call on
> *I **called on** some friends in Plymouth.* (visit)

Come across
> *Joe **came across** this old painting in the attic.* (find by chance)

Come into
> *Sue **came into** a large sum of money.* (inherit)

Count on
> *I'm **counting on** you to help me.* (depend on)

Deal with
> *How would you **deal with** the traffic problem?* (take action about)

Do without
> *We'll have to **do without** a holiday this year.* (manage without)

Get at
> *What are you **getting at**?* (suggest)

Get over
> *Barry has **got over** his illness now.* (recover from)

Go over
> *Let's **go over** our plan once more.* (discuss the details)

Join in
> Try to **join in** the lesson as much as you can.   (contribute to)

Live on
> They **live on** the money her father gives them.   (have as income)

Look into
> The government is **looking into** the problem.   (investigate)

Look round
> Let's **look round** the town today.   (look at everything)

Make for
> Where are you **making for** exactly?   (go in the direction of)

Pick on
> My teacher is always **picking on** me.   (choose a person to punish)

Run into
> I **ran into** Steve in the supermarket yesterday.   (meet by chance)

See about
> We'll have to **see about** getting you an office.   (arrange)

See to
> Can you **see to** the dog's food?   (attend to, take care of)

Stand for
> I won't **stand for** such rudeness!   (tolerate)
> Andrew is **standing for** parliament.   (be a candidate)

Take after
> Helen **takes after** her mother.   (have the same characteristics as)

Activities

1
Rewrite each sentence so that it contains the phrasal verb given, in a suitable form.

a) Sorry, but I haven't found time to fix your bike yet.   (get round to)
...Sorry, but I haven't got round to fixing your bike yet...

b) Oh bother, we don't have any milk left.   (run out of)
....

c) It took me a long time to recover from my illness.   (get over)
....

d) Peter is just like his father!   (take after)
....

e) I think we've found an answer to the problem.   (come up with)
....

f) I don't think I'm well enough to play football today.   (feel up to)
....

g) Ann is someone I really respect.   (look up to)
....

h) I must arrange to have the kitchen painted.   (see about)
....

i) Please help me. I'm relying on you.   (count on)

  ....

j) Julie must be too old to bite her nails.   (grow out of)

  ....

2
Complete the
second sentence
so that it has a
similar meaning
to the first
sentence, using
the word given.
Do not change
the word given.
You must use
between two and
five words.

a) Quite by chance, Brenda met Philip at the station.
  ran
  Brenda ..*ran into Philip*.. at the station.

b) You'll just have to learn to accept the facts!
  face
  You'll just .... the facts.

c) It's time that more women defended their rights!
  stood
  It's time that more .... rights.

d) How can you bear so much traffic noise?
  put
  How can you .... traffic noise?

e) Charles cheated in his exams, and didn't get caught.
  got
  Charles cheated in his exams, and .... it.

f) I visited a few friends while I was in Manchester.
  called
  I .... while I was in Manchester.

g) What are you trying to say?
  getting
  What .... at?

h) I must go to the dentist, and get my teeth taken care of.
  seen
  I must go to the dentist .... to.

i) Do you have a good relationship with your in-laws?
  get
  Do you .... in-laws?

j) You're so lucky to have inherited all that money!
  come
  You're so lucky to .... that money!

3

Complete each sentence with one of the words from the list. Use each word once only.

| across | against | for | in | into | on | round | to | up | with |

a) I'll send someone to call ...*for*....... the parcel on Thursday.

b) You'll have to work hard to keep .... with the rest of the class.

c) Jean didn't expect to come up .... such difficulties.

d) It's not fair. You're always picking .... me.

e) Terry sang the first verse and then everyone joined ....

f) I came .... one of your novels in a second-hand bookshop.

g) I'm not interested in buying anything. I'm just looking ....

h) Don't you think the manager should deal .... this problem?

i) George came .... a lot of money when his uncle died.

j) You look very guilty! What have you been getting up .... ?

4

Complete each sentence with the most suitable word or phrase.

a) There isn't any sugar, I'm afraid. You'll have to ..*C*.. .
A) run out   B) put up with   C) do without   D) make for

b) How much money do you manage to .... ?
A) come into   B) go in for   C) deal with   D) live on

c) The weather was fine, and everyone was .... the coast.
A) going in for   B) making for   C) joining in   D) seeing about

d) I was passing their house, so I .... Claire and Michael.
A) dropped in on   B) came up with   C) got on with   D) ran into

e) I don't really .... winter sports very much.
A) deal with   B) face up to   C) go in for   D) get round to

f) Losing my job was a great shock, but I think I'm .... it.
A) seeing to   B) putting up with   C) standing for   D) getting over

g) Sheila's gone to .... having a new phone installed.
A) see about   B) deal with   C) get round to   D) ask after

h) I've had to .... a lot of insulting behaviour from you!
A) look down on   B) put up with   C) stand up for   D) get on with

i) The hotel was terrible, but the wonderful beach .... our disappointment.
A) got over   B) faced up to   C) saw to   D) made up for

j) Jack has decided to .... the time he spends watching television.
A) run out of   B) see to   C) cut down on   D) come up with

5

Choose the most suitable ending for each sentence. Other meanings of verbs in this unit (possibly in a different category) are included here.

a) I can't put up with ..B... .
   A) you if you should come to London.   B) people who smoke all the time.
   C) the plates onto the top shelf.

b) The chairperson of the committee then called on Tony ....
   A) but his line was engaged.   B) to make a speech in reply.
   C) so that his voice could be heard above the crowd.

c) Mary has been chosen to stand for ....
   A) the bad behaviour of her colleagues.   B) herself in future.
   C) Parliament in the next election.

d) After my holidays it takes me a few days to catch up with ....
   A) the people running in front of me.   B) all the news I've missed.
   C) a really bad cold.

e) Small children soon grow out of ....
   A) their shoes.   B) all the good food they eat.
   C) the habits they have when they get older.

f) I've decided to go in for ....
   A) eating fruit for breakfast.   B) a few days rest in the country.
   C) a photography competition in *Photographer's Weekly*.

g) I'm afraid that our plans to open a new factory have run into ....
   A) some old friends.   B) a tree by the side of the road.
   C) a few unexpected difficulties.

h) We find that this type of tyre makes for ....
   A) safer driving in wet weather.   B) the first place it can stop.
   C) all smaller types of car.

i) I saw my old friend John last week. I couldn't get over ....
   A) my cold before I saw him, though.   B) near enough to talk to him though.
   C) how young he looked.

j) In this part of town, people are only worried about keeping up with ....
   A) others who are faster.   B) late-night television programmes.
   C) the Joneses.

KEY POINTS

1   Check any new phrasal verb with a dictionary, to be sure what type it is.

2   Bear in mind that many phrasal verbs have more than one meaning.

3   Phrasal verbs tend to be more common in spoken language and informal written language.

SEE ALSO

Unit 30
Progress test

Unit 27 Phrasal verbs 2

Explanations

1
Verbs with two parts: transitive and separable

These verbs take an object, and the object (especially *it* and *them*) can be put between the verb and the preposition. Object phrases tend to be put after the preposition. The pronouns *him, her, it, us, them* are put after the verb. Verbs marked * have an intransitive form with a different meaning.

> *We **brought up** this child.   We **brought** her **up**.*

Call back and *show around* always put the object between the verb and the preposition.

Other meanings of the verbs listed here are included in the activities.

Bring up
> *We **brought up** this child.*   (look after and educate)

Carry out
> *You haven't **carried out** my instructions.*   (act upon)

Call off
> *We have decided to **call off** the match.*   (cancel)

Clear up*
> *Could you **clear up** your room please?*   (make tidy)
> *The weather is **clearing up***.*   (improve)

Fill in*
> *Can you **fill in** this form please?*   (complete)
> *Our teacher was ill, so Mrs Frost **filled in***.*   (take someone's place)

Find out
> *I want to **find out** what happened.*   (learn about)

Give away
> *The millionaire **gave** all his money **away**.*   (make a gift of)
> *Jill asked me not to **give** her secret **away**.*   (make something known)

Give up*
> *I've decided to **give up** eating meat.*   (stop)
> *After trying hard, George finally **gave up**.*   (stopped trying)

Hold up
> *Two masked men **held up** the bank.*   (rob)

Knock out
> *The blow on the head **knocked** me **out**.*   (make unconscious)

Leave out
> *I always **leave out** the difficult exercises.*   (not include)

Look up*
> *I have to **look** this word **up** in my dictionary.*   (locate)
> *Things are **looking up***.*   (appear better)

Make up*
   *I think you **made** this story **up**.*   (invent)
   *The couple quarrelled but then **made up**.*   (become friends again)
Pick up
   *I'll **pick** you **up** at six.*   (collect)
Put aside
   *Harry **puts** money **aside** every week for his*   (save)
   holiday.
Put off
   *They **put** the meeting **off** until Thursday.*   (postpone)
   *The smell of fish **put** me **off** my tea.*   (discourage from)
Put up
   *If you come to Florence I can **put** you **up**.*   (provide
                                                                            accommodation)
Show around
   *Let me **show** you **around** the new building.*   (give a guided tour)
Take over*
   *A German company **took** us **over** last year.*   (buy a company)
   *If you are tired, I'll **take over***.*   (take someone's place)
Take up
   *I've decided to **take up** tennis.*   (start a hobby)
Tear up
   *Wendy **tore up** Alan's letters.*   (tear into pieces)
Think over
   *Please **think over** our offer.*   (consider)
Try out
   *Have you **tried out** the new computer?*   (use for the first time)
Turn down
   *Paul was offered the job but he **turned it down**.*   (refuse an offer)
Wear out
   *All this work has **worn** me **out**.*   (make tired)
Work out
   *This is a difficult problem. I can't **work it out**.*   (find a solution)

2
Verbs with two
parts: intransitive

These verbs have no object. Verbs marked * have a transitive form with a
different meaning. There are other meanings, not included here.
Break down
   *The car **broke down** on the motorway.*   (stop working)
Break out
   *The war **broke out** unexpectedly.*   (begin suddenly)
Come out
   *Her new book **came out** last week.*   (be published)
Draw up*
   *Suddenly an ambulance **drew up** outside.*   (come to a stop)
   *My lawyer is **drawing up** a contract for us***.*   (write a legal document)

Fall out
  *Charles and Diana have **fallen out** again.*   (quarrel)
Get away
  *The bank robbers **got away** in a stolen van.*   (escape)
Give in
  *She pleaded with me, and I finally **gave in**.*   (yield)
Go off
  *Everyone panicked when the bomb **went off**.*   (explode)
Look out
  ***Look out**! There's a car coming!*   (beware)
Set in
  *I think the rain has **set in** for the day.*   (begin as if to continue)
Show off
  *You always **show off** at parties.*   (behave to attract attention)

Take off
  *Your plane **takes off** at 6.00.*   (leave the ground)
Turn up*
  *Guess who **turned up** at our party?*   (arrive, often unexpectedly)

  *Can you **turn up** the sound*?*   (increase)
Wear off
  *When the drug **wears off** you may feel pain.*   (fade away)

Activities

1

Rewrite each sentence so that the meaning stays the same, using one of the verbs in the list in a suitable form. Use each verb once only.

call off   draw up   give in   look up   put aside
put up   turn down   turn up   wear off   work out

a) Jack always arrives late for work.
   ...*Jack always turns up late for work.*...

b) See if their number is in the phone directory.
   ....

c) I'm saving up to buy a new bike.
   ....

d) A large black limousine stopped outside the house.
   ....

e) I'm afraid the match has been cancelled.
   ....

f) The government refused to yield to the demands of the terrorists.
   ....

g) We offered them £100,000 for the house but they refused our offer.
   ....

h) You can stay with us if you come to Cambridge.

....

i) I can't calculate how much the whole trip will cost.

....

j) After a few days the pain in Dave's leg went away.

....

2

Put **one** word in each space.

a) Why don't you let me show you ...*round*............. London?
b) Jane is coming to pick us .... after work.
c) Have you found .... what time the train leaves?
d) We had to wait for an hour before the plane took ....
e) Harry was brought .... by his grandparents.

f) A shelf fell on my head and knocked me ....
g) I was so angry when I saw the parking ticket that I tore it ....
h) A fire has broken .... in an office block in central London.
i) Julian always talks loudly and shows ....
j) If you don't like this part you can leave it ....

3

Complete the second sentence so that it has a similar meaning to the first sentence, using the word given. Do not change the word given. You must use between two and five words.

a) I think it's going to rain all day.
    in
    I think the ...*rain has set in for*.. the day.
b) I don't know what to write on this form.
    in
    I don't know .... this form.
c) I started doing this job when Janet left.
    over
    I .... when Janet left.
d) This story of yours isn't true!
    up
    You .... story!
e) I haven't made a decision, but I'm considering it at the moment.
    over
    I haven't made a decision, but I'm .... at the moment.
f) We believe that it was you who robbed the Post Office.
    up
    We believe that .... the Post Office.

g) Tina's car stopped working on the way to Scotland.
   down
   Tina's car .... on the way to Scotland.

h) It would be a good idea to stop drinking coffee.
   up
   It would be a good idea .... coffee.

i) Ruth's party has been postponed until next month.
   off
   Ruth's party .... next month.

j) Our company has just been bought by a multinational.
   over
   Our company .... by a multinational.

4

Put **one** suitable word in each space.

a) In the army, all orders have to be ...*carried*...... out!

b) Why don't you .... up golf? It's a good pastime.

c) If I won a lot of money, I would .... some of it away.

d) Let's .... out the new food processor.

e) This room is a mess. Why don't you .... it up?

f) I've been walking all day. I feel .... out.

g) Joe is very quarrelsome, he .... out with everyone.

h) Where were you exactly when the bomb .... off?

i) When does your new record .... out?

j) Can you .... in for me while I go to the bank?

5

Complete each sentence with the most suitable word or phrase.

a) Brian ..*C*.. at our dinner party wearing a pink bow tie.
   A) wore out   B) showed off   C) turned up   D) tried out

b) David's wife is bound to .... the truth sooner or later.
   A) find out   B) come out   C) make up   D) give up

c) You don't have to decide now, you can ....
   A) put it aside   B) call it off   C) tear it up   D) think it over

d) Pat was caught by the police, but Martin ....
   A) gave in   B) gave up   C) got away   D) held up

e) After the quarrel, we kissed and ....
   A) cleared up   B) looked up   C) made up   D) put up

f) Why exactly did war .... between the two countries?
   A) break out   B) set in   C) go off   D) call off

g) After a long day at work most people feel ....
   A) broken down   B) worn out   C) knocked out   D) turned down

h) I've just been offered a new job! Things are ....
   A) turning up   B) clearing up   C) making up   D) looking up

i) In the end I .... the form in disgust, and threw it away.
   A) filled in   B) worked out   C) tore up   D) put off

j) I was interested in buying the car, but a friend ....
   A) put me off   B) turned me down   C) showed me around   D) gave me away

6

Replace the word
underlined with
a suitable phrasal
verb listed in this
unit.

a) I think that you <u>invented</u> this story. ..*made up*.......
b) When do you think your book will <u>be published</u>? ....
c) I think that the weather is <u>improving</u>. ....
d) I can't <u>find an answer to</u> this problem. ....
e) <u>Be careful</u>! You're going to fall! ....
f) I'm afraid William tends to <u>stop trying</u>. ....
g) If you want a rest, I'll <u>carry on for you</u>. ....
h) The plane is going to <u>leave the ground</u>. ....
i) I think that Sue and Neil have <u>quarrelled</u>. ....
j) Why do you have to <u>make people admire you</u>! ....

7

Choose the best
meaning for the
phrase
underlined in
each sentence.
Other meanings
for verbs listed in
this unit are
included (some
with a change of
category).

a) At half past six, the alarm clock <u>went off</u>. ..*B*....
   A) exploded   B) rang   C) disappeared
b) Jim is very good at <u>taking off his teacher</u>. ....
   A) flying with his teacher   B) getting rid of his teacher
   C) imitating his teacher
c) Please <u>give in</u> your papers at the end of the lesson. ....
   A) give them back   B) put them inside the desk
   C) accept whatever they say
d) Please don't <u>bring up that subject</u> again! ....
   A) start shouting about it   B) mention it   C) talk about it for hours on end
e) There is one small matter I would like to <u>clear up</u>. ....
   A) find an explanation for   B) make clean and tidy
   C) get rid of once and for all
f) Shirley spends hours <u>making up</u> before she goes out. ....
   A) thinking of a good story   B) trying to get on better with her friends
   C) putting cosmetics on her face
g) Jean is really good at <u>picking up languages</u>. ....
   A) choosing languages   B) learning languages by being in a country
   C) learning languages by heart
h) All my old clothes need <u>taking up</u>. ....
   A) taking to the cleaners   B) to be replaced   C) to be made shorter
i) The whole cost of the equipment <u>works out at</u> £450. ....
   A) comes to   B) can be reduced to   C) will involve an extra
j) Jackie <u>broke down</u> and everyone felt sorry for her. ....
   A) injured herself   B) caused an accident   C) started crying

KEY POINTS

1 Check any new phrasal verb in a dictionary, to be sure what type it is.

2 Bear in mind that many phrasal verbs have more than one meaning.

3 Phrasal verbs tend to be more common in spoken language and informal written language.

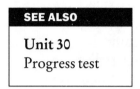

SEE ALSO

Unit 30
Progress test

Unit 28 Verbs followed by infinitive or gerund and *that* clause

Explanations

1
Verbs followed
by *-ing* or a noun

*avoid, be worth, dislike, enjoy, fancy, help, keep, mind, miss, practise, risk,
can't stand*
> Try to **avoid walking** as much as possible.
> I managed to **avoid an argument**.
> It's not **worth waiting** for a bus at this time of day.
> I **dislike having** to get up early.
> Do you **enjoy meeting** people from other countries?
> I don't **fancy going out** this evening.
> George can't **help laughing** when he sees you!
> I wish you wouldn't **keep interrupting**.
> I don't **mind helping** you do the washing-up.
> Jane **misses going** for long country walks.
> You should **practise introducing** yourself.
> We can't **risk starting** a fire in the forest.
> I **can't stand going** to office parties.

2
Verbs followed
by *-ing*, a *that*
clause, or a noun.

admit, consider, deny, imagine, recollect, report, suggest
> Jack **admitted stealing** the money.
> Jack **admitted that** he had stolen the money.
> When accused of stealing the money, Jack **admitted it**.
> Have you **considered taking up** jogging?
> You must **consider that** Jim has never driven abroad before.
> Peter **denied stealing** the money.
> Can you **imagine living** in California?
> I don't **recollect meeting** you before.
> Suddenly I **recollected that** I had another appointment.
> Helen **reported losing** her watch to the director.
> I **suggested going** to the beach.
> I **suggested that we went** to the beach.

3

Verbs followed by either infinitive with to or -ing with little or no change of meaning.

attempt, begin, continue, dread, not bear, hate, intend, like, love, prefer, start
> I **attempted to leave/leaving** but the police stopped me.

For some speakers, *like to* describes a habitual action.
> *On Sundays I* **like to get up** *early and go for a swim.*

Would like, would love and *would prefer* are followed by infinitive with *to.*
> *I'd* **like to come** *to your party, but I'll be away then.*

4

Verbs followed by either infinitive with *to* or -*ing* or a *that* clause, with change of meaning.

forget
> *I* **forgot to buy** *any coffee.*   (I didn't remember)
> *I* **forgot the coffee.**
> *I won't* **forget to go** *there.*   (I'll remember)
> *I won't* **forget meeting** *you.*   (It will stay in my memory.)
> *I* **forgot that I had invited** *ten people to lunch.*

go on
> *Diana* **went on working** *all night.*   (continue)
> *The director* **went on to say** *that the strike was over.*   (add)

mean
> *I* **meant to phone** *you but I forgot.*   (intend)
> *This* **means leaving** *at 6.00.*   (involve)
> *This* **means that** *we will have to leave at 6.00!*

regret
> *I* **regret to tell** *you that you have failed.*   (a formal statement)
> *Kate* **regretted not buying** *the house.*   (be sorry about the past)
> *Kate* **regretted that** *she hadn't bought the house.*
> *Kate* **regretted her decision.**

remember
> *Please* **remember to lock** *the door.*   (don't forget a future action)
> *I* **remember locking** *the door.*   (remember a past action)
> *I* **remembered Sue's birthday.**
> *I* **remembered that I had left** *my keys behind.*

stop
> *I* **stopped going** *to evening classes.*   (give up)
> *I* **stopped to buy** *some coffee.*   (in order to do something)
> *I* **stopped the car.**

try
> *I* **tried to get up** *early, but I couldn't.*   (try and fail)
> *Why don't you* **try getting up** *early?*   (suggesting an action)
> *I* **tried a new kind of toothpaste.**

5

Verbs followed by infinitive without *to*, or *-ing* with change of meaning.

feel, hear, notice, see, watch

Notice can also be followed by a *that* clause.

*I felt the train **moving**.*	(continuing action)
*I felt the train **move**.*	(completed action)
*I **noticed** people **waving** outside.*	
*I **noticed that there were** people waving outside.*	

Some of these verbs can be used with a *that* clause with a change of meaning.

*I **feel that** you should look for another job.*	(believe)
*I've just **heard that** the match is off.*	(receive news)
***See that** you lock up when you leave.*	(make sure)

6

Verbs followed by infinitive with *to*.

afford, appear, ask, choose, fail, happen, help, long, manage, offer, prepare, refuse, tend, wait, want

*I can't **afford to go** on holiday abroad this year.*
*The car **appears to have broken down**.*
*David **asked me to give** this to you.*
*I **chose not to go** to university.*
*Gerry **failed to arrive** on time.*
*I **happened to be passing** so I dropped in.*

7

Verbs followed by infinitive with *to*, or a *that* clause.

agree, arrange, decide, demand, desire, expect, hope, intend, learn, plan, pretend, promise, seem, threaten, wish

*Tom **agreed to meet** us outside the cinema.*
*Tom **agreed that** he would meet us outside the cinema.*
*We **arranged to leave** at 5.30.*
*We **arranged that** we would leave at 5.30.*
*John **decided to** take the bus.*
*John **decided that** he would take the bus.*

Activities

1

Complete each sentence with a suitable form of the verb in brackets.

a) I really miss (play) ..playing.... tennis like I used to.
b) I'm sorry. I meant (write) .... to you, but I've been busy.
c) Harry says he doesn't remember (meet) .... Sally before.
d) Martin failed (pay) .... the rent on time yet again.
e) It's not worth (buy) .... a return ticket.
f) Have you ever considered (work) .... as a teacher?
g) I promise I won't forget (feed) .... the cat.
h) We've arranged (meet) .... outside the school at 4.30.
i) If you've got a headache, why don't you try (take) .... an aspirin?
j) I can't imagine (not have) .... a car!

2

Complete the second sentence so that it has a similar meaning to the first sentence, using the word given.

a) Jack said that he hadn't cheated in the exam.
   cheating
   Jack ..*denied cheating*.. in the exam.

b) It was difficult for me not to laugh at Wendy's letter.
   help
   I .... at Wendy's letter.

c) I'm sorry but you have not been appointed to the post.
   regret
   I .... you have not been appointed to the post.

d) I needed a drink of water and so I stopped running.
   to
   I stopped running .... water.

e) Luckily Peter didn't pay a fine.
   paying
   Luckily Peter .... a fine.

f) I think it would be a good idea to take the train.
   taking
   I .... the train.

g) Don't forget the lights when you leave.
   off
   Don't forget .... when you leave.

h) I can hear voices upstairs.
   talking
   I .... upstairs.

i) I think Derek has forgotten the meeting.
   appears
   Derek .... the meeting.

j) My neighbour said he would call the police!
   threatened
   My neighbour .... the police.

3

Complete each sentence with a suitable form of the verb in brackets.

a) Pauline couldn't manage (eat) ..*to eat*......... all the ice cream.

b) I've decided (not sell) .... my bike after all.

c) A witness reported (see) .... Terry at the scene of the crime.

d) William pretended (not notice) .... the 'No Parking' sign.

e) One of the boys finally admitted (start) .... the fire.

f) I suppose I tend (buy) .... more books than I used to.

g) Bill told Christine that he couldn't go on (live) .... without her.

h) Sometimes I regret (move) .... to this part of the country.
i) Did you notice anyone (wait) .... outside when you left?
j) Mark expects (finish) .... work round about 6.00.

4

Complete each sentence with a suitable form of one of the verbs in brackets.

a) Mary was so angry that she ...*demanded*.. to see the manager.
   (demand, hope, risk, stop)
b) The weather is so awful that I don't .... going out this evening.
   (fancy, like, try, want)
c) The children could hardly .... to leave their pets behind.
   (bear, forget, regret, seem)
d) You don't .... looking after the baby, do you?
   (agree, stand, mind, notice)
e) Do you .... to know when this castle was built?
   (ask, happen, imagine, like)
f) John .... to let his children go to the concert.
   (afford, avoid, refuse, stop)
g) If I give you the information, I .... losing my job!
   (expect, mean, prepare, risk)
h) What do you .... to be doing in ten years time?
   (begin, expect, remember, suggest)
i) Do you .... to tell the police about the missing money?
   (admit, confess, deny, intend)
j) Why does Basil .... looking at his watch?
   (appear, attempt, keep, mean)

KEY POINTS

1 Check new verbs in a dictionary to be sure how they are used.

2 Note that some verbs can be used in different ways with changes of meaning.

SEE ALSO
Unit 30
Progress test

Unit 29 Prepositions following verbs and adjectives

Explanations

Prepositions following verbs

1 About
agree about, argue about, boast about, dream about, know about, laugh about, read about, talk about

2 At
guess at, laugh at, look at

3 For
apply for, arrange for, ask for something, blame someone for, care for, forgive someone for, look for, pay for something, search for, vote for, wait for

4 In
believe in, confide in someone, involve someone in something, specialise in, succeed in, take part in

5 Of
accuse someone of something, (dis)approve of, die of something, dream of, remind someone of something, rob someone of something, smell of, taste of, warn someone of something

6 On
blame something on someone, concentrate on, congratulate someone on something, depend on, insist on, rely on.

7 To
add something to, admit to, apologise to someone for something, be accustomed to, be used to, belong to, confess to, explain something to someone, lend something to someone, listen to, object to, reply to, talk to someone about something

8 With
agree with, argue with, begin with, charge someone with a crime, deal with, discuss something with someone, provide someone with something, share something with someone, trust someone with something

Prepositions
following
adjectives

1 About
annoyed about, anxious about, certain about, excited about, happy about, pleased about, right about, sorry about, upset about

2 At
angry at, annoyed at, bad/good at, surprised at

3 By
bored by, shocked by, surprised by

4 For
famous for, late for, ready for, sorry for

5 From
absent from, different from, safe from

6 In
interested in

7 Of
afraid of, ashamed of, aware of, capable of, fond of, full of, it is good of you (to do something), jealous of

8 On
keen on

9 To
grateful to, kind to, married to

10 With
angry with, annoyed with, bored with, happy with, pleased with

Activities

1
Put **one** suitable word in each space.

a) A lot of people I know really believe ..in........... ghosts.
b) Martin grew to be very fond .... his pet snake.
c) This bread tastes .... fish!
d) Everyone was shocked .... Susan's strange appearance.
e) The company blamed the drop in sales .... the economic situation.
f) Brenda decided to discuss her problems .... a psychiatrist.
g) When Harry made his speech, everyone laughed .... him.
h) Robert has been married .... Deborah for over a year.
i) You were right after all .... the result of the election.
j) The woman who lived next door admitted .... the robbery.

2

Rewrite each sentence beginning as shown, so that the meaning stays the same.

a) Two men stole the old lady's handbag.
The old lady was ..*robbed of her handbag*...

b) John finds photography interesting.
John is ....

c) Helen has a good knowledge of car engines.
Helen knows a lot ....

d) The food in France is famous.
France is ....

e) I'd like to thank your brother for his help.
I am very grateful ....

f) Can you and Stephen share this book, please?
Can you share this book ....

g) I find studying all night rather difficult.
I'm not used ....

h) Harry feels frightened when he sees a snake.
Harry is afraid ....

i) I'm sorry about breaking your camera.
Please forgive me ....

j) Peter knows how to draw well.
Peter is good ....

3

Put **one** suitable word in each space.

a) David was ..*ashamed*... of what he had done, and he blushed.

b) I'm not very .... on the idea of going climbing.

c) Mary is always .... about all the famous people she has met.

d) Jim was often .... for work, and lost his job as a result.

e) There were no empty seats on the train, which was .... of soldiers.

f) Bill decided not to .... Bob with his secrets.

g) The two boys were .... of stealing a sports car.

h) We .... in persuading Carol to lend us her boat.

i) You have worked very hard! I am very .... with you!

j) I can't remember her name, but it .... with 'J'.

4

Complete the
second sentence
so that it has a
similar meaning
to the first
sentence, using
the word given.
Do not change
the word given.
You must use
between two and
five words.

a) William could do better work.
   capable
   William ..is.capable.of.. doing better work.

b) I own this car.
   belongs
   This car .... me.

c) The job received over a hundred applications.
   applied
   Over a hundred people .... the job.

d) Mrs Jones' death was caused by old age.
   died
   Mrs Jones .... old age.

e) 'Well done, Tony, you have passed the exam,' said Joe.
   congratulated
   Joe .... the exam.

f) Jean borrowed Shirley's camera.
   lent
   Shirley .... camera.

g) I'm not sure exactly when the train leaves.
   certain
   I'm .... when the train leaves.

h) Graham found the film very boring.
   by
   Graham .... the film.

i) We all pitied Stephen.
   sorry
   We all .... Stephen.

j) People should treat animals well.
   kind
   People .... animals.

5

Put **one** suitable
word in each
space.

a) My boss shouted at me – he was really ..angry........ with me!

b) I can see your point, but I just don't .... with you.

c) Terry doesn't .... of his children going to rock concerts.

d) George and I .... about politics all night!

e) Can I have a .... at the evening paper?

f) This story .... me of a novel by Dickens.

g) Peter feels .... of anyone who talks to his girlfriend.

h) I didn't expect you to behave like that! I'm .... at you!

i) Oh dear, I forgot to .... any baking powder to the cake.

j) I think you should .... your boss for a rise.

6

Complete each sentence with the most suitable word or phrase.

a) Thank you very much. It's very ..B... you to help me.
    A) good with   B) good of   C) good for   D) good about

b) The bad weather was .... the series of power cuts.
    A) blamed for   B) blamed on   C) blamed with   D) blamed by

c) I'm sorry, but I .... seeing the manager at once!
    A) arrange for   B) look for   C) agree with   D) insist on

d) Why do you spend all your time .... your sister!
    A) arguing about   B) arguing for   C) arguing with   D) arguing at

e) Helen is very .... going to work in Germany.
    A) excited about   B) excited for   C) excited with   D) excited to

f) The tourists were not .... the danger of bandits in the hills.
    A) known about   B) aware of   C) provided with   D) guessed at

g) I understood the problem after it had been .... me.
    A) explained to   B) admitted to   C) confessed to   D) replied to

h) I wish you wouldn't show off and .... your success so much!
    A) full of   B) bored by   C) boast about   D) congratulate on

i) If you listen to music you can't .... your homework.
    A) read about   B) arrange for   C) specialise in   D) concentrate on

j) We thought we would be .... the storm if we sheltered under a tree.
    A) happy about   B) safe from   C) depended on   D) cared for

7

Look carefully at each line. Some lines are correct, but some have a word which should not be there. Tick each correct line. If a line has a word which should not be there, write the word in the space.

Brothers and Sisters

When I was young I had argued with my	..had....
brothers and sisters all the time. I used to	...✓......
share with most of my toys with my brother,	1) ....
but he specialised in to keeping them for	2) ....
himself. When I asked about him for anything	3) ....
he simply used to refuse to give it to me, and	4) ....
then I became and very angry with him. Our	5) ....
sisters blamed for everything on us when our	6) ....
parents accused us of quarrelling all the time.	7) ....
My brother and I got up annoyed about this,	8) ....
but only succeeded them in making matters	9) ....
worse. Our parents didn't approve of our	10) ....
quarrelling so much, and insisted us on	11) ....
not taking sides. They either laughed about	12) ....
it, or told us to forgive and each other for	13) ....
everything. Soon we became ashamed of	14) ....
quarrelling, and became good at last getting	15) ....
on well with each other.	

KEY POINTS

1 Check verbs and adjectives in a dictionary to be certain which prepositions follow them.

2 In some cases different prepositions give different meanings.

3 Note the difference between *used to* (see Unit 1) and *be used to:*
   *I **used to have** a bike, but I sold it.*
   This is a contrast between past and present. *To have* is an infinitive in this sentence.
   *I **am not used to** getting up so early in the morning.*
   To is a preposition, and *getting up* is the noun form of the verb (gerund).

> **SEE ALSO**
>
> **Unit 30**
> Progress test

Unit 30 Progress test

(Units 26, 27, 28, 29)

1

Put **one** suitable word in each space.

Parents and children

I was reading an article last week in which the writer described how her children had changed as they (1) .... up. When they were small she had to (2) .... up with noisy games in the house, or (3) .... in their interminable games of football in the garden which (4) .... her out. If the house went quiet, she wondered what the monsters were (5) .... up to, or what crisis she would have to (6) .... with next. She dreaded the fact that they might (7) .... after her husband, who admitted having been an uncontrollable child who (8) .... most of the time (9) .... off to his friends by breaking things or (10)....... into fights. What was worse was that everyone else thought he was a sweet child, and he (11) .... away with terrible things! However, she had experienced an even greater shock with her children. They had (12) .... out of all their naughty behaviour, and (13) .... up serious hobbies such as chess and playing the piano. They never did anything without (14) .... it over first, and coming to a serious decision. She had to (15) .... up to that fact that they made her feel rather childish, and that in some ways she preferred them when they were young and noisy!

2

Complete each sentence with an expression formed from *get*.

a) When are you going to .... to writing to the bank?
b) I'm afraid I don't .... very well with my teacher.
c) I don't understand what you are .... What do you mean?
d) How are you feeling? Have you .... your cold yet?
e) Jim chased the burglar, but unfortunately the burglar.......... .

3

Complete each sentence with an expression formed from *come*.

a) Has the new book of tests .... yet?
b) It's a difficult situation and we haven't .... a solution yet.
c) I .... these old photographs in my desk yesterday.
d) Julie became rich when she .... a fortune.
e) I'm afraid we've .... a lot of problems in this project.

4
Complete the second sentence so that it has a similar meaning to the first sentence, using the word given. Do not change the word given. You must use between two and five words.

a) I wish I could work in the evenings as I used to.
   miss
   I .... in the evenings.

b) If I take the job I'll have to move to London.
   mean
   Taking the job .... London.

c) Neil wishes he hadn't sold his car.
   having
   Neil .... car.

d) Please see that you post all the letters.
   to
   Please don't .... all the letters.

e) Sheila has decided to take driving lessons.
   how
   Sheila has decided .... drive.

f) Jim said he hadn't stolen the jewels.
   stealing
   Jim .... the jewels.

g) How about going to the theatre tonight?
   like
   Would .... the theatre tonight?

h) Peter will look after the children – he has no objection.
   looking
   Peter doesn't .... children.

i) 'I'll definitely be here by eight,' Ann promised.
   would
   Ann .... by eight.

j) We met in 1978. Do you remember?
   our
   Do you remember .... 1978?

5
Put **one** suitable word in each space.

a) Don't go so fast! I can hardly .... up with you.

b) Don't be such a coward! .... up for yourself!

c) Please don't let me down. I'm .... on you.

d) We don't know who started the fire, but we're .... into it.

e) I must go to the dentist's and have my teeth .... to.

f) It's raining now, but I think it'll .... up later.

g) Ronnie hit his head on the shelf and .... himself out.

h) Tony's application for the job was .... down.

i) Steve woke up when the effect of the sleeping pill .... off.

j) The efforts of the United Nations could not stop war .... out.

6

Decide which answer A, B, C or D best fits each space.

I don't believe in ghosts!

Last year I stayed for a few days in an old house in Scotland which was famous (1) .... its ghost. I don't really believe (2) .... ghosts, so I'm not afraid (3) .... them of course. So when my hosts suggested (4) .... up all night to see their ghost, I simply laughed (5) .... them. Then they told me (6) .... the woman who haunted their house. She had been accused (7) .... murdering her husband in the eighteenth century because she had been jealous (8) .... him, but she had avoided (9) .... tried, and had disappeared. She appeared quite regularly, walking through the house as if she was searching (10) .... something. I agreed to watch that night, although it would (11) .... sitting for hours in the cold. I expected one of my friends to appear dressed (12) .... the ghost, and so when the figure of a woman finally came (13) .... me, I (14) .... to be terrified. You can imagine my surprise when the figure took a knife from her dress, and then vanished. I decided to disappear myself, and drove home to London as (15) .... as I could.

1)	A) with	B) for	C) from	D) as
2)	A) for	B) to	C) at	D) in
3)	A) with	B) for	C) of	D) by
4)	A) waking	B) getting	C) staying	D) coming
5)	A) at	B) with	C) about	D) to
6)	A) for	B) that	C) with	D) about
7)	A) that	B) of	C) for	D) while
8)	A) of	B) by	C) to	D) for
9)	A) and	B) being	C) but	D) having
10)	A) like	B) after	C) with	D) for
11)	A) mean	B) be	C) have	D) uncomfortable
12)	A) with	B) for	C) as	D) in
13)	A) about	B) towards	C) round	D) through
14)	A) wanted	B) imagined	C) pretended	D) supposed
15)	A) quickly	B) then	C) well	D) though

7

Complete each sentence with an expression containing *of*.

a) Jim's boss didn't think he was .... working on his own.
b) Mrs White is very .... animals, and has six cats.
c) I know I shouldn't have stolen the money. I'm .... myself.
d) It was very .... you to help me carry my shopping.
e) Georgina is very .... anyone who dances with her husband.

8

Complete each sentence with an expression containing *about*.

a) I knew I'd really seen a ghost. I was .... it!
b) Bill was very .... missing my birthday party.
c) You were .... the film. It was awful, just as you said.
d) I always get worried at airports. I feel .... missing the plane.
e) Poor Lucy has lost her job. She's very .... it.

9

Complete each sentence with a word ending in *-ing*.

a) That's all right, I don't mind .... up the dirty dishes.
b) Most people try to avoid .... up words in the dictionary.
c) Can you imagine .... up six small children?
d) I was considering .... up golf, actually.
e) We're rather hard up. It means .... without a holiday this year.

10

Put **one** suitable word in each space.

a) Have you ever thought of .... up cycling?
b) Harry had a serious illness, but he has .... over it now.
c) We have decided to .... off our holiday until next month.
d) I think that you .... up the whole story!
e) What are the children .... up to in the garden?
f) Everyone says that Chris .... after his father.
g) You'll never guess who .... up at the end-of-term party!
h) Please .... over our offer before you make a decision.
i) After the party, John had to .... up all the mess.
j) Nigel found it difficult to .... up with the rest of the class.

11

Complete the second sentence so that it has a similar meaning to the first sentence, using the word given.

a) The minister responsible has promised to investigate the problem.
into
The minister responsible has promised .... the problem.
b) Sorry, we must end there, as there is no more time.
run
Sorry, we must end there, as .... time.
c) All passengers are asked to complete this immigration form.
in
All passengers are asked to .... this immigration form.
d) The war began when the army crossed the border.
out
The war .... when the army crossed the border.
e) I don't understand what Ann is trying to say in this letter.
at
I don't understand what Ann is .... in this letter.
f) Your behaviour is intolerable! I won't tolerate it!
for
Your behaviour is intolerable! I .... it!
g) I always omit the garlic from this recipe.
out
I always .... the garlic from this recipe.
h) Have you ever discovered a writer called Jack Common?
across
Have you ever .... a writer called Jack Common?
i) I'll do some of the driving, when you feel like a rest.
over
I'll .... , when you feel like a rest from driving.

j) I'll do the garden soon, but I just haven't found the time yet.
got
I'll do the garden soon, but I just haven't .... yet.

Unit 31 Inversion and question tags

Explanations

Inversion after
negative adverbs

Inversion in this case means that the verb is in a question form and is necessary if a negative adverb (or one with negative meaning) begins the sentence. This only occurs in formal speech, and writing.

1 *Not only*
   Harry **not only missed** the train, but also lost his case.
   Not only did Harry miss the train, but (he) also lost his case.

2 *No Sooner*
   The main verb is always in the past perfect.
   Tim **had** no sooner **left**, than the phone rang.
   No sooner had Tim left, than the phone rang.

3 *Under no circumstances*
   You shouldn't touch these wires **under any circumstances**.
   Under no circumstances should you touch these wires.

4 *Seldom*
   I have seldom watched a better match.
   Seldom have I watched a better match.

5 Other expressions which are followed by inversion are:
   little, never, not once, only then, only after, rarely

Inversion for
emphasis

The verb comes before the subject if the adverb begins the sentence.

1 *Come* and *Go*
   These are mainly used with adverbs of place.
   In this way more emphasis is put on the subject in an exclamation.
   Here **comes** Jack!   There **goes** my money!
   Up **went** the plane into the clouds!   Along the road **came** Jim.

2 Other expressions
   Live and *stand* are used in formal writing. *Now* is used with *to be*.
   In this house **lived** Charles Dickens.
   On a hill outside the town **stands** the castle.
   Now is the best time to visit the Channel Islands.

Question tags

1 Tags are a way of adding a question to a statement, so that it becomes a question. If the intonation of the tag rises, it may be a genuine question, or a request for confirmation. If the intonation falls, the speaker expects agreement.

yes **2** A positive statement has a negative tag, and expects the answer 'Yes'.
  You agree *with me,* ***don't you?***

No A negative statement has a positive tag, and expects the answer 'No'.
  You don't *take sugar,* ***do you?***

3 It is possible for a positive tag to follow a positive statement, to express interest, or ask for confirmation. These are less common.
  So ***you like*** *working here,* ***do you?***

  Tags with *will* and *won't* can be used after imperatives.
  Don't drive too fast, ***will you?***

  Let's … has a tag formed with *shall.*
  Let's have a drink, ***shall we?***

4 Tags generally repeat auxiliaries, or *do/did.*
  Helen lives here, doesn't she?
  You left early, didn't you?
  Jack was born in Italy, wasn't he?
  You will help me, won't you?
  Someone's got to pay, haven't they?

Activities

1
Choose the most suitable words in each sentence.

a) Let's go to London next weekend, shall we/won't we?
b) You shouldn't have told me, <u>did you/should you</u>?
c) Jim hasn't been waiting long, <u>was he/has he</u>?
d) You won't tell anyone about this, <u>do you/will you</u>?
e) You're not doing what I told you, <u>do you/are you</u>?
f) Answer the phone for me, <u>will you/do you</u>?
g) George can't have noticed, <u>can he/has he</u>?
h) You've got to leave now, <u>don't you/haven't you</u>?
i) Pam and Tim got married last year, <u>didn't they/haven't they</u>?
j) I don't think John's very friendly, <u>does he/is he</u>?

2

Add a question
tag to each
sentence. (Do
not use positive
tags for positive
statements here.)

a) Don't leave anything behind, ...will you......... ?
b) David is bringing some wine, ... ?
c) You'll be home before midnight, ... ?
d) Harry was working in Bristol then, ... ?
e) Nobody knows who invented the wheel, ... ?
f) You don't need me any more, ... ?
g) The ticket to London doesn't cost a lot, ... ?
h) Let's invite the Smiths from next door, ... ?
i) You aren't too busy to talk, ... ?
j) Jean owns a restaurant, ... ?

3

Rewrite each
sentence,
beginning as
shown, so that
the meaning
stays the same.

a) Tony was not only late, but he had left all his books behind.
Not only ...was Tony late, but he had left all his books behind.......................

b) I had no sooner gone to bed than someone rang my doorbell.
No sooner ....
c) I have seldom stayed in a worse hotel.
Seldom ....
d) I have never heard such nonsense!
Never ....
e) I realised only then that I had lost my keys.
Only then ....
f) The economic situation has rarely been worse.
Rarely ....
g) The manager not once offered us an apology.
Not once ....
h) You should not send money to us by post under any circumstances.
Under no circumstances ....
i) I understood *Hamlet* only after seeing it on the stage.
Only after seeing *Hamlet*. ....
j) The embassy staff little realised that Ted was a secret agent.
Little ....

4

Rewrite each
sentence so that
it begins with the
word or words
underlined.

a) The best time to buy a house is <u>now</u>.
...Now is the best time to buy a house..
b) The bus came <u>round the corner</u>.
....
c) The price of petrol went <u>up</u>.
....

    d) The Parthenon stands <u>on the top</u> of the Acropolis.

....

    e) The wheels of the engine went <u>round and round</u>.

....

    f) Winston Churchill lived <u>in this house</u>.

....

    g) The flag went <u>down</u>.

....

    h) The best part of the story comes <u>now</u>.

....

5
Decide which
answer A, B, C
or D best fits
each space.

Asking for Advice

You don't happen to know how this computer works, (1) ..... ? (2) ..... had I
bought it (3) ..... I regretted spending so much money! I haven't got an
instruction manual. (4) ..... did I completely fail to understand the instructions,
(5) ..... then I accidentally threw the manual away. Now I'll never understand it,
(6) ..... , I said to myself. (7) ..... my weekend, I thought, but then I remembered
you. You've done a course on computers, (8) ..... ? Let's look at it together,
(9) ..... , and try to understand it. You press this button first, (10) ..... ? Then
(11) ..... this little light, and a message that says 'Error'. It shouldn't do that,
(12) ..... ? You can fix it, (13) ..... ? Don't do that! This label says: '(14) ..... should
an unqualified person remove this panel'. Well, you are unqualified, (15) ..... ?
What do you mean, do it yourself ....

1) A) are you	B) is it	C) do you	D) isn't it
2) A) No sooner	B) After	C) Not only	D) As soon as
3) A) that	B) but	C) and	D) than
4) A) Not only	B) Seldom	C) Not once	D) Only then
5) A) than	B) but	C) so	D) and
6) A) can't I	B) won't I	C) will I	D) can I
7) A) It goes	B) Goes it	C) Goes there	D) There goes
8) A) isn't it	B) haven't you	C) didn't you	D) don't you
9) A) do we	B) don't it	C) shall we	D) aren't we
10) A) don't you	B) isn't it	C) can't you	D) won't you
11) A) on comes	B) comes on	C) it comes on	D) comes it one
12) A) does it	B) should it	C) shouldn't it	D) won't it
13) A) isn't it	B) don't you	C) can't you	D) can't it
14) A) Not only	B) Only then	C) Never	D) Under no circumstances
15) A) isn't it	B) are you	C) don't you	D) aren't you

KEY POINTS

1 Inversion after negative adverbs is more common in formal speech and writing. The adverb has to be at the beginning of the sentence or clause.

2 Intonation carries important meaning in question tags. Rising tags are questions, level tags are checking information.

   Your name's Pauline, isn't it? (question)

   Your name's Pauline, isn't it? (checking)

3 Inversion with *come* and *go* is informal.
   Look out, here comes the teacher!

SEE ALSO

Unit 35
Progress test

Unit 32 Expressing reason, text organisers

Explanations

Reason

1 *As, since* and *for*
As and *since* have the meaning of *because* and can begin a sentence.
For also has the meaning of *because* but cannot begin a sentence and is followed by a clause. It is only used in written language.

> **As/since** *it was late, we decided to go home.*
> *Peter has given up sailing,* **for** *he doesn't have the time.*

2 *On account of, owing to* and *due to*
On account of has the meaning of *because of.*

> *Everyone was depressed* **on account of** *the bad weather.*

Due to and *owing to* also have the meaning of *because of*, and can be used in the same way as *on account of*. However, some grammars make this difference between them:

> *Sue's success was* **due to** *her hard work.*   (noun + *to be* + *due to*)
> *Sue succeeded* **owing to** *her hard work.*   (verb + *owing to*)

Text organisers

This term covers words and phrases which make clear the organisation of what we say or write. Most of the expressions listed are more commonly used in writing, or formal speech. The activities give examples of how these words and phrases can be used.

1 Sequencing
In writing, we often order the points we are making by showing their order or sequence. Points can be introduced by:

> *first (of all) … , secondly … , next … , then … , finally/lastly/last of all …*

In narrative, the sequence of events can be introduced by:

> *first … , then … , after that … , finally/in the end …*

2 Adding
In writing, we can introduce additional points with these words and phrases. These are all formal in use.

> *furthermore … , moreover … , in addition to this … , as well as this … , besides this …*

3 Giving opinions
Personal opinions can be introduced in writing by:

> *Personally … , in my own opinion/view …*

4 Giving examples
   Examples are introduced by:
   > *For example ... , for instance ...*
   Such as is another way of giving examples. It is not used at the beginning of a sentence.
   > *The factory produces electrical goods,* **such as** *food mixers and other kitchen appliances.*

5 Showing result
   Some formal ways of showing result are:
   > *Consequently ... , as a result ... , thus ...*

6 Making contrasts
   In writing, a contrasting point can be introduced by:
   > *On the other hand ... , however ... , nevertheless ...*
   Other contrasts can be made with:
   > *In contrast ... , in comparison ...*

7 Summing up
   We can introduce a summing up of our points with:
   > *In conclusion ... , to sum up ...*

Activities

1
Choose the most suitable word or phrase underlined in each sentence.

a) Many people feel nervous about flying, and worry about the possibility of an accident. Furthermore/However, according to statistics, flying is actually safer than walking down the street.

b) Our local supermarket no longer opens every day, as/on account of very few people live in our village.

c) There are a number of objections to the planned motorway. As well as this/First of all, the new road will destroy valuable farming land. In contrast/In addition to this, it will bring thousands of vehicles to our quiet area, and flood the countryside with tourists. As a result/For example, our peaceful way of life will be destroyed for ever.

d) We conducted a survey of accommodation in the town, and came up with some interesting results. The hotels we saw were rather expensive, and consequently/moreover the actual facilities on offer were not always impressive. Besides this/In contrast, there were many guest houses, offering just bed and breakfast, which were not only good value but also had much better rooms than the hotels did. Finally/Personally, I would recommend 'The Oaks', a particularly impressive guest house in Long Harbour Road.

e) Owing to/Since the increased demand for parking spaces, the company has decided to enlarge the car park behind the main building. Consequently/Nevertheless the exit road on the west side of the car park will be closed from Monday 5th November to allow building work to begin.

2

Put **one** suitable word in each space.

a) ..**In**.. conclusion, I would like to thank everyone for all the help they have given me.

b) .... it's too late to finish the work today, we'll come back tomorrow.

c) The flight was delayed .... a result of the high winds.

d) This radio is expensive, but .... the other hand it has very good reception.

e) First ...... all, I would like to welcome everyone to our annual dinner.

f) John is a hard worker. As ...... as this, he is completely reliable.

g) Science has not entirely changed the way we think. ...... instance, we still speak of the 'sunrise' although we know it is the earth that is moving.

h) Although this building project seems attractive, in my ...... it would be a mistake to spend so much money on it.

3

Decide which answer A, B, C or D best fits each space.

Owning a car has several advantages. (1) ...**A**..... you can go wherever you want, whenever you want. You don't have to depend on public transport and (2) .... you feel more independent. (3) .... you are able to give lifts to friends, or carry heavy loads of shopping. (4) .... , there can be problems, especially if you live in a city. Running a car can be expensive, and you have to spend money on items (5) .... petrol, servicing the car, and repairs. You might also have problems with parking, as everywhere is becoming more and more crowded with cars. (6) .... , most people feel that the advantages of owning a car outweigh the disadvantages. (7) .... most young people of my age start driving as soon as they can. (8) .... , I think that cars nowadays have become essential, but I also feel that they cause a lot of problems, (9) .... they are noisy and dirty. (10) .... , the large number of cars on the road means that most towns and cities are organised for the convenience of cars, and the needs of pedestrians are ignored.

1) A) First of all   B) As a result   C) Personally   D) Besides this
2) A) however   B) personally   C) since   D) as a result
3) A) In contrast   B) In my view   C) Besides this   D) However
4) A) On the other hand B) To sum up   C) Thus   D) For example
5) A) as   B) such as   C) owing to   D) then
6) A) Finally   B) Secondly   C) However   D) As
7) A) For   B) Next   C) As well as this D) Consequently

8) A) For example   B) Personally   C) Nevertheless   D) In comparison
9) A) for example   B) however   C) thus   D) since
10) A) As a result   B) Moreover   C) Personally   D) In comparison

KEY POINTS

1 Text organisers help readers (and listeners to formal speeches) to follow the organisation of the text. They make argumentative writing easier to understand.

2 These expressions should be studied in context so that the meaning is clear. Most of the expressions listed are formal in use.

Unit 33 *It* and *there*, *it* and adjectives, *one*, *someone* etc, *what*, *whatever*, possessives and reflexives

Explanations

It and *there*

It generally refers to something already mentioned, but is also used in some phrases which do not have a grammatical subject. *There* is used with *to be* to describe the existence of something.

> *There is **a good film** on tonight. **It** stars Kim Basinger.*
> *It's raining again.*   *It's half past six.*
> *It doesn't matter.*   *It's time to go.*

It and adjectives

It is also used in patterns with an adjective followed by an infinitive or *-ing* form. In colloquial speech, *it* and the verb *to be* are often left out.

> *It's good to see you.*   **Good** *to see you.*
> *It was nice meeting you.*   **Nice** *meeting you.*

One

1 *One* can be used as a pronoun, and has a plural *ones*.
> *I don't like **this one**. I only like **green ones**.*

2 *One* can also be used with *another* to refer to both subjects.
> *Martin and David can't stand **one another**.*
> This means that Martin can't stand David, and David can't stand Martin.

3 In formal speech and writing, *one* can be used instead of *you* to refer to 'anybody'. This use of *one* is considered over-formal by many speakers.
> *What does **one** wear to a dinner of this kind?*
> *It's not pleasant to hear **oneself** described by **one's** employees.*

Someone, everyone, anyone, everyone, somewhere etc

1 *-body* can be used instead of *-one* without change in meaning.

2 Words beginning *some* or *any* follow the usual patterns for these words, with '*any*' words normally used in questions and after negatives.
> *There's **something** under the desk. Can you see **anything**?*

3 '*Some*' words can be used in questions when these refer to a definite idea.
> *Are you looking for **somewhere** to stay?*
> *Could **someone** help me, please?*

4 Words beginning *any* can be used in positive statements when they refer to 'every possibility'.

*Please sit **anywhere** you like.*   ***Anyone** who's tall will do.*

What as pronoun

What can be used as a pronoun meaning 'the thing or things which'.

***What** we need is a spanner.*

Whatever, whoever, wherever, whenever, why ever, however

1 These are used to add emphasis to the question word.

What are you doing? becomes ***Whatever** are you doing?* (with surprise)

2 Another use adds the meaning of 'any at all'.

***Whatever** you say is wrong!*   ***Anything at all** you say is wrong!*

Reflexives

1 These can be used for emphasis.

*Why don't you do it **yourself**?*   *I paid for the tickets **myself**.*

2 These also include actions which involve doing something to yourself.

*Sue **cut herself**.*   *I have **hurt myself**.*   *Did you **enjoy yourself**?*

Possessives: parts of the body

Parts of the body can be described without using a possessive adjective in some expressions after prepositions:

*Jack gave Bill a punch **on the nose**.*   *I grabbed him **by the arm**.*
*Jack punched Bill **on the nose**.*   *I looked him **in the eyes**.*

Activities

1

Rewrite each sentence, beginning as shown, so that it has the same meaning.

a) I don't mind what you do, but don't tell Jane I was here.
Whatever ...*you do, don't tell Jane I was here.*..

b) The person who stole the painting must have been tall.
Whoever ....
c) What on earth is the time!
Whatever ....
d) I'd like to know why you told me a lie.
Why ever ....

173

e) Every time I go on holiday, the weather gets worse.
Whenever ....

f) Tell me where you have been!
Wherever ....

g) How on earth did you know I was going to be here?
However ....

h) Any place I hang my hat, I call home!
Wherever ....

i) I won't believe you, no matter what you say.
Whatever ....

j) If you are going to do something, do it now!
Whatever ....

2

Complete the second sentence so that it has a similar meaning to the first sentence, using the word given. Do not change the word given. You must use between two and five words.

a) John patted my back.
gave
John *...gave me a pat on*.. the back.

b) Don't hold a rabbit's ears and pick it up.
by
Don't .... the ears.

c) I'll never be able to look at Tanya's face again.
in
I'll never be able to look .... again.

d) Sue grabbed the thief's arm.
by
Sue .... arm.

e) Helen took the baby's hand.
by
Helen .... hand.

f) The bee stung my arm.
me
The bee .... arm.

g) Somebody gave me a black eye.
punched
Somebody .... eye.

h) Jane patted the dog's head.
on
Jane .... head.

i) 'It's my arm! I'm hit!' said Billy the Kid.
wounded
'I'm .... ,'said Billy the Kid.

j) I felt someone pat my shoulder.
me
I felt someone .... shoulder.

3

Complete each sentence so that it has a similar meaning to the first.

a) The local cinema has a good film on at the moment.
There ..*is a good film on at the local cinema*.......................... at the moment.

b) I can't drink coffee so late at night.
It's.. so late at night.

c) Don't worry if you can't answer all the questions.
It doesn't ....all the questions.

d) A storm is coming, I think.
There .... I think.

e) The fridge is empty.
There .... fridge.

f) This journey has been tiring.
It .... journey.

g) If you don't hurry all the beer will be gone.
There .... if you don't hurry.

h) The station is far away.
It .... station.

i) Let's have a break now.
It's .... for a break now.

j) I enjoyed seeing you.
It .... you.

4

Rewrite each sentence, beginning as shown, so that the meaning stays the same.

a) Was it enjoyable at the beach, Joe?
Did you ..*enjoy yourself at the beach, Joe?*...............

b) We really need a new fridge.
What ....

c) There's a lot of fog today.
It's ....

d) People who believe in ghosts are a bit crazy!
Anyone ....

e) Just call me any time you need me.
Whenever ....

f) I was very interested in what we talked about.
It was interesting ....

g) John is hurt.
John has ....

h) Why did you do that?
Whatever ....

i) Never mind.

It ....

j) These bookshelves are my own work.

I made ....

5

Complete each sentence with the most suitable word or phrase.

a) I like this painting but I don't think much of those ...ᒐ... .

A) rest   B) other   C) ones   D) besides

b) What would .... like to do this morning?

A) someone   B) one   C) yourself   D) you

c) Did you enjoy ....

A) at the party   B) the party   C) yourself the party   D) with yourself at the party

d) .... nothing much to do in this town.

A) There's   B) It's not   C) There's not   D) It's

e) .... you do, don't tell Harry that we've lost his camera.

A) Anything   B) What   C) Whatever   D) It's better

f) One prefers to shop at Harrods, ... ?

A) doesn't one   B) isn't it   C) don't you   D) isn't one

g) .... didn't you tell me that you felt too ill to work?

A) Whoever   B) Whatever   C) However   D) Why ever

h) Then George punched the policeman .... the face!

A) at   B) on   C) to   D) in

i) Harry shook my hand and said, 'Pleased .... you.'

A) to meet   B) to introduce   C) to shake   D) to acquaint

j) Please invite .... you like to the reception.

A) one   B) anyone   C) ones   D) all

KEY POINTS

1   In some cases, *it* does not refer to another noun, but stands as the subject of verbs such as *to be* and *rain*.

2   It is possible to use *some* and words made from it in interrogative sentences, where a definite idea is referred to.

> *Are you looking for **someone**?*

3   Some verbs (*cut, enjoy, hurt*) require a reflexive (*myself* etc.) if there is no other object.

> *I enjoyed the party.*
> *I enjoyed **myself**.*
> *Martha cut her finger.*
> *Martha cut **herself**.*

SEE ALSO

Unit 35
Progress test

Unit 34 Spelling and pronunciation

Explanations

Common spelling problems

1 Words that end in *-ful*
These have only one 'l' when *-ful* is a suffix.
useful   helpful

2 Doubling of consonants
Adjectives form adverbs by adding *-ly*.
usefully   helpfully
Words with one syllable, ending in one vowel and one consonant double the consonant when adding *-ing, -ed* or *-er.*
swim swimming   fit fitted   thin thinner
Most two-syllable words ending in one vowel and one consonant also double the last consonant, especially when the stress is on the second syllable.
prefer preferred but **bother bothering**
A common exception is *travel traveller*

3 Words ending in 'y'
(Plurals, present simple, past simple, *-ful, -ness*)
One-syllable words ending in one vowel and 'y' do not change.
try tries tried but *boy boys*
One-syllable words do not change when adding *-ful* and *-ness*.
joy joyful   shy shyness
All two-syllable words change except ones with one vowel before 'y'.
reply replies replied   happy happiness   beauty beautiful
but *destroy destroyed*
These rules do not apply to adding *-ing*.
try trying   study studying   annoy annoying

4 Words with *ie* and *ei*
The general rule is 'i' before 'e' except after 'c', as long as the sound is 'ee'.
receive   relief   feign (the sound is not 'ee')

Spelling and pronunciation

Note the ways of spelling the underlined sounds in each list, and that the ways of spelling these sounds may represent different sounds in other words. Note that schwa /ə/ is an unstressed sound.

1 Vowel sounds.
/ʌ/ l<u>o</u>ve s<u>u</u>dden bl<u>oo</u>d c<u>u</u>ff r<u>ou</u>gh L<u>o</u>ndon br<u>o</u>ther
/əʊ/ b<u>oa</u>t p<u>o</u>st alth<u>ou</u>gh kn<u>ow</u> t<u>oe</u>
/eə/ <u>air</u> th<u>ere</u> b<u>are</u> w<u>ear</u>
/ɑː/ h<u>ear</u>t p<u>ar</u>t st<u>a</u>ff <u>a</u>sk

/ɜː/ w<u>or</u>d h<u>ear</u>d f<u>ur</u>ther exp<u>er</u>t h<u>ur</u>t
/aʊ/ n<u>ow</u> sh<u>out</u> pl<u>ough</u> dr<u>ow</u>n
/ɒ/ l<u>o</u>t st<u>o</u>p <u>o</u>ff
/eɪ/ w<u>ai</u>t g<u>a</u>te w<u>ei</u>ght gr<u>ea</u>t l<u>ay</u>
/aɪ/ br<u>igh</u>t h<u>eigh</u>t s<u>i</u>te <u>eye</u>
/ɔː/ d<u>oo</u>r p<u>our</u> d<u>au</u>ghter
schwa /ə/ p<u>o</u>tato <u>a</u>round s<u>u</u>ggest p<u>er</u>haps neckl<u>a</u>ce

2 Consonant sounds
/ʃ/ <u>sh</u>ame deli<u>ci</u>ous posi<u>ti</u>on in<u>s</u>urance
/tʃ/ <u>ch</u>urch furni<u>t</u>ure wa<u>tch</u>es
/ʒ/ lei<u>s</u>ure confu<u>s</u>ion mea<u>s</u>ure

3 Words ending in -*ough*
Like 'now' *plough bough*   Like 'cuff' *enough rough tough*
Like 'toe' *though dough*   Like 'off' *cough*

4 Words containing -*st* where *t* is not pronounced
listen glisten hasten fasten
castle whistle bristle mistletoe

5 Words containing -*mb* and -*bt* where *b* is not pronounced
plumber thumb comb lamb dumb tomb
debt doubt subtle

Activities

1
Correct any words spelled incorrectly.

a) studing ...*studying*.........   reciept ....
b) destroying ....   wonderfull ....
c) donkies ....   swiming ....
d) flys ....   regreted ....
e) niece ....   hopefuly ....
f) hurryed ....   applying ....
g) furnichure ....   heard ....
h) enough ....   inshurance ....
i) wellcome ....   happily ....
j) hotter ....   advertisment ....

2
Find a word from the list which rhymes with each word given.

| home go white search store |
| stuff come plumber wait cow |

a) church ...*search*.......   f) dumb ....
b) hate ....   g) plough ....
c) rough ....   h) height ....
d) throw ....   i) summer ....
e) comb ....   j) pour ....

3

Write the word ending in the suffix given.

a) supply (ing) ...*supplying*........
b) destroy (ed) ....
c) apply (ed) ....
d) lonely (ness) ....
e) employ (s) ....

f) cry (s) ....
g) silly (ness) ....
h) annoy (s) ....
i) beauty (ful) ....
j) pretty (ness) ....

4

Find one word in each group of words which does not have the same vowel sound (sounds are underlined in two-syllable words).

a) become sung c<u>o</u>mpany cold flood ...*cold*.....
b) plate treat wait weight great ....
c) lose used choose blouse few ....
d) doubt bough ought now shout ....
e) lost post toast ghost host ....
f) mist missed list iced kissed ....
g) love done gone sunk won ....
h) bird search heart word church ....
i) two show though go owe ....
j) <u>a</u>bout wond<u>er</u> s<u>u</u>ppose ref<u>er</u> col<u>our</u> ....

5

Correct any words spelled incorrectly.

a) sincerly ...*sincerely*..........
b) different ....
c) loverly ....
d) writting ....
e) pulover ....
f) freind ....
g) holliday ....
h) likelihood ....
i) impatient ....
j) finaly ....

dictionry ....
intresting ....
necessary ....
unninteresting ....
definitly ....
responsable ....
quantity ....
lugage ....
student ....
pavement ....

6

Correct any words spelled incorrectly.

a) tomorow ...*tomorrow*..........
b) conversation ....
c) atmosfere ....
d) sandwits ....
e) gaurd ....
f) recomend ....
g) tobaco ....
h) recieve ....
i) chimney ....
j) electrisity ....

glases ....
magasine ....
pacient ....
bicycle ....
running ....
skillfull ....
acquaintance ....
attatch ....
cuboard ....
expencive ....

Unit 35 Progress test

(Units 31, 32, 33, 34)

1
Put **one** suitable word in each space.

The first day in the job

I will always remember my first day working at the Excelsior Food Company. First of (1) ..... , I was given a greasy overall. (2) ..... had worn it before had certainly never washed it! When I mentioned this to the foreman he said, 'You're not afraid of a bit of dirt, (3) ..... you?' I wanted to say that I thought (4) ..... was supposed to be a high standard of cleanliness in a food factory, but I managed to control (5) .... Then I was given my first job, (6) ..... involved sweeping the floor. (7) ..... only was my overall filthy, but the whole factory looked as if (8) ..... had ever cleaned it properly. (9) ..... were also (10) ..... I later discovered to be pigs' ears scattered around the place. (11) ..... it was my first day, I didn't say anything about this. (12) ..... that I had to put pies into boxes for the rest of the morning. (13) .... was supposed to put them into the cold-store, but (14) .... this person was, they had obviously forgotten about it. As a (15) ...., there was soon a huge pile of boxes waiting to be moved. Then I discovered that I was supposed to be moving them!

2
Complete the second sentence so that it has a similar meaning to the first sentence.

a) Under no circumstances should you press both buttons at once.
   You ....

b) It was cold, so I decided to wear two pullovers.
   As ....

c) Did you have a good time at the party?
   Did you enjoy ....

d) Outside the cinema somebody grabbed my arm.
   Outside the cinema I ....

e) The army's defeat was due to poor organisation.
   The army was defeated ....

f) Jean not once offered her boss a word of apology.
   Not once ....

g) There's no food in the house, I'm afraid.
   There's nothing ....

h) It's pointless going on any further tonight.
   There's ....

i) It's difficult to describe what Sally saw.
   What ....

j) I have seldom had a more relaxing holiday.
   Seldom ....

3

Complete each sentence with the most suitable word or phrase.

a) One really shouldn't drink too much, ... ?

   A) does one   B) should you   C) do you   D) should one

b) ...., I would like to propose a toast.

   A) For example   B) In conclusion   C) On the other hand   D) Thus

c) Do you think .... could help me choose a pair of trousers?

   A) someone   B) anyone   C) whoever   D) there

d) .... doesn't seem to be anyone at home.

   A) It   B) One   C) There   D) Whenever

e) .... did I realise that the murderer was still in the house!

   A) Seldom   B) Under no circumstances   C) Only after   D) Only then

f) ...., I don't believe that prices will rise next year.

   A) In contrast   B) Personally   C) Not only   D) Whatever

g) You're covered in mud! .... is your mother going to say!

   A) Rarely   B) Furthermore   C) Whatever   D) On account of

h) Oh bother, ... the bus I wanted to catch!

   A) wherever   B) it's left   C) there goes   D) owing to

i) Please help yourselves to .... you like.

   A) whoever   B) nothing   C) everywhere   D) anything

j) Nobody's got to stay late this evening, ... ?

   A) is it?   B) have they   C) isn't it?   D) don't they

4

Look carefully at each line. Some lines are correct, but some have a word which should not be there. Tick each correct line. If a line has a word which should not be there, write the word in the space.

Kidnapped by aliens

I am sure you have heard of Marion Taylor,	....✓......
haven't you? Marion was the young girl she	..she....
kidnapped by aliens in 1993. Not only that was	1) ....
she given a ride to a distant planet, but whether she	2) ....
also managed to take some photos of the aliens	3) ....
who they had taken her prisoner, since she had been	4) ....
carrying herself a camera when they captured her.	5) ....
Whenever I hear stories like this I assume so	6) ....
that they have been made them up. It is hard to believe	7) ....
Marion's story, owing to the fact that she was	8) ....
only ten years old at the time. Besides this, it was	9) ....
turned out that she spent most of her time watching	10) ....
science fiction videos. One cannot really believe in	11) ....
that there are really little green aliens who they fly	12) ....
all the way to our planet just so that they can kidnap	13) ....
people. Nevertheless, although Marion became	14) ....
famous and her photos were bought by a newspaper	15) ....
for a great deal of money.	

Unit 36 Final test

1

Put each verb in brackets into a suitable tense.

a) I (wait) .... for you for the past hour! What (you do) .... all this time?

b) While I (walk) .... to the bus-stop, I realised I (leave) .... the cooker on.

c) Why didn't you phone me? If I (knew) .... you were ill, I (come) .... to see you.

d) Hello, Pat. I (phone) .... to ask if you (do) ...... anything this Saturday.

e) By the time Big Jim (become) .... heavyweight boxing champion he (win) .... over thirty fights.

f) I (not see) .... you for ages. What (you do) ....?

g) Hurry up! I (think) .... you (be) .... ready by now.

h) If I (be) .... you, I (not spend) .... so much money.

i) Danny's train (arrive) .... tomorrow evening at 6.00 so we (meet) .... him at the station.

j) Wish me luck! If I (get) .... the job I (let) .... you know.

2

Complete the second sentence so that it has a similar meaning to the first sentence, using the word given. Do not change the word given. You must use between two and five words.

a) I'd prefer you not to wear jeans to the office.

rather

I'd .... wear jeans to the office.

b) We won't get there on time without taking a taxi.

unless

We won't get there on time .... a taxi.

c) 'I wouldn't go swimming after dark, if I were you, Tom.'

advised

Brian .... swimming after dark.

d) Although she had twisted her ankle, Sally still won the race.

twisting

Sally still won the race, ... her ankle.

e) Mike enjoys playing golf more than I do.

as

I don't enjoy playing golf .... does.

f) I regret selling my car.

wish

I .... my car.

g) Nobody has cut the lawn for weeks!

hasn't

The lawn .... for weeks.

h) I'm sure Dick didn't mean to offend you.

have

Dick .... offend you.

i) Have you got a smaller size than this?

the

Is .... you have got?

j) Would you like to go out for a drink?
   like
   Do you .... out for a drink?

3

Look carefully at each line. Some lines are correct, but some have a word which should not be there. Tick each correct line. If a line has a word which should not be there, write the word in the space.

Foreign travel

Nowadays more and more people enjoy	...✓........
foreign travel, and take up their holidays in	...up.......
the distant countries. However, not everyone	1) ....
has had the same reason for travelling. Some	2) ....
of people travel so that they can practise	3) ....
foreign languages, or because they want to	4) ....
visit the well-known sights in other countries.	5) ....
Lots of young people just want to have relax	6) ....
and make up new friends. Personally, I would like	7) ....
to travel abroad for the excitement! I have never	8) ....
been visited to a foreign country before, but I have	9) ....
been planning a trip around Europe by the train with	10) ....
some friends of mine. As we are students, and so we can	11) ....
buy cheaper tickets. One of my friends went on	12) ....
having this kind of trip a few years ago. She stayed in	13) ....
youth hostels, and managed to spend a very little	14) ....
money. I think that this would be an exciting holiday.	15) ....

4

Complete the second sentence so that it has a similar meaning to the first sentence, using the word given. Do not change the word given. You must use between two and five words.

a) I don't play tennis as well as you do.
   better
   You .... do.

b) You ought to have your house painted.
   be
   Your house .... painted.

c) I haven't been to the dentist's for two years.
   since
   It's .... to the dentist's.

d) The film was so funny that I burst out laughing.
   a
   It was .... that I burst out laughing.

e) I've never flown in a helicopter before.
   first
   This is .... flown in a helicopter.

f) 'You stole the money, Joe, didn't you!' said the inspector.
   accused
   The inspector .... the money.

g) It is essential that this letter is posted today.
   must
   This letter .... today.

h) 'Is the train on time?' asked one of the people waiting.
whether
One of the people waiting wanted to.. on time.

i) My advice is to inform the police.
better
I think .... inform the police.

j) They believe a single gunman carried out the attack.
believed
A single gunman .... carried out the attack.

5
Decide which
answer A, B, C
or D best fits
each space.

The school sports

Our school sports were held last week, and the whole afternoon was a disaster. For a start, very (1) ..... people bothered to turn (2) ..... , and there is nothing (3) ..... than trying to win a race with only three or four people cheering you on. It rained (4) ..... afternoon, from the moment the first starting pistol (5) ..... fired, until the last medal had (6) ..... presented. I was in the high jump, (7) ..... meant running up to do my best jump and then landing (8) ..... a pool of cold muddy water. It was raining (9) ..... hard that we couldn't see the runners in the 5000 metres, and it (10) ..... out that they had all stopped (11) ..... the other side of the field to shelter under a tree. My other event was the javelin, but (12) ..... time I tried to throw, the javelin kept slipping from my hand. In (13) ..... case, I couldn't see where I was throwing, and when I (14) ..... finally manage to launch my javelin into the air, it disappeared in the direction of the railway line, and was never seen (15) ..... .

1) A) little	B) small	C) few	D) rare
2) A) up	B) about	C) round	D) over
3) A) like	B) better	C) left	D) worse
4) A) by	B) the	C) entire	D) all
5) A) had	B) was	C) has	D) been
6) A) to	B) had	C) been	D) itself
7) A) which	B) and	C) so	D) nevertheless
8) A) on	B) at	C) in	D) to
9) A) so	B) as	C) and	D) very
10) A) worked	B) found	C) looked	D) turned
11) A) under	B) on	C) through	D) about
12) A) first	B) in	C) every	D) a
13) A) this	B) the	C) whatever	D) any
14) A) did	B) had	C) should	D) have
15) A) there	B) again	C) to	D) back

6

Complete the second sentence so that it has a similar meaning to the first sentence, using the word given. Do not change the word given. You must use between two and five words.

a) A year ago we hadn't even met!
   last
   This .... even met.

b) Without your help, I wouldn't have passed the exam.
   for
   If it .... I wouldn't have passed the exam.

c) Nobody knows anything about the whereabouts of the President.
   about
   Nothing .... the whereabouts of the President.

d) My teachers made me work hard at school.
   was
   I .... hard at school.

e) 'I'm awfully sorry, Carol, but I've broken your watch,' said Jim.
   to
   Jim .... her watch.

f) Please see that you close the door when you go.
   open
   Please don't .... when you go.

g) Your hair needs cutting.
   had
   It's .... cut.

h) Do you own these two fields?
   belong
   Do .... you?

i) Business hasn't been so bad for a long time.
   has
   Rarely .... been so bad.

j) I won't sell the painting, no matter how much you offer me.
   price
   Whatever .... the painting, I won't sell it.

Vocabulary

1 Travel and Holidays

1
Complete each sentence with a word from the list.

> buffet   coach-station   departure-lounge   harbour   **quay**
> cabin   deck   destination   platform   runway

a) Most of the young people on the boat slept on the .... in their sleeping bags.

b) As the train **drew** in to the station, Terry could see her sister waiting on the ....

c) I was so nervous about flying that I left my bag in the ....

d) By the time I got to the .... , the express bus to Scotland had left.

e) As soon as the boat left the .... , the storm began.

f) We hadn't had anything to eat, but luckily there was a .... on the train.

g) I'm afraid there is only one first-class .... free on the boat.

h) Tim reached Paris safely, but his luggage didn't reach its ....

i) There was a queue of cars on the .... , waiting for the car-ferry to the island.

j) Our plane nearly crashed into a fire-engine on the ....

2
Choose the most suitable word or words underlined.

a) David's plane was cancelled/delayed by thick fog.

b) The ship's owner agreed to give the crew/passengers a pay-rise.

c) The plane from Geneva has just grounded/landed.

d) We hope that you will enjoy your flight/flying.

e) Because of heavy snow in London, their plane was diverted/deviated to Manchester.

f) I won't be long. I'm just packing my last luggage/suitcase.

g) A sign above the seats in the plane says 'Fasten your life belt/seat belt'.

h) You have to check in/check up an hour before the plane leaves.

i) All duty free goods must be declared/surrendered at the customs.

j) On the plane a stewardess/waitress brought me a newspaper.

k) The plane took off/took up and was soon high over the city.

l) I bought a simple/single ticket, as I was going to return by car.

3
Use a word or words from **1** or **2** to complete each sentence. The word may be in a different form.

a) I had to .... my tickets, because I was ill and couldn't travel.

b) The train for London is now arriving at .... three.

c) The plane .... on time but arrived half an hour late.

d) We finally reached our .... after travelling all day.

e) It was hard to find a seat on the train as there were so many ....

f) While we were waiting at the station we had a bite to eat in the ....

g) I felt seasick so I went to my .... and tried to sleep.

h) Do you want a return ticket, or a .... ?

i) The customs officer asked Bill if he had anything to ....

j) There is a small .... here for fishing boats and yachts.

k) How much .... am I allowed to take with me on the plane?

l) The 8.55 from Hull will be 30 minutes late. We apologise for the ....

4
Match these words with the definitions given.

| an expedition a flight a tour a voyage a package tour |
| an itinerary a trip travel a cruise a crossing |

a) A journey by ship for pleasure. ....

b) A journey by plane. ....

c) The plan of a journey. ....

d) An informal word for journey. Sometimes meaning a short journey.

....

e) A journey for a scientific or special purpose. ....

f) A holiday which includes organised travel and accommodation.

....

g) Taking journeys, as a general idea. ....

h) A journey by sea. ....

i) An organised journey to see the sights of a place. ....

j) A journey from one side of the sea to the other. ....

5
Use a word from 4 in each sentence.

a) The travel agent will send you the .... for your trip.

b) My neighbours went on a guided .... of Rome.

c) The first time I went from England to France we had a very rough

....

d) The first prize in the competition is a luxury Mediterranean ....

e) When you go on a/an .... , you pay one price which covers everything.

f) The college organised a/an .... to search for the ancient ruins.

g) Olympic Airways announces the arrival of .... OA 269 from Athens.

h) The Titanic sank on its first .... in 1912.

i) .... is one of my main interests.

j) Mr Dean is away on a business .... at the moment. Can I help you?

6
Replace the words underlined in each sentence with a word from the list.

| camp-site book hostel accommodation double |
| hitch-hike a fortnight guest-house vacancy porter |

a) I stayed in France for <u>two weeks</u> last year. ....

b) It's difficult to find <u>anywhere to stay</u> in this town in the summer. ....

c) We were short of money so we decided to <u>get lifts in other people's cars</u>.

....

d) I'd like a room for the night please. A <u>room for two people</u>. ....

e) The place where we stayed wasn't a hotel but a <u>private house where you pay to stay and have meals</u>. ....

f) I'd like to <u>reserve</u> three single rooms for next week, please. ....

g) It was raining, and we couldn't find a <u>place to put our tent</u>. ....

h) I'd like a room for the night please. Do you have a <u>free one</u>? ....

i) The school has its own <u>place for students to stay</u>. ....

j) We gave a tip to the <u>person who carried our bags in the hotel</u>. ....

7

Use a dictionary to find compound words beginning *sea-*. Complete each sentence with one of these words.

a) Last year we decided not to spend our holidays in the country as usual, and we went to the .... instead.

b) There's a restaurant near the harbour that serves wonderful ....

c) The beach was covered in piles of smelly green ....

d) This town is very high up. It's over a thousand metres above ....

e) We drove along the .... but we couldn't find anywhere to park.

f) Tourists were throwing bread to the .... flying behind the ship.

g) Luckily I had taken some travel pills so I didn't feel ....

h) Children were building sand castles on the ....

8

Choose the most suitable word or phrase to complete each sentence.

a) They .... all day swimming and sunbathing at the beach.
   A) did   B) used   C) spent   D) occupied

b) The hotel room .... over a beautiful garden.
   A) viewed out   B) faced up   C) opened up   D) looked out

c) We didn't .... to the station in time to catch the train.
   A) get   B) reach   C) arrive   D) make

d) I was in such a hurry that I left one of my bags ....
   A) out   B) aside   C) on   D) behind

e) Mr Hill had his money stolen and couldn't .... his hotel bill.
   A) pay up   B) pay   C) pay for   D) pay out

f) Jane lost her case because it did not have a/an .... with her name on.
   A) ticket   B) poster   C) label   D) identification

g) Take the bus, and .... at Oxford Circus.
   A) get out   B) get off   C) get down   D) get away

h) I was too tired to .... my suitcase and hang my clothes in the wardrobe.
   A) unpack   B) empty   C) put out   D) disorder

i) On the first day of our holiday we just .... by the hotel pool.
   A) enjoyed   B) calmed   C) comforted   D) relaxed

j) The wind was blowing so much that we couldn't .... our tent.
   A) raise   B) put up   C) make up   D) build

9

Rewrite each sentence, beginning as given, so that it contains an expression with *have*.

a) I sunbathed for a while, and then went swimming.
   I sunbathed for a while, and then ....

b) I really enjoyed my holiday last year.
   I ....

c) David crashed his car while he was driving to Spain.
   David ....

d) When we left, Maria wished us a safe journey.
   'Goodbye,' said Maria, 'and .... '

e) Most of the people on the beach were wearing very little.
   Most of the people on the beach ....

f) We couldn't decide about our holiday but then Sue thought of something.
   We couldn't decide about our holiday until Sue ....

g) There was a party at Martin's house last night.
   Martin ....

h) Brenda couldn't go away for the weekend because she was busy.
   Brenda couldn't go away for the weekend because she ....

i) Ian didn't know how to water-ski, but he gave it a try.
   Ian didn't know how to water-ski but he ....

j) Laura suspected that the hotel food was going to be bad.
   Laura ....

10

Decide which
answer A, B, C
or D best fits
each space.

Holidays

Is it better to go on a package (1) ..... , or to (2) ..... on your own? I suppose the
answer depends on what kind of (3) ..... you are. A complicated tour organised
by a travel (4) ..... has some advantages. You have a/an (5) ..... , which gives you
definite (6) ..... and arrival dates, and a list of all your (7) ..... . The (8) ..... may be
cheaper, as it has been (9) ..... in advance, so you spend less time worrying about
where you are going to (10) ...... If you book your own hotel, you might have
trouble finding a/an (11) ..... , unless you are going to stay for a (12) ..... , for
example. On the other hand, organising your own (13) ..... can be fun. Many
students (14) ..... or buy cheap train tickets, and (15) ..... the night in student
hostels or guest-houses.

1) A) travel	B) tour	C) journey	D) cruise
2) A) travel	B) trip	C) voyage	D) tourist
3) A) voyager	B) passenger	C) tourist	D) mover
4) A) office	B) agent	C) tour	D) operation
5) A) timetable	B) scheme	C) notice	D) itinerary
6) A) departure	B) parting	C) leave	D) quitting
7) A) cancellations	B) expeditions	C) organisations	D) destinations
8) A) bedrooms	B) staying	C) flat	D) accommodation
9) A) preserved	B) booked	C) reservation	D) hotels
10) A) stay	B) pass	C) live	D) cross
11) A) empty	B) free	C) vacancy	D) available
12) A) fortnight	B) daytime	C) fifteen) days	D) passage
13) A) voyage	B) expedition	C) trip	D) package
14) A) auto-stop	B) hitch-hike	C) lift	D) journey
15) A) have	B) at	C) for	D) spend

2 Work and Employment

1

Match each job in list A with a place in list B. More than one answer may be possible.

A	cashier farmer mechanic photographer typist cook hairdresser miner pilot vicar dentist librarian musician porter waiter

B	bank garage studio kitchen coal-mine cockpit hotel office surgery salon field concert hall restaurant church library

cashier/bank

2

Match each job from the list with the sentence which best refers to the job.

accountant chef estate agent plumber architect refuse collector firefighter postman/woman carpenter electrician optician vet

a) Yesterday I had to give an injection to an injured bull. ..*vet*..........

b) I get rather tired of picking up rubbish all day. ....

c) I can help you sell your house. ....

d) I can make new doors for the wardrobe if you like. ....

e) Make sure that the fish is fresh by looking at the eyes. ....

f) I'll come round and replace all the pipes in the kitchen. ....

g) Unless you keep the receipts you'll pay more tax. ....

h) The cause was either an electrical fault or a cigarette. ....

i) Always turn the power off at the mains before you start. ....

j) You can see the balcony on the plan for the second floor. ....

k) It's a registered parcel. Can you sign here? ....

l) This pair also protects your eyes from the sun. ....

3

Which person from **1** and **2** would you need in each situation?

a) One of the radiators has burst and flooded your bedroom. ....

b) You are very short-sighted and get headaches when you read. ....

c) You have to carry a lot of heavy bags at the airport. ....

d) You think you need three fillings ....

e) Your fringe is too long and you want a perm. ....

f) The floorboards in the living room need replacing. ....

g) Your pet goat has started sneezing. ....

h) You have read the menu twice and you are feeling hungry. ....

i) When you turn on your cooker, the fridge turns off. ....

j) Your car makes a funny whistling noise. ....

4

Complete each sentence with a word from the list. The words can be used more than once.

| business job living work |

a) Jack makes his .... working as a journalist.
b) She has just left to go to .... , I'm afraid.
c) They worked very hard and now have their own ....
d) There are still nearly two million people without ....
e) The cost of .... has risen greatly over recent years.
f) Stop interfering! This is none of your ....
g) Lucy has a very good .... in an international company.
h) I can't come out tonight. I've got too much .... to do.
i) Some ....-men came and dug a hole in the road outside.
j) An early .... by Picasso was sold for £2,000,000.

5

Complete each sentence with a word from the list. Use each word once only.

| call draw fall get take come face fill go turn |

a) I think we should .... over our plan again before we tell the managing director.
b) Have you .... up with any new ideas for advertising the new products?
c) Our deal with the Chinese company may .... through, but we can sell the machinery to the German firm if necessary.
d) You have to .... in this form, and return it to the personnel manager.
e) She didn't .... on with her boss, so she left the company.
f) If they don't give us a better price, we'll .... down their offer.
g) I'm afraid we have to .... up to the fact that the company is losing money.
h) Our lawyers are going to .... up a new contract tomorrow.
i) A multinational company is trying to .... over our firm, but we want to stay independent.
j) We had to .... off the office party because of the economic situation.

6

Complete each sentence a) to j) with one of the endings 1) to 10). Use each ending once only.

a) If you work hard, the company will give you ....
b) In a different job I could get a higher ....
c) The best way to find new staff is to put a/an ....
d) Because he had stolen the money, we decided that ....
e) She has a pleasant personality but hasn't got the right ....
f) In the meeting we are going to discuss the ....
g) As he has three young children he doesn't want ....
h) I think it would be a good idea to send in your ....
i) I'm afraid that in this job there aren't very good ....
j) We cannot give you the job without ....

1) .... qualifications for a job of this kind.
2) .... advertisement in the local press on Friday.
3) .... application for the job as soon as possible.
4) .... promotion to a more responsible position.
5) .... full-time employment at the moment.
6) .... references from your previous employer.
7) .... dismissing him was the only possible action we could take.
8) .... prospects for the future at the moment.
9) .... salary and better conditions of employment.
10) .... appointment of a new sales representative.

7

Use the word in capitals at the end of each line to form a word that fits in the space in the same line.

Leaving a job

I recently left my job in an (1) .... agency   ADVERTISEMENT
after a disagreement with my boss. She accepted my
(2) .... but warned me that because of the   RESIGN
(3) .... situation, I might have to get used to the   ECONOMY
idea of being (4) .... for a while. I thought that she   EMPLOY
was trying to make a point, but after I had made over
fifty (5) .... to other companies, I realised that she   APPLY
was right. Although I am a (6) .... designer, I   QUALIFICATIONS
didn't receive any offers of a job. After that I tried
working from home, but it was not very (7) .... Then   PROFIT
I became an (8) .... in a fast-food restaurant,   EMPLOY
even though my (9) .... were extremely low.   EARN
I wish I had accepted early (10) .... from my old job.   RETIRE
That is what I disagreed with my boss about!

8

Choose the most suitable word or phrase underlined in each sentence.

a) The building workers were paid their <u>income/salary/wages</u> every Friday.
b) She's only here for three weeks. It's a/an <u>full-time/overtime/temporary</u> job.
c) When he retired he received a monthly <u>bonus/pension/reward</u>.
d) Apparently she <u>earns/gains/wins</u> over £20,000 a year.
e) While the boss is away, Sue will be <u>in charge/in control/in place</u> of the office.
f) Could I have two days <u>away/off/out</u> next week to visit my mother?
g) Paul was always arriving late, and in the end he was <u>pushed/sacked/thrown</u>.
h) When I left the job, I had to hand in my <u>application/dismissal/notice</u> three weeks beforehand.
i) How much exactly do you <u>do/make/take</u> in your new job?
j) If you have to travel on company business, we will pay your <u>costs/expenses/needs</u>.

9

Rewrite each sentence so that it contains the word or words given, and so that the meaning stays the same. Do not change the words given in any way.

a) Terry works in a different place now.   JOB
....

b) A good boss looks after everyone in the company.   EMPLOYER
....

c) I am sure you will learn a lot in this job.   EXPERIENCE
....

d) This job is a good way to earn money, but that's all.   LIVING
....

e) The firm gave me a rise after I had worked there a year. RAISED
....

f) The company was profitable last year.   MADE
....

g) I had to be interviewed at the head office.   ATTEND
....

h) My monthly salary is £1000.   A YEAR
....

i) Jill is employed by a firm of accountants.   WORKS
....

j) We advertised the job in the paper.   PUT
....

10

Decide which answer A, B, C or D best fits each space.

Choosing a job

One of the most difficult decisions is choosing what to do for a (1) .... For example, do you want to follow a definite (2) ..... , and (3) ..... a low (4) ..... at the beginning, but have good (5) ..... in a company that trains its (6) ..... ? Or are you more interested in taking any kind of work, because you need a/an (7) ...... ? You may have to (8) ..... the fact that a good (9) ..... can be difficult to find. In that case, why not take a (10) ..... one? You will gain some useful (11) .... Remember that even if you have the right (12) ..... , you may have to (13) ..... lots of application forms before you are asked to (14) ..... an interview. But don't worry if you don't know what you want to (15) ..... exactly. You'll enjoy finding out!

1) A) salary	B) living	C) employee	D) work
2) A) company	B) training	C) business	D) career
3) A) earn	B) gain	C) win	D) take
4) A) money	B) profit	C) cheque	D) salary
5) A) hopes	B) prospects	C) futures	D) promotions
6) A) employers	B) crew	C) staff	D) persons
7) A) money	B) cash	C) account	D) income
8) A) face up to	B) go over	C) come up with	D) call off
9) A) work	B) labour	C) job	D) seat
10) A) temporary	B) overtime	C) profitable	D) short
11) A) experiences	B) experienced	C) experience	D) experiencing
12) A) qualifications	B) exams	C) letters	D) degrees

13) A) fall through B) get on C) turn down D) fill in
14) A) be B) attend C) make D) advertise
15) A) work B) job C) do D) employ

3 Sport and Leisure

1
Complete each sentence with a word from the list. Use each word once only.

handlebars racket rope glasses net costume whistle saddle gloves rod club ice

a) When Brenda entered the swimming competition she bought a new ....

b) I learned to ride a horse without using a ....

c) Gemma tried to hit the golf-ball with her .... , but missed it.

d) After the tennis match, one of the players jumped over the ....

e) Diana's bike crashed into a tree, and she was thrown over the ....

f) A mountain-climber's life may depend on their ....

g) Open-air skating can be dangerous if the .... is too thin.

h) Peter put his .... in front of his face to protect himself from his opponent's punches.

i) Suddenly the referee blew his .... and pointed to the penalty spot.

j) Skiing can be dangerous if you don't wear dark ....

k) I had to play the doubles match with a borrowed ....

l) Terry went fishing with the new .... his parents gave him.

2
Match these words with the comments given.

billiards crossword embroidery hiking camping draughts gambling jigsaw cards do-it-yourself gardening model-making

a) Catherine dealt, and gave me the ace, king and queen of hearts. ....

b) You need a small needle, and threads of different colours. ....

c) I couldn't find ten down, so I looked for words in the dictionary. ....

d) Ian glued the parts together wrongly because he didn't read the instructions. ....

e) When Ellen is losing, she tries to knock the pieces off the board. ....

f) The path we want doesn't seem to be on the map. ....

g) Nigel missed the red, and put the pink in the pocket by mistake. ....

h) I want to put £50 on 'Ealing Comedy' to win in the 4.30 at York. ....

i) These pieces with flowers on all look the same, don't they. ....

j) Graham papered the hall while I was painting the doors. ....

k) When I woke up there was a chicken inside the tent. ....

l) The daffodils I put in haven't come up this year. ....

3

Choose the most suitable word underlined in each sentence.

a) Sue came first in the 5000 metre <u>competition/game/race</u>.

b) Jack and Eddie arranged to meet outside the football <u>ground/field/pitch</u>.

c) Brenda goes jogging every morning to keep <u>exercised/fit/trained</u>.

d) Our team <u>beat/defeated/won</u> the match by two goals to nil.

e) The local stadium isn't large enough for so many <u>audience/viewers/spectators</u>.

f) I'm afraid I don't find basketball very <u>interested/interesting</u>.

g) Collecting matchbox labels is Rebecca's favourite <u>leisure/occupation/pastime</u>.

h) Norman won first <u>medal/prize/reward</u> in the cookery competition.

i) All <u>competitors/rivals/supporters</u> for the relay race should make their way to the track.

j) The final result was a/an <u>draw/equal/score</u>.

4

Replace the word or words underlined in each sentence with a word from the list. Use each word once only.

arranged	outdoors	record	second	captain	postponed
referee	side	champion	professionally	score	spare

a) Mary plays tennis <u>as a way of earning her living</u>.

b) Tomorrow's hockey match has been <u>put off for another time</u>.

c) In motor racing last year William Green was the <u>best driver of all</u>.

d) The player with the lowest <u>number of points</u> wins the game.

e) A match between the Dutch and German teams has been <u>fixed</u> for next month.

f) I like going swimming in my <u>free</u> time.

g) Jane Briggs was <u>the runner-up</u> in the 100 metres hurdles.

h) Who is the <u>player in charge</u> of your football team?

i) She won all her matches this season, which is a <u>best ever performance</u>.

j) Charles was sent off for punching the <u>person who controls the match</u>.

k) We decided to hold this year's dancing competition <u>in the open air</u>.

l) Everyone agreed that United were the best <u>team</u>.

5

Use the word in capitals at the end of each line to form a word that fits in the space in the same line.

How a hobby can make you angry!

Recently I decided to take up (1) .... as a hobby. I have   PHOTOGRAPH
always taken snapshots, but I have never been very (2) .... SKILL
My snaps were either a complete (3) .... for   FAIL
technical reasons, or were just not very (4) .... First   IMAGINE
I decided that to be (5) .... , I would have to buy new   SUCCESS
equipment. Just then I had an (6) .... piece of good   EXPECT
luck. A friend who works in a camera shop said she
could sell me a (7) .... camera. A customer had   VALUE

left it at the shop to be repaired, but there had been
a (8) .... , and it was actually for sale.
I thought this was a rather (9) .... explanation
and so I asked her some more questions. It turned out
that she had had a (10) .... with the customer and he
had thrown the camera at her in anger because she had
disliked his photos!

UNDERSTAND
BELIEF

AGREE

6

Complete the
compound word
in each sentence
using a word
given in the list.

| board   court   jacket   repairs   collection   field |
| making   site   course   hooligan   pools   track |

a) Everyone who goes sailing must wear a life-................... .
b) Karen's hobby is doing her own car................... .
c) I'm afraid that Ruth doesn't have the patience for model-................... .
d) People look bored when I talk about my stamp................... .
e) Bring your racket and I'll meet you at the tennis................... .
f) Because Bill wears a scarf everyone thinks he is a football................... .
g) The school has sold its playing................... to a property company.
h) Violet won half a million pounds on the football................... .
i) I enjoy walking around the golf................... and watching people play.
j) Every morning I jog round the running................... opposite my house.
k) Steve jumped from the diving................... wearing all his clothes!
l) We stayed on a lovely camp................... just outside Paris.

7

Choose the most
suitable word or
phrase to
complete each
sentence.

a) Mary stopped swimming and just .... on the surface.
   A) sank   B) floated   C) dived   D) poured
b) Jack turned the last corner and .... for the finishing line.
   A) approached   B) arrived   C) waited   D) headed
c) David was trying to .... another cyclist when he crashed.
   A) overpass   B) overcome   C) overtake   D) overcharge
d) You have to .... the person with the ball until you catch them.
   A) chase   B) rush   C) jump   D) drop
e) The fans climbed over the fence to .... paying.
   A) avoid   B) prevent   C) abandon   D) refuse
f) I fell over while skiing and my sister had to .... a doctor.
   A) bring   B) take   C) fetch   D) carry
g) It's very easy to .... over when the snow is hard.
   A) slide   B) skid   C) skate   D) slip
h) Don't .... the road until all the runners have gone by.
   A) pass   B) cross   C) across   D) pass by
i) The swimmers .... forward as they waited to begin the race.
   A) fell   B) crawled   C) rolled   D) leaned
j) When I was hiking in the mountains I .... on a snake.
   A) tripped   B) stepped   C) surprised   D) carried

8

Complete each sentence with a word from the list. Use each word once only.

anywhere	dinner	ready	through	back	lost
right	together	better	off	stuck	used

a) After Paul's leg was injured, it took him a long time to get ....

b) Unfortunately Sally rode her bike into the mud and got ....

c) An hour before the race I went to the stadium and started to get........ .

d) Some of the competitors got .... because of the thick fog.

e) I tried learning to do embroidery but I didn't get ....

h) Jean worked on her stamp collection while Barry was getting the ....

g) I didn't get .... from the match till late because of the crowds.

h) David practised hitting the golf ball until he got it ....

i) Kate enjoyed riding the horse but found it hard to get ....

j) I tried to phone the tennis club but I couldn't get ....

k) We have a great time whenever our rugby team gets ....

l) I can't get .... to playing football on plastic grass!

9

Rewrite the sentences in **8** so that each one contains *one* of the words in the list, and does *not* contain a form of *get*.

answer	dismount	perfected	strange	became	home
prepare	succeed	cooking	meets	recover	way

a) ....

b) ....

c) ....

d) ....

e) ....

f) ....

g) ....

h) ....

i) ....

j) ....

k) ....

l) ....

10

Decide which answer A, B, C or D best fits each space.

Sport

Someone once said that there are three kinds of people who are (1) ..... in sport: people who (2) ..... part, people who watch, and people who watch (3) ..... television. It's very easy to make fun of stay-at-home sports (4) ..... , but on the other hand, television does enable us to enjoy all kinds of (5) ..... events. We can watch a racing car (6) ..... another, see a cyclist (7) ..... the finishing line, or enjoy the goals of our favourite football (8) ..... . The first time I watched a tennis (9) ..... was on television, and I found it (10) ..... interesting. It's not always easy to (11) ..... long distances to football (12) ..... , and television is a good solution. Of course, you can (13) ..... used to sitting indoors all the time, and this is dangerous. We should all try to (14) ..... fit, and have other interests and (15) ..... .

1) A) playing	B) really	C) interested	D) succeed
2) A) take	B) have	C) make	D) get
3) A) on	B) with	C) by	D) from
4) A) people	B) centres	C) programmes	D) fans
5) A) the	B) future	C) sports	D) athlete
6) A) cross	B) overtake	C) or	D) from
7) A) overtake	B) and	C) cross	D) professional
8) A) group	B) class	C) band	D) team
9) A) match	B) it	C) which	D) that
10) A) valuable	B) imaginatively	C) unexpectedly	D) real
11) A) trip	B) tour	C) pass	D) travel
12) A) areas	B) grounds	C) teams	D) fans
13) A) or	B) which	C) get	D) is
14) A) keep	B) make	C) do	D) have
15) A) customs	B) habits	C) pastimes	D) leisure

4 Clothes and Appearance

1

Choose words from the list to complete the labels for the illustrations. Not all words given are suitable.

belt   costume   handbag   shoes   suit   blouse   dress
jacket   skirt   suitcase   boots   earrings   sandals   socks
tie   briefcase   glasses   shirt   stockings   waistcoat

2

Choose the most suitable word or phrase underlined in each sentence.

a) At Harry's school, the children have to wear a special appearance/style/uniform.

b) If we go to the Embassy ball we'll have to wear fashion/formal/polite clothes.

c) I really like Jack's new dress/suit/trouser.

d) In the summer I always wear shirts with short collars/cuffs/sleeves.

e) Paul answered the door wearing his pyjamas and his <u>dressing gown/ nightdress</u>.

f) You get really dirty repairing a car unless you wear <u>a jumper/overalls/ underwear</u>.

g) I didn't get wet in the rain because I put on my plastic <u>mac/overcoat/tights</u>.

h) When it snows Freda always wears a/an <u>anorak/glove/scarf</u> around her neck.

i) David had to stop three times to tie up his small daughter's <u>heels/shoelaces/ soles</u>.

j) My hands were cold so I put them in my <u>jacket/pockets/turn-ups</u>.

k) I don't like that dress, it isn't in <u>fashion/mode/style</u>.

l) Julie was given a lovely <u>fur/hair/skin</u> coat for her birthday.

m) All the men at the wedding were wearing top <u>caps/hats/helmets</u>.

n) The waitresses in this restaurant all wear white <u>aprons/dungarees/robes</u>.

o) When Tom goes to a party he always wears a <u>bow/butterfly/knot</u> tie.

3

Use the word in capitals at the end of each line to form a word that fits in the space in the same line.

Father and son

My next-door neighbour has a very unusual (1)	APPEAR
He has long hair with a (2) .... in the middle, and	PART
usually wears an old pair of jeans and a (3) .... shirt.	STRIPE
His clothes are very (4) .... for working in a bank, but	SUIT
that is what he does! Unless he (5) .... when he gets to	DRESS
work and changes his clothes! His clothes are usually filthy	
and I am sure he never washes them or takes them to	
the (6) .... When he wears a coat it is always	CLEAN
old and (7) .... , and even on very cold days it is	WEAR
(8) .... all down the front. The funny thing is that his	BUTTON
son is very (9) .... , always wears the latest styles, and	FASHION
never wears casual clothes, even on an (10) .... occasion.	FORMAL

4

Correct any errors in these sentences. Some sentences contain no errors.

a) This shirt is too small, it's not my number.

b) You have so many clothes. Why did you buy this cloth as well?

c) What costume did you wear to the fancy dress party?

d) Joan was dressed completely in white.

e) I like your new trouser. How much was it?

f) Excuse me for a moment. I have to wear some different clothes.

g) As far as I can see, the man in this photograph wears a suit.

h) The blouse is a good fit, but it isn't a very good suit.

i) What are you wearing to the party this evening?

j) You're soaked! Put out your clothes immediately!

5

Choose the most suitable word or phrase to complete each sentence.

a) When you saw Jack at the dance, what did he .... ?
   A) wear   B) have on   C) dress   D) put on

b) My hands were so cold that I couldn't .... my coat buttons.
   A) open   B) remove   C) put out   D) undo

c) Those trousers are far too big. Why don't you have them ....
   A) taken in   B) let out   C) taken up   D) let in

d) I don't think that purple shirt .... with your yellow skirt.
   A) suits   B) fits   C) goes   D) wears

e) This jacket is the kind of thing I want. Can I .... ?
   A) wear it   B) dress it   C) take it off   D) try it on

f) You look really silly! Your pullover is on ....
   A) upside down   B) inside out   C) round and round   D) side by side

g) I don't want a pattern. I prefer just a/an .... colour.
   A) plain   B) simple   C) clear   D) only

h) You look hot in that coat. Why don't you .... ?
   A) put it on   B) take it off   C) put it away   D) take it out

i) Your diet was a success! You look wonderfully ....!
   A) skinny   B) thin   C) slim   D) underweight

j) I went shopping today and bought a new winter ....
   A) costume   B) outfit   C) suit   D) clothing

6

Complete the word in each sentence. Each space represents one letter.

a) It's cold today. I'm going to put on a thick s _ _ _ _ _ _ .

b) When they go to church the women wear lace s _ _ _ _ _ over their heads.

c) Graham usually wears a leather j _ _ _ _ _ _ .

d) My trousers are falling down! I must buy a b _ _ _ .

e) It's too hot for trousers. I'm going to wear my s _ _ _ _ _ .

f) Let's roll up our shirt s _ _ _ _ _ _ and start work.

g) I can't wear these jeans! They are too t _ _ _ _ .

h) I bought this lovely s _ _ _ scarf in Japan.

i) Don't forget to put your clothes away in the w _ _ _ _ _ _ _ .

j) I'm never cold as long as I wear my woolly u _ _ _ _ _ _ _ _ .

7

Choose the most suitable word or phrase to complete each sentence.

a) If I wear a long-sleeved shirt, I usually ...... the sleeves.
   A) put up   B) take up   C) roll up   D) get up

b) You're too fat! You have definitely ...... that roll necked jumper!
   A) grown out of   B) put away   C) worn out   D) tried on

c) That skirt is very short. Why don't you have it ......?
   A) left out   B) set in   C) let down   D) taken round

d) The thief wore gloves so that his fingerprints didn't ......
   A) give him in   B) give him away   C) give him out   D) give him up

e) I can't walk in these high-heeled boots. I keep ......
   A) falling off   B) falling back   C) falling out   D) falling over

f) What do you mean, my swimming costume is too small? What are you ......
   A) seeing to   B) getting at   C) making up   D) putting out

g) I'm ...... money every week to buy a new sports jacket.
   A) making for   B) getting over   C) putting aside   D) turning in

h) Some of the young people in my town ...... very strange haircuts!
   A) go out with   B) go in for   C) go through with   D) go back on

i) Before we choose a dress for you, let's ...... all the shops.
   A) look into   B) look through   C) look up   D) look around

j) If you work in a bank, you can't ...... wearing an open-necked shirt.
   A) get round to   B) get into   C) get away with   D) get out of

8
Decide which answer A, B, C or D best fits each space.

Choosing Clothes

Are you one of the thousands of people who eagerly follow every new (1) ....
that appears? Or are you one of those who go to the shops and just buy
whatever they can find in their (2) .... that (3) .... them? Or perhaps you
order from a mail-order catalogue, and then have to send everything back
because nothing (4) .... ? Whatever (5) .... of shopper you are, one thing is
certain. Everyone finds (6) .... important. According to a recent survey,
people spend more time either buying clothes, or thinking about buying them,
or looking at them in shop (7) .... , than they do on most other products,
(8) .... from food. And the reason is obvious. Clothes are an important part
of our (9) .... At work, you may need to impress a customer, or persuade the
boss that you know what you are doing, and clothes certainly help. (10) ....
dressed people, so they say, get on in the world. And as far as attracting the
opposite sex is concerned, clothes also play a vital role. If a friend who has been
(11) .... the same old jacket or the same old dress suddenly appears in the
(12) .... fashion, you can be sure that romance is in the air. And apart from
work and romance, there are the influences of sport, music and leisure on the
way we (13).......... . So excuse me while I (14) .... on my tracksuit and
training (15) .... I'm just dashing off for some fast window-shopping.

1) A) appearance	B) fashion	C) uniform	D) dress
2) A) place	B) price	C) size	D) self
3) A) suits	B) makes	C) takes	D) likes
4) A) sizes	B) styles	C) fits	D) measures
5) A) means	B) typical	C) idea	D) kind
6) A) out	B) clothes	C) dresses	D) vests
7) A) centres	B) sales	C) times	D) windows
8) A) apart	B) or	C) according	D) taken
9) A) nowadays	B) appearance	C) looking	D) events
10) A) well	B) good	C) best	D) fancy
11) A) dressing	B) putting) on	C) carrying	D) wearing
12) A) last	B) minute	C) latest	D) complete
13) A) clothes	B) have	C) dress	D) go
14) A) put	B) dress	C) wear	D) have
15) A) fit	B) shoes	C) tonight	D) again

5 Towns and Buildings

1
Choose the most suitable word underlined in each sentence.

a) As you can see, the garden has two ornamental iron doors/gates and there is a stone path/pavement leading to the house.

b) This is the front entry/entrance, but there is another door at the edge/side of the house.

c) All the rooms have covered/fitted carpets.

d) All the cupboards/wardrobes in the kitchen and the bookshelves/library in the living room are included in the price.

e) There is a beautiful stone chimney/fireplace in the living room, and there are sinks/washbasins in all the bedrooms.

f) At the top of the stairs/steps there is a 19th century coloured/stained glass window.

g) The bathroom has a shower/washer and modern mixer pipes/taps.

h) At the top of the house there is a/an attic/cellar and the garden contains a glasshouse/greenhouse and a garden hut/shed.

i) There is a wooden fence/wall on one side of the garden, and a bush/hedge on the other.

j) All in all, this is a fine single/detached house in a quiet residential neighbourhood/suburb.

2
Match these words with an explanation. Not all words given are possible.

| aerial   curtains   drive   parking   shelf   central heating   dishwasher |
| furniture   radiator   stool   cook   doormat   landing   stove/cooker |
| rug   door knocker   letter box   settee/sofa   washing machine |

a) Rectangular hole in the front door. ....

b) Kitchen appliance running on gas or electricity. ....

c) Long narrow rectangular piece of wood or metal fixed to the wall. ....

d) Short road between the street and a house or its garage. ....

e) Use this if you want someone to open the front door. ....

f) Put the dirty dishes in this. ....

g) This system makes the house warm. ....

h) A small carpet. ....

i) More than one person can sit on this. ....

j) This helps a radio or television to receive a broadcast. ....

k) An area at the top of some stairs. ....

l) Wipe your feet on this before you enter the house. ....

m) Pull these to cover the windows. ....

n) Small seat without back or arms. ....

o) Put your dirty washing in this. ....

3

Complete each sentence a) to j) with one of the endings 1) to 10) so that the meaning of the word underlined is clear. Use each ending only once.

a) I would prefer to live in a <u>cottage</u> ....
b) The shopping centre has a <u>multi-storey car-park</u> ....
c) My grandmother bought a <u>bungalow</u> ....
d) Jenny lives in a small <u>flat</u> ....
e) This street is only for <u>pedestrians</u> ....
f) Helen and John live in a <u>square</u> ....
g) Peter has moved to a London <u>suburb</u> ....
h) This village is surrounded by lovely <u>countryside</u> ....
i) Sue's new house is <u>unfurnished</u> ....
j) My house is <u>semi-detached</u> ....

1) .... on the third floor of a modern block.
2) .... and he commutes to work in the centre.
3) .... with room for over 2000 vehicles.
4) .... but the rent is so high that she cannot afford much furniture.
5) .... which has a beautiful garden in the middle.
6) .... in a small village in the country.
7) .... and the neighbours often bang on the wall.
8) .... because she had difficulty climbing stairs.
9) .... with fields, woods, streams and a small lake.
10) .... and cars and lorries are not allowed.

4

Complete each sentence with the words *home, house* or a word formed from one of these words.

a) The old couple decided to live in an old people's ....
b) Jane can't stand washing and ironing and other ....
c) Graham bought a terraced .... in a quiet city street.
d) Many .... people sleep in the streets in London.
e) Jack was unable to look after his children so he employed a ....
f) I come from Newcastle. It's my .... town, you could say.
g) Paul used to live on the river on a ....boat.
h) When I went to boarding school I felt very ....sick at first.
i) Our first home was on the ....estate on Oakwood Hill.
j) Pour yourself a drink and make yourself at ....

5

Choose the most suitable word or phrase to complete each sentence.

a) The view from the skyscraper .... over New York harbour.
   A) shows up   B) sees about   C) stands up   D) looks out
b) The old houses opposite are going to be ....
   A) broken down   B) knocked down   C) put down   D) taken down
c) .... ! You're about to push the wheelbarrow over my foot!
   A) hang up   B) stop off   C) get away   D) look out
d) Please .... the rubbish because the dustman is coming tomorrow.
   A) take in   B) make up   C) put out   D) tie down
e) Please come and unblock our drains! I'm .... you!
   A) doing without   B) counting on   C) seeing to   D) waiting for

f) I can't put these plants in pots. I've .... earth.
   A) run out of   B) put up with   C) given up   D) come up with

g) We .... through the window by climbing up a ladder.
   A) fell out   B) got in   C) ended up   D) set off

h) I've been planting trees all day and I'm ....
   A) worn out   B) taken in   C) run down   D) grown up

i) A lot of tiles .... our roof after the high wind.
   A) came off   B) took off   C) put off   D) got off

j) The car went out of control and .... hitting a lamp-post.
   A) speeded up   B) ran up   C) turned up   D) ended up

6

Use the word in capitals at the end of each line to form a word that fits in the space in the same line.

A house in the country

When Ann decided to move house, it was mainly because
she was tired of the (1) .... she lived in. It was crowded,   NEIGHBOUR
there was a (2) .... of parking places, and   SHORT
the view from her (3) .... windows was of distant   STAIRS
factory chimneys. Luckily she arranged the (4) ....   SELL
of her house very easily, and with a small (5) .... from   LEND
the bank, was able to buy a house in the country. It was an
old farm building, which had been (6) .... and turned into   BUILD
a modern house. After loading all her belongings into a van,
Ann managed to get them into the new house (7) ....   DAMAGE
She (8) .... most of the rooms with what she already   FURNITURE
owned. Even her curtains were the right (9) .... for the   LONG
windows and she only had to buy a new (10) .... for   COOK
the kitchen. It seemed too good to be true. Surely
something was bound to go wrong!

7

Choose the most suitable word or phrase underlined in each sentence.

a) Laura was sitting beside the fire in a comfortable <u>armchair/sofa</u>.
b) We drove out of the village along a winding <u>lane/path</u>.
c) Steve redecorated his room with flowery <u>posters/wallpaper</u>.
d) Put the meat in the <u>cooker/oven</u> for two hours.
e) These plums are ripe. They need <u>picking/picking up</u>.
f) Peter was in the garden mowing the <u>flowers/lawn</u>.
g) We used to keep the coal downstairs in the <u>cave/cellar</u>.
h) Why don't you put the car in the <u>car park/parking</u>?
i) Kate lives in a flat on the first <u>floor/storey</u>.
j) Put your wet socks on the <u>central heating/radiator</u> to dry.
k) Let's take the <u>runway/motorway</u>, we'll get there faster.
l) Go and get the lawnmower. The grass <u>is/are</u> very long.
m) I like the painting but I don't like the <u>frame/surrounding</u>.
n) Mary has a lot of small ornaments on her window <u>shelf/sill</u>.
o) There's someone <u>at/on</u> the door. Can you see who it is?

8

Match these words with the explanations given.

| shutters ceiling chimney pillow kennel blind cushion roof |
| rubbish urban bunk eiderdown kerb litter rural |

a) Put this over you if you are cold in bed.
b) Put this behind your back if you are sitting uncomfortably.
c) This describes city places.
d) These protect your windows outside and can be closed in bad weather.
e) This is paper dropped in the street.
f) This is the top of the room.
g) This is a bed with others above it.
h) This describes country places.
i) This is the top of the house.
j) Put this under your head when you go to sleep.
k) Close this to keep the sunlight out of your room.
l) This is anything you throw away in the dustbin.
m) This is home for your pet dog.
n) This is the stone edge of the pavement at the side of the road.
o) The smoke goes up this from the fireplace.

9

Decide which answer A, B, C or D best fits each space.

Moving In

The entrance to the flat was at the (1) ..... of the house. Jane had to walk along a (2) ..... across the lawn and past a (3) ..... full of gardening equipment. Inside the back door there was a flight of (4) ..... and then another door on the (5) .... It was a (6) ..... flat with a bedroom, living room, kitchen and bathroom. There was not a lot of (7) ..... but certainly enough for a student like Jane. There was a/an (8) ..... with an electric fire, and the kitchen had a small (9) ..... and a fridge. The bathroom did not have a bath, only a (10) ..... and a basin, but Jane didn't mind. She was thinking about other problems. There wasn't a washing (11) ..... , and there was no (12) ..... heating. It was raining outside, and the flat felt damp and chilly. On the bed there were some (13) ..... and an eiderdown , but no (14) .... It was lucky that Jane had brought a sleeping bag. As she was wondering what to do next, there was a knock (15) ..... the door.

1) A) side   B) inside   C) beginning   D) garden
2) A) road   B) way   C) path   D) stairs
3) A) room   B) shed   C) cellar   D) floor
4) A) ladder   B) upstairs   C) rooms   D) stairs
5) A) roof   B) landing   C) balcony   D) bottom
6) A) multi-storey   B) semi-detached   C) furnished   D) cottage
7) A) furniture   B) rent   C) neighbours   D) housing
8) A) oven   B) chimney   C) radiator   D) fireplace
9) A) cook   B) cookery   C) cooker   D) cooking
10) A) waterfall   B) shower   C) splash   D) sink
11) A) machine   B) up   C) room   D) powder

12) A) central   B) much   C) radiator   D) good
13) A) wrappings   B) rugs   C) carpets   D) blankets
14) A) whites   B) sheets   C) spreads   D) cloths
15) A) for   B) behind   C) to   D) at

6 Vehicles and Transport

1
Choose the most suitable word or phrase underlined in each sentence.

a) I enjoy taking the baby out in its cart/pram/trailer.
b) The train fare is expensive, it's cheaper to go by carriage/coach/waggon.
c) Terry and Bill rode around the island on their bicycle/trolley/tandem.
d) A farmer gave me a lift across the muddy field on his dustcart/lorry/tractor.
e) Cars made between 1916 and 1930 can be called racing/sports/vintage cars.
f) The first person who arrived at the scene of the accident phoned for a/an ambulance/stretcher/trolley.
g) Lorries, motorbikes and sports cars are all kinds of cars/motors/vehicles.
h) Jack was nearly run over by a fire engine/hosepipe/tanker on its way to a put out a serious blaze.
i) You need a powerful car to tow a camping/caravan/sleeper in the mountains.
j) Most buses in London are double decks/decked/deckers and you can see the sights from upstairs.

2
Complete each sentence with a word from the list. Use each word once only.

| captain   crew   guard   pedestrian   chauffeur   cyclist   mechanic |
| steward   conductor   driver   motorist   traffic warden |

a) The company chairman has a Rolls-Royce driven by a ....
b) When my car broke down a passing .... towed it to a garage.
c) The police wanted me to describe the .... of the car.
d) The four passengers on the ship had dinner with the ....
e) The train couldn't leave until the .... waved his green flag.
f) Hilary was given a parking ticket by a ....
g) Before take-off, the .... told me to fasten my seat belt.
h) When I got on the ship, one of the .... helped me find my cabin.
i) There isn't a .... on this bus, you pay the driver.
j) Eddie is a keen .... and rides his bike to work every day.
k) The bus mounted the pavement and injured a ....
l) Jim works as a .... in a local garage.

3

Choose words from the list to complete the labels for the illustration.

| roof rack   bonnet   bumper   tyre   exhaust   windscreen   wheel |
| engine   headlight   mirror   steering wheel   aerial   boot   wiper   wing |

4

Choose the most suitable word or phrase to complete each sentence.

a) The ship stopped because two passengers had fallen ....
   A) upside down   B) overboard   C) underground   D) inside out

b) The .... was crowded with passengers waiting for the train.
   A) platform   B) quay   C) runway   D) pavement

c) We had to stop for petrol at a filling ....
   A) garage   B) service   C) pump   D) station

d) Mary looked up the fastest train to Glasgow in the ....
   A) catalogue   B) timetable   C) dictionary   D) programme

e) The train was very crowded because there were only four ....
   A) coaches   B) waggons   C) trucks   D) cars

f) Peter's car .... off the icy road and fell into a ditch.
   A) crashed   B) collided   C) hit   D) skidded

g) I dropped my wallet from the boat but luckily it ....
   A) drifted   B) floated   C) sank   D) rescued

h) Everything went dark when the train entered a/an ....
   A) underground   B) tunnel   C) tube   D) metro

i) David missed his train because of the queue in the ticket ....
   A) office   B) agency   C) room   D) lounge

j) To get to our hotel we had to cross the railway ....
   A) road   B) route   C) rails   D) line

5

Use the word in capitals at the end of each line to form a word that fits in the space in the same line.

A letter of apology

I am writing to apologise for the (1) .... of your Happy Holiday Coach Tour to Aberdeen. (2) .... our luxury coach was involved in a (3) .... in France a week ago, and our driver has been (4) .... obliged to remain there for the moment. The coach was travelling on a road (5) .... for heavy traffic, and the accident was (6) .... Luckily none of the passengers suffered any (7) .... , and we have complained to the authorities that the road needs (8) .... Our new coach will be fitted with (9) .... seat belts for the safety and comfort of passengers. We will of course return the (10) .... you have made for your holiday as soon as possible.

CANCEL
FORTUNE
COLLIDE
EXPECT
SUIT
AVOID
INJURE
WIDE
ADJUST

PAY

6

Complete each sentence with the word *sail* or *ship*, or a word formed from one of these words.

a) Jack has been working as a .... for ten years.
b) We're all flying home but our furniture is being ....
c) What time does the ferry set .... ?
d) We are expecting a .... of coffee from Brazil this week.
e) We have decided to go for a .... tomorrow afternoon.
f) When Paul was young he .... round the world.
g) It's time you were aboard .... We're leaving soon.
h) Do you like .... ? Or do you prefer water-skiing?
i) Graham works in the harbour as a .... clerk.
j) The boats on the lake had brightly coloured ....

7

Match these words with the description given.

accelerator   chain   gear   parachute   bonnet   cockpit
handlebars   reverse   brakes   deck   oars   wings

a) An aeroplane has two of these. ....
b) Change this in a car to change speed. ....
c) Hold these when you ride a bicycle. ....
d) This will save your life if you fall from a plane. ....
e) You need these to row a boat. ....
f) This might be on a bicycle or around your neck. ....
g) Put these on if you want to stop. ....
h) Your car engine is usually under this. ....
i) Walk on this when you are on a ship. ....
j) The pilot of a plane sits in this. ....
k) Put your foot on this to make the car go faster. ....
l) Go into this if you want to go backwards. ....

8
Complete each
sentence with
one suitable
word.

a) I'm really .... forward to sailing in Jean's new yacht.
b) In cities, cars and other vehicles .... up most of the space.
c) We'll come with the van and .... up the rest of the furniture.
d) When the storm began, the small boat .... for the nearest harbour.
e) How can you .... up with all those exhaust fumes!
f) We can't .... up with that speedboat in this rowing boat!
g) Jane likes .... off by driving her sports car at 100 miles an hour.
h) A fire engine arrived and soon .... out the fire.
i) Little Johnny is in the garden .... out his new tricycle.
j) One way of .... with the pollution problem is to use unleaded petrol.

9
Decide which
answer A, B, C
or D best fits
each space.

Past, Present and Future

A hundred years ago, most people travelled (1) ..... foot, by train, or on horseback. (2) ..... had made it possible to travel rapidly over long distances. Bicycles were also becoming (3) ..... , after the invention of the air-filled (4) ..... , which made cycling a lot more comfortable. Buses, trams and (5) ..... railways had already been invented, and cities all over the world already had traffic (6) ..... . There were very few private cars, and city (7) ..... were still full of horses. What a difference a hundred years have (8) ..... ! (9) ..... we have got (10) ..... to the problem of private cars, and some cities are so noisy and (11) ..... that in many places (12) ..... have been banned from the city centre. How will we be travelling in a hundred years' time? Perhaps (13) ..... then there will be only personal helicopters. There may be no need to (14) ..... to work or school in the future, since everyone will have a computer at home. There might even be more people walking and horse-riding, for pleasure and (15) ..... .

1)	A) by	B) on	C) with	D) to
2)	A) Tracks	B) Lines	C) Ways	D) Railways
3)	A) popular	B) invented	C) then	D) handlebars
4)	A) boot	B) brake	C) tyre	D) engine
5)	A) metro	B) buried	C) underground	D) submerged
6)	A) blocks	B) sticks	C) knots	D) jams
7)	A) streets	B) pavements	C) lawns	D) carts
8)	A) taken	B) done	C) made	D) got
9)	A) Presently	B) Nowadays	C) Then	D) Later
10)	A) more	B) them	C) motorists	D) used
11)	A) even	B) polluted	C) so	D) poisoned
12)	A) vehicles	B) traffic	C) transport	D) trips
13)	A) cars	B) by	C) even	D) transport
14)	A) have	B) transport	C) decide	D) commute
15)	A) exercise	B) keep) fit	C) energy	D) healthy

7 Food, Restaurants and Cooking

1

Choose the most suitable word or phrase underlined in each sentence.

a) Waiter, could you bring me my <u>account/bill/addition</u> please?
b) It's a very popular restaurant – we should <u>apply for/book/keep</u> a table.
c) If you're hungry, why not ask for a large <u>dish/plate/portion</u>?
d) Please <u>help/serve/wait</u> yourself to salads from the salad bar.
e) Waiter, can I see the <u>catalogue/directory/menu,</u> please?
f) This fish is not what I <u>called/commanded/ordered</u>.
g) This <u>dish/plate/serving</u> is a speciality of our restaurant.
h) Have you tried the <u>crude/raw/undercooked</u> fish at the new Japanese restaurant? It's great!
i) Paul never eats meat, he's a <u>vegetable/vegetarian/vegetation</u>.
j) Have you decided what to have for your main <u>course/food/helping</u>?

2

Complete each sentence a) to j) with one of the endings 1) to 10). Use each ending once only.

a) Dinner's nearly ready. Can you lay ....
b) There's some meat in the fridge. Just warm ....
c) Keep an eye on the milk or it might boil ....
d) Jack likes his steak rare but I prefer mine well ....
e) When we finish lunch, I'll do the washing ....
f) I always cut roast beef with an electric carving ....
g) Mary bought a lovely set of cups and ....
h) They serve a very cheap three course ....
i) I really enjoyed that freshly ground ....
j) If you have finished eating I'll clear ....

1) .... up if you dry and put the dishes away.
2) .... it up in the microwave oven for a few minutes.
3) .... coffee you made for me this morning.
4) .... meal at the pub opposite the supermarket.
5) .... knife as it makes really thin slices.
6) .... the small table in the dining room?
7) .... saucers in the sales last week.
8) .... done, but not burnt if you see what I mean.
9) .... away the plates and bring the next course.
10) .... over and make a mess on the cooker.

3

Complete each phrase with the most suitable word from the list. Use each word once only.

| bacon butter forks pepper beer chips grapes |
| saucers bread chocolate instant coffee wine |

a) cups and ....   e) eggs and ....   i) a can of ....

b) fish and ....   f) salt and ....   j) a bar of ....

c) knives and ....   g) a loaf of ....   k) a jar of ....

d) bread and ....   h) a bottle of ....   l) a bunch of ....

| frying pan saucepan casserole jar kettle |
| jug bowl tin opener mug food mixer |

4

Choose words from the list to complete the labels for the illustrations.

5

Complete each sentence with **one** suitable word.

a) I'm trying to cut down .... fatty food.

b) Don't worry! The smell of garlic wears .... after a while.

c) Let's look .... the market before we buy any vegetables.

d) I can't understand this recipe. Can you work .... what it means?

e) I'm afraid I don't feel up .... eating another cream cake.

f) I visited a farm once, and it put me .... eating meat for a week.

g) I haven't got .... to cleaning the fish yet.

h) Why don't we warm .... last night's leftovers for lunch?

i) Keith usually makes .... his recipes as he goes along.

j) The waiter seemed a bit put .... when we didn't leave a tip.

6

Choose the most suitable word or phrase to complete each sentence.

a) Would you prefer .... potatoes or chips?
  A) poached   B) ground   C) mashed   D) powdered

b) I bought this bread four days ago and now it's ....
  A) stale   B) off   C) bad   D) rotten

c) Don't forget to buy a packet of .... peas.
  A) chilled   B) frozen   C) frosted   D) chilly

d) Can you give me the .... for this pie? It's delicious.
  A) prescription   B) instructions   C) ingredients   D) recipe

e) There was a wonderful smell of .... bread in the kitchen.
   A) cooking   B) roasting   C) baking   D) grilling

f) Don't buy those fish, they aren't very ....
   A) fresh   B) new   C) recent   D) young

g) I'd like to eat more of this cake, but it's very ....
   A) fat   B) fatty   C) fattened   D) fattening

h) Waiter, I can't eat this meat. It's under-........ .
   A) done   B) developed   C) nourished   D) weight

i) Is the hamburger for you to eat here, or to .... ?
   A) go out   B) take away   C) carry on   D) sit down

j) That was fantastic. Could I have a second .... please?
   A) plate   B) course   C) helping   D) service

7

Complete each sentence with a word formed from *cook*. Use each word once only.

a) The hospital has over twenty .... working in the kitchen.

b) We bought David a .... book when he left home.

c) Do you like my new electric .... ?

d) The meals were large but not very well ....

e) I don't mind shopping, but I can't stand ....

f) You can boil these shellfish, or you can eat them ....

8

Complete each sentence with a word from the list. Use each word once only.

| add   beat   cool   grate   heat   melt   peel   pour   slice   sprinkle |

a) .... the potatoes and .... them thinly.

b) .... the eggs in a bowl, and then .... them to the mixture.

c) .... the butter in a saucepan and .... gently for two minutes.

d) .... the mixture into a bowl and leave to ....

e) .... some cheese, and .... over the potatoes.

9

Make a word or compound word to match the description.

a) A spoon used for putting sugar in tea. ...*teaspoon*...............

b) A cloth put on the table at meal times. ....

c) A metal device for opening bottles. ....

d) A pot in which tea is made. ....

e) An electrical appliance for making toast. ....

f) A cup specially made for coffee. ....

g) An omelette containing mushrooms. ....

h) An electrical appliance for mixing food. ....

i) A napkin made of paper. ....

j) The amount contained in a tablespoon. ....

k) An electrical appliance for washing dishes. ....

10

Decide which
answer A, B, C
or D best fits
each space.

Chick Pea Soup

This is just right for a cold winter's day, and is both (1) ..... and cheap. If you use
dried chick-peas, (2) ..... them for at least twelve hours in cold water. Drain them
and put them in a large (3) ..... with plenty of water. Bring them to the boil, and
then let them simmer gently (4) ..... the chickpeas are soft. I find it easier to use
(5) ..... chickpeas, which are already cooked. This (6) ..... time, and also
guarantees that the chickpeas will be soft, since it can take hours of boiling
before they (7) ..... . Two small 450 gram cans are usually (8) ..... . Strain the
chickpeas, but keep some of the liquid for the soup. (9) ..... about three
tablespoons of olive oil in a clean saucepan, and gently heat a chopped (10) ..... ,
two or three cloves of garlic and some (11) ..... carrot. (12) ..... half the chick peas
and turn them in the oil over a low heat. Meanwhile blend the remaining
chickpeas in a food (13) ..... until they make a smooth cream. Add about half a
litre of water to the vegetables and bring to the boil. Mix in the creamed
chickpeas and cook slowly. Add salt and (14) ..... and a pinch of mixed herbs.
You can also add a stock cube or other vegetables. Some (15) ..... add lemon juice
at the end. Serve hot with plenty of bread.

1) A) expensive	B) tasty	C) worth	D) cold
2) A) soak	B) bury	C) wash	D) water
3) A) kettle	B) mug	C) sink	D) saucepan
4) A) when	B) until	C) if	D) enough
5) A) the	B) to	C) canned	D) crude
6) A) makes	B) takes	C) saves	D) gives
7) A) soften	B) harden	C) widen	D) lengthen
8) A) much	B) enough	C) mine	D) few
9) A) Grate	B) Peel	C) Beat	D) Pour
10) A) onion	B) up	C) one	D) water
11) A) melted	B) beaten	C) poached	D) sliced
12) A) One	B) Then	C) Add	D) Serve
13) A) just	B) not	C) dish	D) mixer
14) A) paper	B) puppy	C) pepper	D) poppy
15) A) cookers	B) cooks	C) cookery	D) chiefs

8 Shops and Shopping

1
Choose the most suitable word or phrase underlined in each sentence.

a) That new clothes shop has a lot of very good <u>bargains/sales</u>.
b) On Saturday morning the High Street is full of <u>customers/shoppers</u>.
c) It costs £2.50, so give her £3, and she'll give you 50p <u>change/rest</u>.
d) I don't go to that supermarket, it's a bit <u>priced/pricey</u>.
e) You cannot return goods without the original <u>recipe/receipt</u>.
f) Supasoft Soaps are <u>for sale/on sale</u> here.
g) A carrier bag is free with each <u>buyer/purchase</u> over £5.
h) If you pay cash we can give you a 10% <u>cutting/discount</u>.
i) How much did you <u>pay/spend</u> for your new shoes?
j) This is a good shoe shop, but the <u>costs/prices</u> are very high.

2
Rewrite each sentence so that it includes the word given in capitals.

a) I can't manage to see what the price is. Let's ask inside.   MAKE
....

b) Is this coat the right size? Can I check?   TRY
....

c) Two masked men robbed the supermarket yesterday.   HELD
....

d) You need a new coat. Your old one is too small.   GROWN
....

e) I've been shopping all morning. I feel exhausted.   WORN
....

f) I'll come and collect the goods on Thursday.   PICK
....

g) Sorry, we don't have any bread left.   RUN
....

h) Are you going to the chemist's?   CALLING
....

i) I don't like supermarkets. I can't bear the queues.   PUT
....

j) I don't know whether to buy this car. I'll consider it.   OVER
....

3
Complete each sentence with a word from the list. Use each word once only.

change	deliver	find	fit	go	help
order	pay	queue	serve	try	wrap

a) You have to .... for ages to pay in this supermarket.
b) In the London area, we .... furniture free of charge in our van.
c) The trousers I bought are the wrong size, I'd like to .... them.
d) Could somebody .... me, please? I've been waiting for ten minutes.
e) Is this a present? Would you like me to .... it for you?
f) I like the colour of this skirt, but it doesn't .... me.

g) Good morning, madam. Can I .... you?

h) We don't have your size at the moment, but we can .... it for you.

i) Can you .... at the other cash desk please.

j) Would you like to .... on this green pair?

k) I went shopping but couldn't .... exactly what I wanted.

l) Food is so expensive now. The prices seem to .... up all the time.

4

Complete each sentence a) to j) with one of the endings 1) to 10). Use each ending once only.

a) I bought my new television from a department ....

b) Don't forget to write a shopping ....

c) Can you pay over there? This cash ....

d) Most of the tourists went bargain ....

e) Why don't we go to the new shopping ....

f) Quite late at night the little corner ....

g) It would be much better to buy an economy ....

h) Don't forget that we have to stop at the filling ....

i) There's a very nice suit on display in the shop ....

j) Mary has just started work as a shop ....

1) .... centre near the public library

2) .... register doesn't work.

3) .... window of that new shop next to the post office.

4) .... size box of paper tissues.

5) .... store in the town centre.

6) .... shop down the road is still open.

7) .... assistant in a shoe shop.

8) .... list before we go to the market tomorrow.

9) .... station to get some petrol.

10) .... hunting in the old part of the city.

5

Choose the most suitable word or phrase to complete each sentence.

a) I bought these jeans very cheaply in the ....
   A) bargains B) reductions C) sales D) discounts

b) The washing instructions for this shirt are given on the ....
   A) label B) badge C) notice D) mark

c) All the small .... closed their shops in protest at the price rises.
   A) shop assistants B) shoppers C) shopkeepers D) shop stewards

d) We don't have the cassette, I'm afraid. It's out of ....
   A) order B) stock C) shelf D) sale

e) The street market was full of .... selling fruit and vegetables.
   A) counters B) boutiques C) tables D) stalls

f) The shop opposite my house sells a variety of ....
   A) objects B) purchases C) goods D) productions

g) I'm sorry, but the dress you want is not .... in red.
   A) possible B) economical C) suitable D) available

h) Every Friday you can buy cheap vegetables in the market ....
A) street   B) place   C) store   D) sales
i) I like street markets, because you shop in the open ....
A) prices   B) sunshine   C) bargains   D) air
j) I like your new car. What .... is it?
A) brand   B) make   C) name   D) label

6

Complete each sentence with a word from the list. Use each word once only.

| baked beans   chocolates   jam   orange juice   soap |
| breakfast cereal   flowers   margarine   paper tissues   toothpaste |

a) a tube of ....
b) a bunch of ....
c) a pot of ....
d) a tin of ....
e) a box of ....
f) a box of ....
g) a packet of ....
h) a bar of ....
i) a carton of ....
j) a tub of ....

7

Match these words with the descriptions given.

| advertisement   bargain   catalogue   deposit |
| list   manager   purse   receipt   trolley   wallet |

a) You push this in the supermarket and fill it with food. ....
b) You are given this as proof of buying something. ....
c) This tries to persuade you to buy something. ....
d) You put money, especially banknotes, in this. ....
e) This person is in charge of a shop. ....
f) You might make this before you go shopping. ....
g) Leave this if you can't pay now but want to buy later. ....
h) Do this if you want to get a better price. ....
i) Coins are usually carried in this, especially by women. ....
j) Read this to find descriptions of goods. ....

8

Use the word in capitals at the end of each line to form a word that fits in the space in the same line.

Supermarkets

Nowadays, a great (1) .... of different food is available from large supermarkets. There are rarely any (2) .... of fresh food, and there is far less (3) .... of our having to rely on (4) .... products. Does this mean that supermarkets have become the most (5) .... shops of all time? Certainly they seem to have made some kinds of food less (6) .... and most people enjoy shopping in them. There has been a (7) .... in the number of (8) .... made against supermarkets in recent years. The assistants are no longer (9) .... , but smile and try to be helpful. Above all, supermarkets have shown a (10) .... to listen to their customers, and to adapt to customers' needs.

VARY
SHORT
LIKELY
FREEZE
SUCCESS

EXPENSE
REDUCE
COMPLAIN
POLITE
WILLING

9
Decide which answer A, B, C or D best fits each space.

Street Markets

Most people enjoy looking for (1) ..... in street markets. It can be very enjoyable walking around the (2) ..... , among the crowds of (3) ..... , and trying to spend as (4) ..... as possible. Of course it depends (5) ..... the market. In fruit and (6) ..... markets, there is usually a wide variety of (7) ..... produce, but it may not be cheap. There may be goods at (8) ..... prices at the end of the day, however. Clothes markets can be a problem, as it is difficult to (9) ..... on new clothes in the open (10) ..... ! My favourite are antique markets, where although there is not much (11) ..... of finding valuable objects which are also cheap, you can enjoy yourself looking at all the things for (12) ..... . Whatever kind of market you look (13) ..... , and whether you buy things or not, you usually (14) ..... up feeling completely worn (15) ..... . Still, it is an interesting way of shopping.

1) A) cheap	B) sale	C) inexpensive	D) bargains
2) A) tables	B) stalls	C) boxes	D) stores
3) A) shoppers	B) public	C) buys	D) goods
4) A) little	B) soon	C) late	D) is
5) A) from	B) with	C) on	D) to
6) A) salads	B) green	C) farm	D) vegetable
7) A) new	B) fresh	C) young	D) early
8) A) half	B) bottom	C) reduced	D) down
9) A) look	B) try	C) have	D) take
10) A) time	B) shop	C) light	D) air
11) A) likelihood	B) instead	C) in spite	D) luck
12) A) that	B) all	C) sale	D) others
13) A) round	B) for	C) up	D) out
14) A) shut	B) bring	C) get	D) end
15) A) clothes	B) however	C) out	D) through

9 Crime and the Law

1
Choose the most suitable word or phrase underlined in each sentence.

a) Sally didn't realise that she had broken/countered/denied the law.
b) The police have banned/cancelled/refused parking in this street.
c) I must remember to get a/an agreement/licence/permission for my television.
d) The president admitted that there had been a breakdown of law and crime/government/order.
e) Jim's parents wouldn't agree/allow/let him go to the demonstration.
f) Carlos was arrested because he had entered the country falsely/illegally/wrongly.

g) Talking to other students is against the <u>law/orders/rules</u> of the examination.

h) The two men were arrested before they could <u>commit/make/perform</u> any more crimes.

i) I had to take the company to <u>court/justice/law</u> to get the money they owed me.

j) Smoking is <u>compulsory/prohibited/refused</u> near the petrol tanks.

2

Match each person in the list with the description given.

| blackmailer | forger | hooligan | murderer | shoplifter | vandal |
| burglar | hijacker | kidnapper | pickpocket | smuggler | witness |

a) This person takes control of a plane or boat by force. ....

b) This person sees what happens during a crime or accident. ....

c) This person brings goods into the country illegally. ....

d) This person might steal food from a supermarket. ....

e) This person kills someone on purpose. ....

f) This person takes people and demands money for their return. ....

g) This person makes illegal copies of paintings, documents etc. ....

h) This person damages other people's property. ....

i) This person might steal your wallet in a crowd. ....

j) This person steals from houses. ....

k) This person gets money from others by threatening to tell secrets. ....

l) This person causes trouble at football matches. ....

3

Complete each part sentence a) to j) with one of the endings 1) to 10). Use each ending once only.

a) I decided to buy a burglar alarm after someone broke ....

b) When Alan was stopped outside the supermarket he ended ....

c) As it was Sheila's first offence she was let ....

d) After climbing over the prison wall, Peter managed to get ....

e) The old couple who live opposite were taken ....

f) At the end of the trial Hilary was found ....

g) My neighbours admitted denting my car but got away ....

h) The bank at the end of the street was held ....

i) Nobody saw Jack cheating and he got away with ....

j) The hijackers took fifteen people ....

1) .... in by a salesman who cheated them out of their money.

2) .... away by stealing a car parked nearby.

3) .... up at the police station, charged with shoplifting.

4) .... it, although everyone suspected what had happened.

5) .... into my house and stole my stereo.

6) .... off with only a warning.

7) .... with paying only £50 damages.

8) .... hostage and demanded £1,000,000 from the authorities.

9) .... guilty and sentenced to six months in prison.

10) .... up by two masked men last week.

4
Complete each sentence with a word from the list. Use each word once only.

> accused   evidence   guilty   lawyer   statement
> charged   fine   jury   sentence   suspect

a) The customs officers arrested Bob and .... him with smuggling.
b) The police spent all morning searching the house for ....
c) Jean left her car in a no-parking area and had to pay a/an ....
d) Unfortunately at the end of the trial my brother was found ....
e) The trial took a long time as the .... couldn't reach a verdict.
f) George won his case because he had a very good defence ....
g) The police visited Dawn and asked her to make a/an ....
h) Because of his past criminal record, Brian was the main ....
i) Pauline decided to sue the police because she had been wrongly ....
j) The murderer of the children received a life ....

5
Choose the most suitable word or phrase to complete each sentence.

a) Most schools in my country no longer have ...... punishment.
   A) physical   B) capital   C) bodily   D) corporal
b) The policemen following the robbers were in ...... clothes.
   A) plain   B) ordinary   C) normal   D) simple
c) The two old ladies were ...... of their purses.
   A) stolen   B) attacked   C) robbed   D) snatched
d) At the end of the story, the hero manages to arrest the ....
   A) offenders   B) villains   C) wrongs   D) evils
e) I had to answer question A because it was ....
   A) compulsory   B) necessary   C) a must   D) an obligation
f) Charles could not ...... having been at the scene of the crime.
   A) refuse   B) object   C) deny   D) alter
g) As there was no evidence, the judge dismissed the ....
   A) trial   B) witness   C) court   D) case
h) If your dog damages your neighbour's property, you could be ....
   A) guilty   B) liable   C) payable   D) illegal
i) After ten years in prison, Stephen was ...... and set free.
   A) pardoned   B) released   C) innocent   D) forgiven
j) The detective inspector told the young ...... to make some tea.
   A) officer   B) official   C) guardian   D) police

6
Rewrite each sentence, beginning as shown, so that the meaning stays the same.

a) They said that John had stolen the money.
   They accused ....
b) Ian said that he hadn't punched anybody.
   Ian denied ....
c) 'OK, Andy, you can go now,' said the detective.
   The detective gave Andy ....
d) 'James Frogget, you will go to prison for ten years,' said the judge.
   The judge sentenced ....

e) 'I forged the signature,' said Mary.
   Mary admitted ....

f) Harry stole £30,000 and was arrested.
   Harry was arrested ....

g) 'We saw the accused break into the car,' said the witnesses.
   The witnesses stated ....

h) Graham said that he wouldn't go to the police station.
   Graham refused ....

i) 'It's true,' said Norman, 'I murdered Alan.'
   Norman confessed to ....

j) 'Can you come with me, please,' the detective said to Helen.
   The detective asked ....

7

Use the word in capitals at the end of each line to form a word that fits in the space in the same line.

Arthur's life of crime

At his last trial, nobody believed in Arthur's (1) .... He   INNOCENT
had been accused of the (2) .... of a valuable Chinese vase,   THIEF
and was also charged with ten other (3) .... The value of   OFFEND
the (4) .... goods was said to be over £10,000. Arthur said   STEAL
in his own (5) .... that the vase had been put into his car   DEFEND
(6) .... He also pointed out that the Chinese vase was a   ACCIDENT
fake, and was almost (7) .... The judge did not believe   WORTH
Arthur's story. He told Arthur he was a hardened (8) ....   CRIME
and that he deserved a severe (9) .... Then   PUNISH
the judge sentenced Arthur to five years (10) ....   PRISON
Arthur just smiled. He had spent most of his life in prison
and so he was used to it.

8

Choose the most suitable word or phrase underlined in each sentence.

a) Harry was told that fishing in the lake was against/by/over the law.
b) Catherine led a secret life for/in/of crime before she was caught.
c) Having trouble with your phone? Send at/for/to Fix-a-phone!
d) I regret to tell you that you are for/in/under arrest.
e) I only attacked the young man from/in/with self-defence.
f) David was often at/in/with trouble with the police when he was young.
g) The robbers' car was hidden below/by/from sight behind the bank.
h) The kidnappers have been caught, and the child is no longer at/in/on danger.
i) Tony was caught by a policeman who was off/out/away from duty and cycling to work.
j) The thieves took the wrong painting by/in/under mistake.
k) The suspicious manager left the safe unlocked from/on/with purpose.
l) The robbers met to plan the bank raid from/in/with secret.

9

Decide which answer A, B, C or D best fits each space.

Inspector Crumb Investigates

'I think I know the identity of the murderer,' said Inspector Crumb, 'and at (1) ..... one of the guests in this hotel was a/an (2) ..... to the crime, probably by (3) .... I believe that the same guest is also a (4) ..... , and has been given money by the killer.' 'So whoever (5) ..... this terrible crime is still here,' I said. 'But of course. In (6) ..... he – or she – is in this room, and will soon be (7) ..... arrest.' There was silence for a moment. I noticed that everyone was trying to look (8) ..... , but they all looked guilty instead! 'Do you have any (9) ..... , Inspector,' asked Lady Grimshaw finally, 'or are you simply (10) ..... people for fun? If you intend to (11) ..... someone, you should do it now.' The Inspector smiled. 'I asked you here (12) ..... purpose, Lady Grimshaw. I have been reading your (13) ..... , you see, and it is quite clear that you have told several (14) ....' 'How dare you!' Lady Grimshaw spluttered. 'Do you (15) ..... that you were with Tim Dawson in the garden on the night of the murder?' the Inspector said? 'You forgot about the security cameras, you see...

	A)	B)	C)	D)
1)	last	least	the	school
2)	witness	offender	guilty	verdict
3)	now	damages	law	accident
4)	blackmailer	hostage	hooligan	forger
5)	confessed	committed	admitted	performed
6)	crime	self-defence	fact	danger
7)	to	having	under	my
8)	accused	suspicious	ordinary	innocent
9)	evidence	witness	permission	body
10)	suspecting	suing	denying	accusing
11)	trial	charge	sentence	confess
12)	with	for	on	by
13)	statement	biography	evident	history
14)	people	errors	times	lies
15)	refuse	deny	contradict	suppose

10 Entertainment and the Arts

1

Choose the most suitable word or phrase underlined in each sentence.

a) I like this book, and I've read six capitals/chapters/prefaces already.
b) It's not a proper drawing, only a rough/plan/sketch.
c) The play is very long but there are three breaks/intervals/rests.
d) At the cinema I don't like sitting too near the film/screen/stage.
e) We heard a piece by Mozart performed by a German band/group/orchestra.
f) Her second book was very popular and became a best buy/seller/volume.
g) I like the painting but I can't stand its ugly border/frame/square.
h) Robert's new book will be broadcast/published/typed in August.
i) I liked the acting, and the costumes/dressing/outfits were good too.
j) The best act/place/scene in the film is when Jack meets Kate.

2

Complete each sentence with a word from the list. Use each word once only.

announcer   composer   critic   editor   playwright
author   conductor   director   novelist   sculptor

a) The orchestra would not be so successful with a different ....
b) I want a book on sailing, but I can't remember the name of the ....
c) We must see the new film by that Italian ....
d) The .... said that the sports programme is on after the news.
e) Harry writes for the theatre, but he is not only a ....
f) We saw some interesting metal objects made by a French ....
g) That's a nice piece of music. Who is the .... ?
h) Peter Smith was the only .... who wrote in praise of the film.
i) Charles Dickens is probably the best known British ....
j) The .... of the newspaper usually decides what it contains.

3

Complete each sentence by putting *in, on, at* or *out of* in each space.

a) Harry Potter is hard .... work writing his new screenplay.
b) The music was terrible and the singer was .... tune.
c) I can't tell what that is .... the background of the picture.
d) Jane's new book is coming out .... paperback next year.
e) Is there anything good .... Channel 4 this evening?
f) The school put on *Hamlet* .... modern dress.
g) The critics found Joe's kind of writing rather .... date.
h) In the last scene, all the actors are .... stage together.
i) When David took his place .... the piano the audience went wild.
j) The film stars Doris Fleck .... the part of Queen Elizabeth.
k) I had to read her latest book .... professional interest.
l) Margaret's new sculptures are .... display in the park.

4

Complete each sentence with a word from the list. Use each word once only.

| current electric humorous modern public special |
| dull gripping live popular readable still |

a) No recording can be as good as a .... concert in my opinion.
b) It was a very .... story and made me laugh a lot.
c) I couldn't put that book down, it had such a .... plot.
d) Most people find it difficult to understand .... art.
e) My favourite television programmes are about .... affairs.
f) Of course it's possible to like both classical and .... music.
g) Everyone enjoyed the .... effects in the 'Star Wars' films.
h) I don't buy books because there's a good .... library nearby.
i) We both found it a very .... film I'm afraid.
j) George doesn't paint people, but mainly does .... life paintings.
k) It was an interesting book, and very ....
l) Unfortunately the boy upstairs is learning the .... guitar.

5

Choose the most suitable word or phrase to complete each sentence.

a) Susan's first painting was a/an .... portrait.
    A) self   B) own   C) selfish   D) auto
b) The audience enjoyed the play so much that they .... for ten minutes.
    A) booed   B) screamed   C) applauded   D) handed
c) Peter sings every Sunday in the local church ....
    A) concert   B) chorus   C) opera   D) choir
d) I bought this book mainly because it has a very attractive ....
    A) folder   B) cover   C) coat   D) wrapping
e) The play was a success and had very good .... in the papers.
    A) reviews   B) critics   C) advertisements   D) notes
f) If you can't find what you are looking for in the book, use the ....
    A) preface   B) directory   C) list   D) index
g) The average .... watches television for about 15 hours a week.
    A) viewer   B) audience   C) spectator   D) observer
h) First we see their faces from far away, and then we see a ....
    A) side by side   B) foreground   C) replay   D) close up
i) Please note that the next programme is .... for children.
    A) unusual   B) unsuitable   C) unmistakable   D) unreasonable
j) All the members of the .... had a party after the play was over.
    A) scene   B) cast   C) circle   D) drama

6

Use the word in capitals at the end of each line to form a word that fits in the space in the same line.

The School Play

Congratulations to all involved with the school (1) .... of   PRODUCE
The Woman Next Door. The (2) .... was carried out by the   ADVERTISE
Art Department, and the posters were very (3) .... We   IMAGINE
certainly have some very (4) .... students in our school!   ART
Many people helped with building and painting the (5) ....   SCENE
and the play was written by the English Department, who
managed to create an (6) .... story, with excellent songs.   AMUSE
The music was written by Sue Porter, who also (7) .... the   COMPANY
singers on the piano. Everyone enjoyed a thoroughly (8) ....   ENTERTAIN
evening, and there was a long round of (9) .... at the end.   APPLAUD
Jim Barrett gave a brilliant (10) .... as Sergeant Moss, and   PERFORM
Liz Aitken was a delightful Mrs Jump. Well done everyone!

7

Complete the compound word in each sentence, using a word given in the list. Use each word once only.

| back   book   fair   operas   rehearsal |
| biography   circle   ground   piece   scripts |

a) Edward's third book is usually considered his master.................... .
b) A lot of people enjoy watching soap .... on television.
c) I found the Prime Minister's auto..................... very interesting.
d) Some of the actors still did not know their lines at the dress ....
e) I won't buy the book until it comes out in paper..................... .
f) We had very good seats in the dress ....
g) There is a black cat painted in the fore..................... of the picture.
h) Writing film .... is rather like writing for the theatre.
i) I was fined because I forgot to return my library ....
j) The scene showed them on a roundabout in a children's fun..................... .

8

Replace the verb underlined in each sentence with a verb from the list, so that the meaning stays the same. Change the tense where necessary.

| call off   go over   pick up   take over   turn up |
| come out   look up   put on   take up   work out |

a) My radio doesn't <u>receive</u> the BBC World Service very easily.

....

b) Our school is going to <u>do</u> *The Tempest* next month.

....

c) The management <u>cancelled</u> the performance an hour before the opening.

....

d) I <u>searched for</u> the reference in the index.

....

e) I can't hear the radio. Can you <u>make it louder</u>?

....

f) Colin's new book <u>is published</u> next week.

....

g) The conductor <u>studied</u> the music carefully before the concert.

....

h) The publishing company was <u>bought</u> by a Japanese firm.

....

i) I like detective stories where I can't <u>think</u> who did the murder!

....

j) Jim has <u>started</u> painting as a hobby.

....

9
Decide which
answer A, B, C
or D best fits
each space.

Why Read Books?

Is it worth reading books, (1) ..... nowadays there are so many other forms of (2) ..... ? Some people say that even (3) ..... books are expensive, and not everyone can (4) ..... books from a library. They might add that television is more (5) ..... and that viewers can relax as they watch their favourite (6) .... All that may be true, but books are still very (7) ...... They encourage the reader to use his or her (8) ..... for a start. You can read a (9) ..... of a book, or just a few pages, and then stop. Of course, it may be so (10) ..... that you can't stop! There are many different kinds of books, so you can choose a crime (11) ..... or an autobiography, or a book which gives you interesting (12) .... If you find it hard to choose, you can read (13) ..... , or ask friends for ideas. Personally, I can't (14) ..... without books, but I can (15) ..... up television easily enough. You can't watch television at bus stops!

1) A) in	B) or	C) why	D) since
2) A) entertain	B) entertainment	C) entertained	D) entertaining
3) A) paperback	B) the	C) so	D) when
4) A) borrow	B) buy	C) lend	D) take
5) A) excited	B) excitable	C) exciting	D) excitement
6) A) ones	B) programmes	C) episodes	D) cereals
7) A) too	B) public	C) live	D) popular
8) A) imagination	B) author	C) index	D) amusement
9) A) capital	B) head	C) chapter	D) cover
10) A) current	B) imagined	C) interest	D) gripping
11) A) history	B) novel	C) booklet	D) poetry
12) A) advise	B) idea	C) information	D) fact
13) A) announcements	B) gossip	C) reviews	D) prefaces
14) A) do	B) make	C) have	D) take
15) A) pick	B) look	C) give	D) turn

11 The Natural World

1

Choose the most suitable word or phrase underlined in each sentence.

a) The fields were flooded after the river burst its <u>banks/edges/sides</u>.
b) After the rain the street was full of <u>floods/lakes/puddles</u>.
c) During the storm, the climbers sheltered in a <u>cave/cliff/valley</u>.
d) A small <u>river/stream/torrent</u> runs across the bottom of our garden.
e) It was difficult to swim because the <u>waters/waves/tides</u> were so high.
f) From the <u>peak/summit/top</u> of the hill you can see the sea.
g) You must carry a lot of water when you cross the <u>desert/plain/sand</u>.
h) In the middle of the square there is an old <u>fountain/source/tap</u>.
i) I think it's going to rain. It's very <u>clouded/clouding/cloudy</u>.
j) The church caught fire when it was struck by <u>hurricane/lightning/thunder</u>.

2

Complete each sentence with a word from the list. Use each word once only.

forest	leaves	plant	seeds	trunk	lawn	peel	roots	stone	twig

a) We cut down the tree but then we had to dig up its ....
b) The road goes through a beautiful pine ....
c) When Tom was eating a cherry, he accidentally swallowed the ....
d) In autumn, these paths are covered in fallen ....
e) Who is going to cut the .... while I am away?
f) We bought Diana a beautiful indoor .... for her birthday.
g) A tree fell, and its massive .... blocked the road.
h) Harry buys .... and grows all his own vegetables.
i) The bird was carrying a .... to build its nest.
j) Some people like eating orange ....

3

Complete each sentence a) to j) with one of the endings 1) to 10). Use each ending once only.

a) A large green snake ....
b) A small brown duck ....
c) A large black and yellow wasp ....
d) A shiny green crab ....
e) An enormous black spider ....
f) A bright green frog ....
g) A black and white puppy ....
h) A herd of cattle ....
i) A dirty black lamb ....
j) A small ginger kitten ....

1) .... was spinning its web across the window.
2) .... was plodding across the field, mooing loudly.
3) .... was buzzing around the jar of honey on the table.
4) .... was sitting on a branch and miaowing.
5) .... was slithering across the floor towards me.
6) .... was sitting on a leaf and croaking.
7) .... was following the flock, baaing quietly.

8) .... was swimming on the pond and quacking loudly.
9) .... was barking furiously outside the gate.
10) .... was pinching Fiona's toe as she stood on the sea shore.

4
Match these words with the descriptions given.

| bee   dolphin   giraffe   moth   rabbit   whale |
| camel   fly   leopard   pig   shark   worm |

a) It lives in a hole in the ground and has long ears.   ....
b) It flies at night and is attracted to light.   ....
c) It lives in a hive and makes honey.   ....
d) It has yellow fur and a long neck.   ....
e) It is a large dangerous fish.   ....
f) It lives in the earth and we can use it when we go fishing.   ....
g) It is a large member of the cat family with spotted fur.   ....
h) It is the largest kind of animal in the world.   ....
i) It is used for transport in desert countries.   ....
j) It is a fat pink animal which lives in a sty.   ....
k) It is a large intelligent sea animal.   ....
l) It is an insect which spreads diseases.   ....

5
Choose the most suitable word or phrase to complete each sentence.

a) The dog .... its tail furiously when it saw the children.
    A) shook   B) wagged   C) moved   D) rubbed
b) A large .... of the tree broke off in the storm.
    A) trunk   B) bark   C) twig   D) branch
c) There was field after field of golden .... waving in the wind.
    A) corn   B) bushes   C) grass   D) herbs
d) Before railways were built, many goods were carried on ....
    A) channels   B) water   C) canals   D) river.
e) The children enjoyed rolling down the grassy ....
    A) mountain   B) cliff   C) stone   D) slope
f) What kind of .... is your dog?
    A) breed   B) race   C) mark   D) family
g) Some wild animals will become .... if they get used to people.
    A) peaceful   B) tame   C) organised   D) petty
h) There's a .... of blackbirds at the bottom of the garden.
    A) house   B) home   C) cage   D) nest
i) Many people are interested in watching ....
    A) wildlife   B) wilds   C) wilderness   D) wildly
j) You have to sleep under a net to avoid being bitten by ....
    A) lobsters   B) geese   C) cockroaches   D) mosquitoes

6

Use the word in capitals at the end of each line to form a word that fits in the space in the same line.

A pet parrot

From early (1) .... Jane had always wanted a pet parrot.   CHILD
Her parents told her that a parrot was an (2) .... pet, but Jane   SUIT
insisted. She was worried about the (3) .... of the rainforests   DESTROY
where parrots live, and she felt that parrots needed more
(4) .... Her father argued that a parrot would suffer from   PROTECT
(5) .... if it lived in a house. He also explained that pet parrots   LONELY
are caught by (6) .... , who need money and don't care about   HUNT
protecting species. 'They catch the parrots and send them to
Europe in (7) .... boxes,' he told her. 'And in any case, parrots   WOOD
are very (8) .... and don't make good pets.' Jane soon made   OBEY
an interesting (9) .... , however. She found a pet shop which   DISCOVER
bred parrots instead ofimporting them. So she took all her
(10) .... and bought a tiny S. American parrot, which she   SAVE
called 'Pixie'.

7

Complete the compound word in each sentence, using a word given in the list. Use each word once only.

forecast	hive	house	side	top	fountain	hole	mower	skin	trap

a) There were so many mice we had to buy a mouse.................... .
b) Paula was cutting the grass with an electric lawn.................... .
c) There's a drinking .... on the other side of the park.
d) What's the weather .... for tomorrow?
e) The hill.................... was covered in beautiful wild flowers.
f) You can see the mountain .... among the clouds in the distance.
g) At the end of the field was a large stone farm.................... .
h) We collect honey from our own bee.................... .
i) There's a rabbit.................... in the corner of this field.
j) Martin was wearing imitation snake.................... boots.

8

Complete each sentence with **one** suitable word.

a) I think this fruit juice has gone .... It smells funny.
b) Mind .... ! Our cat has very sharp claws!
c) I keep my dog on a lead, but I let it .... in the park.
d) Would you like me to show you .... the house.
e) I like the idea of camping, but I am put .... by the insects.
f) Our dog never got used .... sleeping in its kennel.
g) I don't think I want to find .... whether that bull has sharp horns!
h) After they made .... , George gave Silvia a bunch of roses.
i) My puppy managed to tear .... three of my school books.
j) I've taken .... going for long walks in the countryside.

9

Decide which answer A, B, C or D best fits each space.

Pets

If you decide to buy a pet, you should (1) ..... out as much as possible about the pet you (2) ..... . Cats are easy to (3) ..... after and seem to be (4) ..... , but also need the company of people. If your cat finds someone who (5) ..... for it more than you do, it will change owners! A small puppy may look like a (6) ..... pet, but don't forget that it will (7) ..... up. You may not be able to (8) ..... up with a very large dog that is too big for its (9) ..... and which (10) ..... on sleeping on your bed! Unless you (11) ..... it, it may attack people, or (12) ..... loudly day and night. Nobody loves a (13) ..... pet. Perhaps this is why so many people (14) ..... in for birds or fish as pets. Whatever you decide in the (15) ..... , think carefully before you make a decision.

1)	A) go	B) look	C) find	D) take
2)	A) choose	B) decide	C) take	D) do
3)	A) run	B) change	C) find	D) look
4)	A) singular	B) depended	C) independent	D) single
5)	A) feeds	B) cares	C) looks	D) loves
6)	A) suited	B) suiting	C) suit	D) suitable
7)	A) grow	B) get	C) stand	D) buy
8)	A) stay	B) live	C) put	D) feed
9)	A) lodging	B) kennel	C) cupboard	D) box
10)	A) relies	B) insists	C) carries	D) concentrates
11)	A) train	B) learn	C) lesson	D) educate
12)	A) wag	B) quack	C) moo	D) bark
13)	A) disobey	B) disobeying	C) disobedient	D) disobeyed
14)	A) go	B) prefer	C) decide	D) take
15)	A) house	B) fact	C) first	D) end

12 People and Behaviour

1

Choose the most suitable word or phrase underlined in each sentence.

a) Please don't push. It's very <u>bad-tempered/rude/unsympathetic</u>.

b) Jack hates spending money. He's rather <u>frank/greedy/mean</u>.

c) Our teacher is very <u>proud/strict/tolerant</u> and won't let us talk in class.

d) Helen never does her homework. She is rather <u>gentle/lazy/reliable</u>.

e) I didn't talk to anyone at the party because I felt <u>ambitious/lonely/shy</u>.

f) When Harry saw his girlfriend dancing with Paul he felt <u>jealous/selfish/sentimental</u>.

g) I don't like people who are noisy and <u>aggressive/courageous/sociable</u>.

h) Thank you for bringing us a present. It was very <u>adorable/grateful/thoughtful</u> of you.

i) Teresa never gets angry with the children. She is very <u>brave/patient/pleasant</u>.

j) Tom always pays for everyone when we go out. He's so <u>cheerful/generous/honest</u>.

2

Match these words with the descriptions given. Use each word once only.

| bad-tempered | determined | lazy | reliable | cheerful | frank |
| mean | selfish | considerate | honest | punctual | sympathetic |

a) You always arrive on time. ....

b) You are always happy. ....

c) You do what you say you will do. ....

d) You say exactly what you think. ....

e) You don't think about the needs of others. ....

f) You have a strong wish to get what you want. ....

g) You are unkind, or not willing to spend money. ....

h) You easily become angry with others. ....

i) You think about the needs of others. ....

j) You tell the truth and obey the law. ....

k) You understand the feelings of others. ....

l) You try to avoid work if you can. ....

3

Complete each sentence with a word from the list. Use each word once only.

| ambitious | greedy | polite | sociable | brave | imaginative |
| proud | stubborn | grateful | kind | snobbish | tolerant |

a) I think I'll stay here on my own, I'm not feeling very .... today.

b) Diana wants to get to the top in her company. She is very ....

c) It's not .... to stare at people and say nothing!

d) I think you have to be very .... to write a novel.

e) Thank you for helping me. It was very .... of you.

f) Peter refuses to change his mind, although he is wrong. He's so ....

g) It was very .... of Sheila to put out the fire on her own.

h) Our neighbours look down on us. They are a bit ....

i) Don't eat all the cakes! You really are becoming .... !

j) If you lend me the money I'll be very ....

k) I am very .... of my new motorbike.

l) My parents don't mind my crazy hair style. They are very ....

4

Use the word in capitals at the end of each line to form a word that fits in the space in the same line.

Jack's real character

How easy is it to understand another person's character?

My friend Jack, was once a rather (1) .... person. He was   ANNOY

always getting into trouble at school because he was so (2) ....   OBEY

In class he was very (3) .... and never stopped making   TALK

jokes. The teachers all told him he was (4) .... because   POLITE

he interrupted them. When I met him he was very (5) ....   FRIEND

and didn't want to talk to me at all. People told me that he
stole things, and that he was (6) .... His school work   HONEST
was terrible. He didn't take any (7) .... in his writing, he   PROUD
never spent enough time doing his homework, and he
was not at all (8) .... One day he saw a gang of boys   CONSCIENCE
attacking an old man. Jack hated (9) .... and he fought   VIOLENT
them all until they ran away. He was awarded a medal
for (10) .... After that, people changed their minds   BRAVE
about him.

5

Choose the most
suitable word or
phrase to
complete each
sentence.

a) You can't tell what someone is like just from their ....
    A) character   B) appearance   C) personality   D) looking
b) I was born in Scotland but I .... in Northern Ireland.
    A) grew up   B) raised   C) brought up   D) rose
c) Edward was named after one of his father's distant ....
    A) family   B) brothers   C) members   D) relations
d) Jane and Brian got married a year after they got ....
    A) divorced   B) proposed   C) engaged   D) separated
e) Graham works well in class, but his .... could be better.
    A) rudeness   B) behaviour   C) politeness   D) acting
f) Julie had a terrible .... with her parents last night.
    A) row   B) discussion   C) argue   D) dispute
g) I got to .... Steve well last year when we worked together.
    A) introduce   B) know   C) meet   D) sympathise
h) Is Brenda married or ....? I don't like to ask her.
    A) spinster   B) alone   C) bachelor   D) single
i) Parents and teachers have to try hard to understand the younger ....
    A) generation   B) people   C) adolescents   D) teenagers
j) My father likes to be called a 'senior citizen', not an old age ....
    A) person   B) relative   C) gentleman   D) pensioner

6

Match each
person from the
list with a
suitable
description. Use
each name once
only.

| adult   colleague   nephew   toddler   best man   fiancé |
| niece   twin   bride   neighbour   sister-in-law   widow |

a) The son of your brother or sister.   ....
b) A woman on the day of her marriage.   ....
c) A young child who is learning to walk.   ....
d) What a woman calls the man she is engaged to.   ....
e) One of two children born at the same time.   ....
f) A person who lives near you.   ....
g) The daughter of your brother or sister.   ....
h) A person who is fully grown.   ....
i) A woman whose husband has died.   ....
j) At a wedding, the friend of the bridegroom.   ....

k) The sister of the person you marry. ....
l) A person you work with. ....

7
Complete each sentence with **one** suitable word.

a) After a few days they realised they were .... love.
b) I went .... with a very interesting girl last week.
c) Andrew acts as .... he was the most important person in the room.
d) After two years, their marriage broke ....
e) John discovered that he was related .... his next door neighbour.
f) My parents keep treating me .... a child, but I'm not one!
g) I was brought .... by my aunt after my parents died.
h) It was very kind .... you to give me a lift.
i) Teachers should be patient .... small children.
j) James was very disappointed .... his new job.
k) It's very .... of character for Bill to behave like that.
l) Most famous people behave quite normally .... private.

8
Complete each sentence by replacing the words underlined with one of the verbs in the list. Use each verb once only.

call in   fall out   give away   put up with   turn down
count on   get on well with   look up to   take after   turn up

a) The wedding was cancelled when the bride failed to <u>arrive</u>. ....
b) Susan feels that her boss is someone to <u>respect</u>. ....
c) I'm sorry, but I just can't <u>stand</u> your behaviour any longer. ....
d) My brother and I really <u>have a good relationship with</u> our parents. ....
e) Why don't you <u>visit my house</u> on your way home from the shops? ....
f) Tony felt that he could <u>rely on</u> his friend Mary. ....
g) The millionaire decided to <u>make a present of</u> his money to the poor. ....
h) Paula and Shirley are good friends but sometimes they <u>quarrel</u>. ....
i) Jean decided to <u>refuse</u> Chris's offer of marriage. ....
j) All three children <u>behave like</u> their father and are very sociable. ....

9
Decide which answer A, B, C or D best fits each space.

Ann Johnson – A Confidential Report

Ann Johnson has worked at this college for three years. She is a (1) ..... employee, and (2) ..... on well with the other members of the department. We have all found her to be an excellent (3) .... She has always been (4) ..... for her lessons, and is an extremely (5) ..... member of staff who is able to work independently. I can always (6) ..... on her to organise the end of term play, and she has put on some extremely (7) ..... productions. Her students often tell me how (8) ..... she is, always ready with a smile, and she has been very (9) ..... to many of them. In (10) ..... she is not very talkative and seems rather (11) ..... at first, and might not show her true (12) ..... in an interview. Her work is excellent, and she is (13) ..... to succeed. She is also quite (14) ..... , and has applied for two other positions as Director of Studies. I think that you can count (15) ..... Ann to make your school a success, and I recommend her for the post of Director.

1) A) conscientious B) conscience C) consciousness D) conscious
2) A) goes B) carries C) gets D) likes
3) A) colleague B) adult C) employer D) fellow
4) A) timed B) late C) hourly D) punctual
5) A) greedy B) reliable C) stubborn D) lazy
6) A) request B) concentrate C) take D) rely
7) A) imaginary B) imagination C) imaginative D) imagined
8) A) tempered B) cheerful C) frank D) proud
9) A) kind B) aggressive C) polite D) mean
10) A) first B) times C) usual D) private
11) A) but B) shy C) however D) alone
12) A) person B) behaviour C) character D) part
13) A) used B) determined C) had D) supposed
14) A) obedient B) disappointed C) grateful D) ambitious
15) A) on B) for C) with D) to

13 Technology and Machines

1

Choose the most suitable word or phrase underlined in each sentence.

a) This is a small car, but it has a powerful <u>engine/machine</u>.
b) Do you use an <u>electric/electrical</u> toothbrush?
c) I can't see anything. Where's the light <u>plug/switch</u>?
d) I've decided to buy a new <u>typewriter/typist</u>.
e) You can't use the lift. It's out of <u>order/work</u>.
f) If you don't press this button the washing machine won't <u>go/move</u>.
g) Use this torch. The other one doesn't <u>act/work</u>.
h) The lights have gone out. It must be a power <u>break/cut</u>.
i) A car <u>factory/industry</u> has just been built in our town.
j) Who exactly <u>discovered/invented</u> the computer?

2
Choose words from the list to complete the labels for the illustrations.

| axe   file   needle   razor   scissors   spade   corkscrew hammer   pin   saw   screwdriver   spanner |

3
Complete each sentence with a suitable word from **2**. Use each word once only.

a) You can cut that plank in half with this ....
b) You need a .... to open this bottle of wine.
c) I've split my trousers. Do you have a .... and thread?
d) I can't open the back of the television without a special ....
e) You can make the edges smooth with a ....
f) I've cut myself shaving again. I think I'll buy an electric ....
g) We could chop this tree down if we had a sharp ....
h) Until I can sew this, I'll fix the edges together with a ....
i) I was going to dig the garden but I can't find the ....
j) Oh bother! I've hit my thumb with the .... instead of the nail!
k) You can cut this cardboard if you have some sharp ....
l) This nut is impossible to undo. I need a larger ....

4
Complete each sentence a) to j) with one of the endings 1) to 10). Use each ending once only.

a) It's very hot in here. Why don't you ....
b) I can't make out what it is. I think I'll ....
c) We haven't got much time but I can ....
d) I need to put up these shelves, so I'm going to ....
e) It's a long way up. I think we should use ....
f) The lamp does work. You'll have to ....
g) The radio isn't very loud. I must ....
h) This would make a nice picture. Hang on while I ....
i) A seat on the morning flight? Let me just ....
j) The tyre's a bit flat. I'll have to ....

1) .... get the pump out of the boot.
2) .... fetch my camera from the living room.
3) .... heat up the food very quickly in the microwave.
4) .... the lift, but we can walk down if you like.
5) .... put on the air conditioning?
6) .... find out from the computer.
7) .... put in a new light bulb.

8) .... borrow William's electric drill.

9) .... go and get my binoculars.

10) .... buy some new batteries.

5

Choose the most suitable word or phrase to complete each sentence.

a) James is going to be late. His car has ....
   A) broken out   B) broken up   C) broken in   D) broken down

b) If your camera is faulty, you should return it to the ....
   A) creator   B) manufacturer   C) inventor   D) builder

c) It is hard to get .... parts for this car if something goes wrong.
   A) extra   B) spare   C) additional   D) emergency

d) I bought this electric drill from a ....-it-yourself shop.
   A) do   B) repair   C) make   D) fix

e) This clock .... on two small batteries.
   A) goes   B) works   C) runs   D) moves

f) Lift the .... and listen for the dialling tone.
   A) microphone   B) dial   C) receiver   D) number

g) Don't touch that wire! You'll get an electric ....
   A) surprise   B) current   C) charge   D) shock

h) It's difficult to repair a car unless you have the right ....
   A) gadgets   B) instruments   C) appliances   D) tools

i) This knife is really .... I'll have to sharpen it.
   A) blunt   B) dull   C) flat   D) frank

j) Don't forget to .... your alarm clock for 6.30.
   A) put   B) set   C) ring   D) go off

6

Use the word in capitals at the end of each line to form a word that fits in the space in the same line.

How does the video work?

When I was young, I always dreamed of becoming a
famous (1) .... When I was at school I decided to study   SCIENCE
(2) .... , and then become a millionaire by inventing   ENGINE
a wonderful new (3) .... which would make the world   PRODUCE
a better place. Unfortunately, I wasn't very good at technical
subjects. Any time I operate any kind of (4) .... ,   EQUIP
something terrible happens. Machines which use (5) .... ,   ELECTRIC
such as computers or televisions, always seem to give me a
(6) .... shock. The instruction booklets are always   POWER
(7) .... They never help me at all. Nowadays you need   USE
to have (8) .... knowledge just to turn on the video. To   SPECIAL
my great (9) .... it is always a child of six who helps me   EMBARRASS
out of my (10) ....   DIFFICULT

7

Complete each sentence by putting **one** word in each space.

a) There's nothing good on the television. Why don't you turn it ....?
b) Can you plug the electric fire .... for me?
c) Hurry up sir. We're just going to lock .... for the night.
d) The machine is quite automatic – it does everything .... itself.
e) We'd better stop for some petrol. We've nearly run ....
f) The parts come from Japan, but we put them .... here in Italy.
g) The word processor consists .... a keyboard, a screen and a printer.
h) This looks like wood but actually it's made .... plastic.
i) What exactly is a file used .... ?
j) These two metal sections are then bolted .... to make one.

8

Replace the words underlined in each sentence with one of the verbs from the list.

break down	go off	keep up with	pick up	run out
do without	hang up	look out	put off	stand for

a) My car isn't as fast as yours. I won't be able to <u>stay near</u> you. ....
b) The torch doesn't work. The batteries must have <u>been used up</u>. ....
c) This radio doesn't <u>receive</u> the BBC World Service very well. ....
d) The car is making a funny noise. I think it's going to <u>stop working</u>. ....
e) I was going to buy a motorbike, but I was <u>discouraged</u> by my parents. ....
f) People call me on the phone, but then <u>put down the receiver</u>. ....
g) <u>Be careful!</u> You're going to give yourself an electric shock! ....
h) It's difficult to <u>manage if you don't have</u> a washing machine. ....
i) The letters CD <u>mean</u> compact disc, actually. ....
j) Without a fridge, fresh food will <u>become bad</u> very quickly. ....

9

Decide which answer A, B, C or D best fits each space.

Do It Yourself

What do you do when something (1) ..... down? Are you the kind of person who knows how things (2) ..... ? Or do you prefer to have it (3) ..... by an expert? Personally, when I use a (4) ..... I always hit my finger, and I can never (5) ..... anything with my screwdriver because I can never find it. Despite having all the wrong (6) ..... , and despite being a useless (7) ..... , I recently decided to take my bike to pieces and (8) ..... it. I had (9) ..... out of money as usual, and as I use my bike (10) ..... getting to college, I had no choice. It was making a terrible noise, and the front tyre was (11) .... I had a few (12) ..... but I didn't have any (13) ..... parts. I managed to (14) ..... the wheel and take it off, but then I lost my (15) ..... , and couldn't put the wheel back on properly. At least I am taking more exercise, as I now have to walk to college.

1) A) falls   B) repairs   C) breaks   D) runs
2) A) do   B) make   C) fix   D) work
3) A) repaired B) out   C) sometimes D) operated
4) A) drill   B) scissors   C) hammer   D) spade

5) A) drive   B) unscrew   C) cut   D) unwind
6) A) equipment   B) contents   C) instruments   D) gadgets
7) A) technician   B) engineer   C) machine   D) mechanic
8) A) make   B) fix   C) build   D) construct
9) A) spent   B) paid   C) run   D) fallen
10) A) and   B) because   C) by   D) for
11) A) flat   B) empty   C) over   D) bad
12) A) chances   B) tools   C) information   D) advice
13) A) spare   B) emergency   C) renew   D) repair
14) A) remove   B) smooth   C) fill   D) undo
15) A) saw   B) plug   C) spanner   D) file

14 Problems

1
Choose the most
suitable word or
phrase
underlined in
each sentence.

a) Many people were injured when the building <u>demolished/collapsed</u>.
b) The ship radioed to say that it was in <u>difficulties/dangers</u>.
c) The government has announced plans to help the <u>poor/poverty</u>.
d) The driver of the bus admitted that he had <u>done/made</u> an error.
e) Everyone agrees that the <u>environment/nature</u> must be protected.
f) There has been another <u>increase/rising</u> in the amount of crime.
g) There are few jobs here and many people are <u>away from work/unemployed</u>.
h) The train was in <u>accident/collision</u> with a bus on a level crossing.
i) No ships are sailing today because of the <u>high/storm</u> winds.
j) There was a large <u>demonstration/manifestation</u> against nuclear power in
    Manchester yesterday.

2
Complete each
sentence with a
word from the
list. Use each
word once only.

| disaster emergency hooliganism living disease famine |
| injuries rubbish earthquake floods invasion slums |

a) Food has been sent to areas in Africa suffering from ....
b) Many people live in overcrowded .... on the edge of the city.
c) The cost of .... has risen steadily this year.
d) Thousands of buildings fell down during a severe ....
e) .... at football matches has been reduced this year.
f) The .... of Ruritania has been condemned by the United Nations.
g) The eruption of the volcano was a terrible ....
h) Hundreds of people were drowned during the .... in China.
i) Two of those involved in the crash had serious ....
j) Large cities face the problem of what to do with household ....

k) Doctors announced that there was now a cure for the ....

l) During the storm there were hundreds of .... calls.

3

Complete each sentence with the best word or phrase.

a) Most young people want to .... more about environmental problems.
A) look up   B) find out   C) deal with   D) make out

b) Everyone knows about pollution problems, but not many people have .... any solutions.
A) thought over   B) got round to   C) looked into   D) come up with

c) Many factories break the anti-pollution laws and ....
A) put up with it   B) take it over   C) get away with it   D) come round to it

d) Disposing of waste and rubbish is a hard problem to ....
A) carry out   B) put up   C) get away   D) deal with

e) More people in cities should .... cycling instead of using cars.
A) rely on   B) take up   C) set up   D) get around to

f) Most governments seem to just .... dealing with environmental problems.
A) put off   B) make up for   C) do without   D) take after

g) In some countries environmental organisations have been .... to inform people and gain their support.
A) set off   B) make up   C) set out   D) set up

h) Unless we .... the problem, many animals could become extinct.
A) face up to   B) look up to   C) turn up to   D) get up to

i) Quite soon, the world is going to .... energy resources.
A) run out of   B) get into   C) keep up with   D) come up against

j) The important thing is to believe that problems can be solved, and not to ....
A) make up   B) look up   C) give up   D) put up

4

Replace the words underlined in each sentence with a word or phrase from the list.

> banned   ignored   increased   polluted   solved   flooded
> improved   overpopulated   protected   unemployed

a) Smoking has been <u>made illegal</u> in public places in some countries. ....

b) Famine is a serious problem, and it hasn't been <u>dealt with</u> yet. ....

c) Many kinds of wild animals need to be <u>guarded by the law</u>. ....

d) Living conditions have been <u>made better</u> in some parts of the world. ....

e) Our local lake has been <u>made dirty</u> by nearby factories. ....

f) A problem which is <u>not thought about</u> does not simply go away. ....

g) A lot of people in industrial areas are <u>without work</u> at the moment. ....

h) After the recent storms, the town was <u>filled with water</u>. ....

i) Some countries are <u>inhabited by too many people</u>. ....

j) Recently the number of people riding bicycles has <u>grown larger</u>. ....

5

Choose the most suitable word or phrase to complete each sentence.

a) I'm glad I .... my plane! I've just heard that it's been hijacked.
   A) lost   B) refused   C) missed   D) altered

b) The cruise ship hit a rock and ....
   A) sank   B) drowned   C) flooded   D) crashed

c) I lost the keys to my house and had to climb in .... the window.
   A) by   B) to   C) through   D) with

d) The village was completely .... in an earthquake.
   A) collapsed   B) destroyed   C) ruined   D) broken

e) The bus driver couldn't .... the accident.
   A) protect   B) control   C) provide   D) prevent

f) After police found drugs there, the disco was ....
   A) closed down   B) banned   C) ignored   D) abolished

g) During the match, someone .... fire to the stadium.
   A) set   B) put   C) opened   D) caught

h) We decided not to go camping because of the .... rain.
   A) great   B) amount   C) heavy   D) extra

i) I had to shut the window because the noise outside was ....
   A) shouting   B) unbearable   C) in danger   D) enormous

j) When the fire broke out, an electronic alarm ....
   A) came in   B) opened up   C) went off   D) put out

6

Use the word in capitals at the end of each line to form a word that fits in the space in the same line.

A modern Robinson Crusoe

After a (1) .... between two ships in the Atlantic, Alan   COLLIDE
Connaught from Dundee ended up (2) .... living on a   EXPECT
desert island. 'I fell (3) .... and no-one noticed.   BOARD
A few hours later I found myself lying (4) .... on a   EXHAUST
beach after swimming for miles. It was (5) .... too, not   FREEZE
warm and sunny, like Crusoe's island. The only (6) ....   SOLVE
I could find was to dig a hole in the sand as a shelter.'
After an (7) .... in the weather, Alan waited to be rescued.   IMPROVE
'There was little food and no fresh water. It was an (8) ....   HEALTH
life, and I felt ill most of the time. I suffered from (9) ....   LONELY
too, but then I found a village on the other side of the island!'
he said. 'The people had moved there after the (10) .... of   DESTROY
their homes by a volcano. Luckily they had a radio, and a ship
soon came to rescue me.'

7

Match these words with the descriptions given.

| aid   conservation   drought   famine   riot   charity |
| demonstration   emergency   pile-up   strike |

a) An organisation which collects money to help those in need. ....

b) When an area is desperately short of water. ....

c) The act of protecting animals, or parts of the environment. ....

d) When people march through the streets to show their opinions. ....
e) A collision involving several vehicles. ....
f) When an area is desperately short of food. ....
g) Something unexpected which must be dealt with quickly. ....
h) When people stop working through disagreement with their employers. ....
i) Help (money, food, etc.) given by governments or other organisations. ....
j) When a crowd of people is violent and out of control. ....

8
Put **one** word in each space in these sentences.

a) The fireman put his life .... risk to rescue the child.
b) Teachers have decided to go .... strike next month.
c) Sue has a lot of work to do and is .... stress at the moment.
d) The coach driver went through a red light .... mistake.
e) Many people are dying .... hunger in the desert area.
f) The boat which sank was crowded .... people.
g) The two countries are now .... war with each other.
h) .... an emergency, break the glass.
i) When the fire brigade arrived, the church was no longer .... fire.
j) When the volcano erupted, a party of tourists was .... danger.

9
Decide which answer A, B, C or D best fits each space.

A Letter to the Editor

Dear Sir,

We are writing to suggest that all cars should be (1) ..... from the centre of the city as soon as possible. The amount of (2) ..... from car exhaust fumes is now (3) ..... , and we believe that the public must be (4) ..... . Apart from this, the streets are crowded (5) ..... cars, and our lives are at (6) ..... when we try to cross the road! There has been a huge (7) ..... in the amount of traffic recently, and the government just seems to put (8) ..... the problem, instead of (9) ..... it. Unless we (10) ..... the traffic problem, and seriously consider some of the (11) ..... , life in our city will become (12) .... Our organisation, Cities for People, has been (13) ..... to make the government do something! We are holding a (14) ..... next week in the city centre, and hope that many people will (15) ..... us.

Yours Faithfully,
Mary Kingwood, Secretary, Cities for People

1) A) stopped   B) banned   C) removed   D) altered
2) A) this   B) problem   C) driving   D) pollution
3) A) unbearable   B) much   C) overcrowded   D) exceeded
4) A) preserved   B) saved   C) exhausted   D) protected
5) A) from   B) in   C) with   D) between
6) A) risk   B) danger   C) urgent   D) problem
7) A) size   B) number   C) growing   D) increase

8	A) out	B) away)	C) up	D) off
9	A) going through	B) dealing with	C) closing down	D) keeping up with
10	A) look for	B) make out	C) face up to	D) come round to
11	A) solutions	B) errors	C) suggestions	D) matters
12	A) lifeless	B) uninhabitable	C) impossible	D) destruction
13	A) taken after	B) set up	C) carried out	D) looked into
14	A) pile-up	B) riot	C) organisation	D) demonstration
15	A) join	B) bear	C) increase	D) agree

15 Health and the Body

1
Choose the most suitable word or phrase underlined in each sentence.

a) There were ten people waiting in the doctor's office/surgery/ward.
b) After I ate the shellfish I experienced/fell/happened ill.
c) George's cut arm took over a week to cure/heal/look after.
d) David fell down the steps and twisted his ankle/heel/toe.
e) Everyone admired Lucy because she was tall and skinny/slim/thin.
f) I've been digging the garden and now my back aches/pains/injures.
g) Whenever I travel by boat I start feeling hurt/sick/sore.
h) The doctor can't say what is wrong with you until she cures/examines/recovers you.
i) Use this thermometer and take his fever/heat/temperature.
j) I seem to have caught/infected/taken a cold.

2
Replace the words underlined in each sentence with one of the words from the list. Use each word once only.

agony	body	breath	look	stomachache
beard	brains	heart	spine	tongue

a) Janet fell from her horse and injured her backbone. ....
b) I had a very bad toothache, and was in great pain all night. ....
c) The police discovered the dead person buried in the garden. ....
d) One thing you can say about Ann, she has certainly got intelligence. ....
e) They have a new house right in the centre of the countryside. ....
f) Italian is actually Mary's native language. ....
g) Before I dived in the water, I took a deep mouthful of air. ....
h) After dinner, Jack had a pain from eating too much. ....
i) Shirley had a strange expression on her face. ....
j) David managed to grow a lot of hair on his face. ....

3

Complete each sentence with a word from the list. Use each word once only.

cheek	knees	neck	throat	waist	chin	lips	nose	thumb	wrist

a) After speaking for two hours, the lecturer had a sore ....
b) Terry was on his hands and .... , looking for the fallen coin.
c) Paul gave his aunt an affectionate kiss on the ....
d) There was such a terrible smell that I had to hold my ....
e) Stan is deaf, but he can understand people by reading their ....
f) I never wear a watch because I don't like the weight on my ....
g) One of the boxers punched the other on the .... and knocked him out.
h) When Diane was a baby, she used to suck her ....
i) I've lost a lot of weight, especially around the ....
j) Norma wears a heart on a gold chain around her ....

4

Complete each sentence a) to j) with one of the endings 1) to 10). Use each ending once only.

a) I think we should send for an ambulance ....
b) Some people go jogging every morning ....
c) It would be a good idea for you to go to the dentist's ....
d) The doctor gave Andy an injection ....
e) I'm going into hospital tomorrow ....
f) We took the cat to the vet ....
g) Susan took two aspirins ....
h) Nobody could find a stretcher ....
i) The doctor gave Helen a prescription ....
j) I bought some special cream ....

1) .... to have that bad tooth of yours taken out.
2) .... to check whether it had recovered from its accident.
3) .... to take old Mrs Jones to hospital.
4) .... to put on my sunburnt arms and legs.
5) .... to get rid of her headache.
6) .... to reduce the pain and help him sleep.
7) .... to take to the chemist's.
8) .... to keep fit, or to lose some weight.
9) .... to carry the injured man out of the building.
10) .... to have an operation on my foot.

5

Choose the most suitable word or phrase to complete each sentence.

a) Martin hasn't quite .... his illness yet.
   A) recovered   B) got over   C) looked after   D) suffered
b) Pauline .... birth to a baby girl yesterday afternoon.
   A) was   B) put   C) had   D) gave
c) Your leg isn't broken but it is badly ....
   A) fractured   B) bruised   C) bandaged   D) bent
d) Several angry drivers shook their .... at me as I drove away.
   A) fists   B) arms   C) hands   D) elbows

e) That was a bad fall! Have you .... yourself?
   A) harmed   B) damaged   C) wounded   D) hurt
f) Each time I sneezed, everyone said, '........... you!'
   A) cough   B) bless   C) cold   D) thank
g) Stop making that noise! You're getting on my ....!
   A) muscles   B) brains   C) nerves   D) blood
h) As the little boy cried, large .... rolled down his cheeks.
   A) drips   B) tears   C) puddles   D) streams
i) I had severe toothache and half my face was badly ....
   A) swollen   B) rounded   C) exploded   D) injured
j) I've got a headache, and I don't feel very ....
   A) healthy   B) fit   C) sane   D) well

6

Use the word in capitals at the end of each line to form a word that fits in the space in the same line.

A visit to the doctor's

Jim decided to visit the doctor after his trip to the jungle.
He was normally a tall (1) .... person, but over the past   MUSCLE
month he had lost a lot of (2) .... He had also noticed   WEIGH
that his ankles and knees had become rather (3) ....   PAIN
He thought that he might have eaten or drunk something (4) .....   POISON
or caught some kind of (5) .... disease. The doctor   INFECT
took some blood for tests and told Jim to go back a week
later. This time the doctor had an optimistic (6) .... on her   EXPRESS
face, and Jim felt quite (7) .... 'Don't worry,' said the   HEART
doctor, 'it's nothing serious. You haven't caught an (8) ....   CURE
disease, or anything terrible like that. It's a simple virus, and
you will need some (9) .... Take these tablets twice a   TREAT
day for two weeks, and you'll make a full (10) .... '.   RECOVER

7

Match each sentence a) to j) with a sentence from 1) to 10) which has the same meaning.

a) Henry's heart was in the right place.   ....
b) Paul held his tongue.   ....
c) Richard jawed away for at least an hour.   ....
d) Dave had a lot of cheek to talk like that.   ....
e) Keith couldn't stomach his new boss.   ....
f) Harry backed his boss.   ....
g) William kept poking his nose in.   ....
h) Graham thumbed a lift to work.   ....
i) Charles put his foot in it.   ....
j) Jack's heart ached to be where he belonged.   ....

1) He talked.
2) He supported him.
3) He said the wrong thing.
4) He was kind.
5) He was rather rude.

6) He didn't say anything.
7) He interfered in other people's business.
8) He hitch hiked.
9) He missed home.
10) He didn't like him.

8

Complete each sentence with **one** suitable word.

a) I am afraid she is suffering .... an incurable disease.
b) I was .... agony all night with earache.
c) I think you've put .... a lot of weight lately.
d) The effect of this drug will slowly wear ....
e) You really get .... my nerves sometimes!
f) After Jack fainted it was several minutes before he .... round.
g) Is Coral being operated .... tomorrow?
h) Harry went .... with flu during his holiday.
i) Peter was treated .... minor injuries and shock.
j) Don't worry. I'll take care .... you myself.

9

Decide which answer A, B, C or D best fits each space.

A Disastrous Holiday

The day Gerald arrived at the Almara Beach Hotel, he fell (1) ..... the stairs. The manager called a/an (2) ..... , but fortunately Gerald's leg was only badly (3) ..... , and not broken. The doctor (4) ..... swimming as further (5) ..... but gave Gerald a/an (6) ..... for some tablets in case his leg became (7) ..... . The next day Gerald sunbathed by the pool, and then took a deep (8) ..... and dived into the water. There was not very much water in the pool, and he (9) ..... one of his arms when he hit the bottom. This time he complained to the hotel manager, who sent a special meal to Gerald's room. Later that night, Gerald was (10) ..... from a (11) ..... back, the injuries to his arm and leg, and also had a terrible (12) ..... . He had a high (13) ..... and felt terrible. Luckily he had the tablets the doctor had given him to (14) ..... the pain. As he reached for them, he fell out of bed and broke his (15) ..... . He spent the rest of his holiday in bed.

1) A) down   B) to   C) with   D) for
2) A) stretcher   B) prescription C) ambulance   D) emergency
3) A) sick   B) bruised   C) hurt   D) infected
4) A) went   B) prevented   C) said   D) recommended
5) A) medicine   B) cure   C) drugs   D) treatment
6) A) recipe   B) paper   C) prescription D) order
7) A) painful   B) pained   C) painless   D) pain
8) A) end   B) breath   C) mouthful   D) water
9) A) hurt   B) injury   C) ached   D) sore
10) A) ill   B) injured   C) suffering   D) damaged
11) A) sunny   B) sunburnt   C) sunshine   D) grilled
12) A) agony   B) hurt   C) heat   D) stomachache
13) A) pain   B) temperature C) ache   D) degree

14) A) hold   B) check   C) rid   D) reduce
15) A) waist   B) lips   C) wrist   D) throat

16 Money

1
Choose the most suitable word or phrase underlined in each sentence.

a) I haven't got enough money, I'm afraid. Could you <u>borrow/lend</u> me some?
b) It's a good school, but the <u>fares/fees</u> are rather high.
c) This car is too expensive. We can't <u>afford/pay</u> it.
d) It was a very good meal. Can we have the <u>account/bill</u> please?
e) There's a small flat to <u>hire/let</u> in Bridge Street.
f) How much do you <u>earn/gain</u> in your new job?
g) She's a good dentist, but she doesn't <u>charge/spend</u> too much.
h) I bought this coat in the sales. It was <u>decreased/reduced</u> a lot.
i) Jack made his <u>fortune/treasure</u> buying and selling property.
j) How much do you <u>reckon/value</u> that house would cost?

2
Replace each word or phrase underlined with a word or phrase from the list which has the <u>opposite</u> meaning.

> cash   generous   profit   save   well off   expensive
> poverty   purchase   take out   worthless

a) I was surprised by how <u>mean</u> Charles was. ....
b) Janet says that she is very <u>hard up</u> at the moment. ....
c) Last year their business made a huge <u>loss</u>. ....
d) I'd like to <u>pay in</u> £100 please. ....
e) That part of Spain always seems very <u>cheap</u> to me. ....
f) Most people in the city live in great <u>prosperity</u>. ....
g) The manager insisted that I paid <u>by cheque</u>. ....
h) Some people manage to <u>spend</u> most of their money. ....
i) Jean was able to make only one <u>sale</u> during the morning. ....
j) The old painting I found in the loft turned out to be <u>valuable</u>. ....

3
Complete each sentence with a word from the list. Use each word once only.

> coin   guarantee   pension   rent   tip
> credit card   loan   receipt   safe   wealth

a) The old couple had only a small .... to live on.
b) My uncle Sam acquired his considerable .... selling cars.
c) David never carries cash with him and pays for everything by ....
d) I wouldn't have been able to buy my boat without a bank ....
e) The shop won't change any goods without the original ....
f) Keith didn't like the waiter so he didn't leave a ....

g) The house is not in very good condition so the .... is low.

h) The food mixer has a twelve month ....

i) We keep all our money and valuables in this .... in the floor.

j) The five pence .... is so small that everyone dislikes it.

4

Choose the most suitable response to each sentence a) to j) from the sentences 1) to 10). Use each response once only.

a) Who do I make the cheque out to?   ....

b) We seem to be spending a lot of money lately.   ....

c) The house has burnt down! What are we going to do?   ....

d) How much do you want for this drawing?   ....

e) Did you inherit this house?   ....

f) Your dog must have cost a lot of money.   ....

g) Do we still owe the bank any money?   ....

h) How much do you make a year?   ....

i) Can we change money at the hotel to pay the bill?   ....

j) Why are you putting so much money in the bank?   ....

1) Sorry, but it's not for sale.

2) I'm saving up to buy a new motorbike.

3) Perhaps we should try to economise a bit.

4) Yes, my Aunt Clara left it to me.

5) Well, we've nearly paid it all back.

6) To JB Woolbury PLC.

7) Actually I got it for nothing.

8) I think they accept travellers cheques anyway.

9) I've got quite a good salary actually.

10) Don't worry, we're insured.

5

Choose the most suitable word or phrase to complete each sentence.

a) I bought these shoes in the sales. They were a real ....
   A) cheap   B) economy   C) bargain   D) purchase

b) If you put your money in the bank, it will earn ten per cent ....
   A) interest   B) profit   C) deposit   D) investment

c) John asked his parents if they would pay off his ....
   A) rents   B) debts   C) accounts   D) credits

d) Adults have to pay £2.50 to get in, but children under 14 get in ....
   A) free   B) nothing   C) penniless   D) open

e) I'm interested in this old car. Is it .... ?
   A) selling   B) a sale   C) to sell   D) for sale

f) I'm trying to save for my holidays so I'm .... some money each week.
   A) putting in   B) putting aside   C) putting behind   D) putting up

g) Just a minute! You've forgotten to .... your cheque!
   A) mark   B) make   C) place   D) sign

h) I like your typewriter. How much did it .... exactly?
   A) pay   B) cost   C) afford   D) spend

i) The blackmailer asked for the money in used ....
   A) notes   B) cheques   C) paper   D) cash

j) I gave the assistant £10 and she gave me four pounds ....
   A) rest   B) money   C) coins   D) change

6

Use the word in capitals at the end of each line to form a word that fits in the space in the same line.

Money! Money! Money!

Helen had always dreamed of becoming a (1)	WEALTH
woman, and imagined living in a (2) .... mansion,	LUXURY
and how her friends would praise her (3)	GENEROUS
when she gave them expensive presents. In reality she	
was usually hard up. She had some (4) .... and a	SAVE
small life (5) .... , but her antique shop was not really	INSURE
very (6) .... Every time she took money out of the bank,	PROFIT
the (7) .... checked her account, and told her how little	CASH
there was in it! Helen had taken out a (8) .... a month	LEND
before. How could she repay it? Then one day she noticed	
an old painting in her shop. She had thought it was (9)	WORTH
but as she brushed away the dust , she saw the (10)	SIGN
at the bottom. It said 'Renoir'! She was rich at last!	

7

Complete each sentence with a word or phrase formed from *pay*. Each space represents one word.

a) You can pay the full price now, or make six monthly ....
b) If you lend me the money, I'll .... next week.
c) I haven't got enough money to .... the suit now.
d) We .... a lot of money on the decorating for this house.
e) Whenever Alan loses a bet he refuses to ....
f) Thank goodness it's Friday today. It's ....
g) I must do something about all these .... bills.
h) Please make the cheque .... R.D. Smith.
i) Take this money and .... to the bank.
j) I like my job, and it's very ....

8

Match each person from the list with a suitable description. Use each name once only.

accountant	cashier	heir	manager	pensioner
agent	customer	investor	miser	swindler

a) Someone who likes to keep money and not spend it.   ....
b) Someone who inherits money or property.   ....
c) Someone who runs a bank.   ....
d) Someone who has retired.   ....
e) Someone who keeps or checks financial records.   ....
f) Someone who buys things in a shop.   ....
g) Someone who pays out money in a bank.   ....
h) Someone who represents others in business.   ....
i) Someone who puts money into a business.   ....
j) Someone who cheats people out of money.   ....

9
Decide which answer A, B, C or D best fits each space.

Money Matters

Are you always (1) ..... up? Do you often have to (2) ..... money from friends, or from your parents, whenever you need a little extra (3) ..... ? If you (4) ..... too much, and save too little, you will end up with more (5) ..... than friends. You know the solution, of course: just save a small (6) ..... every month. Most banks will pay (7) ..... on your savings, and you will soon be able to (8) ..... all those things which seemed to cost too much before. The trouble is, you're a university student, and many banks treat you like a child. But not us. If you open a/an (9) ..... with Smith Fulton Bank before October 31st, we'll not only send you your own (10) ..... book and credit (11) ..... , but you'll also receive a copy of our booklet 'Putting Money (12) ..... for Your Future'. Smith Fulton can pay your (13) ..... , help you with special student (14) ..... , and your friendly branch (15) ..... can give you advice for the future. We believe in you. Why not believe in us and open an account?

1) A) shut	B) hard	C) debt	D) money
2) A) borrow	B) lend	C) save	D) pay
3) A) cheque	B) pension	C) wealth	D) cash
4) A) sign	B) spend	C) cost	D) cheat
5) A) owe	B) loans	C) debts	D) profits
6) A) amount	B) number	C) note	D) rest
7) A) receipts	B) credits	C) rents	D) interest
8) A) lend	B) economise	C) afford	D) spend
9) A) cheque	B) customer	C) bill	D) account
10) A) loan	B) cheque	C) cash	D) money
11) A) plastic	B) tip	C) card	D) cheque
12) A) aside	B) up	C) inside	D) work
13) A) sales	B) bets	C) bargains	D) bills
14) A) coins	B) loans	C) fortunes	D) pensions
15) A) miser	B) swindler	C) manager	D) cashier

17 Feelings and Opinions

1
Choose the most suitable word or phrase underlined in each sentence.

a) When Dick saw his neighbour kick his dog he became <u>angry/nervous</u>.
b) Sue wasn't really <u>interested/interesting</u> in the film.
c) We were both <u>afraid/anxious</u> that we would miss the plane.
d) Please accept our <u>faithful/sincere</u> congratulations.
e) I wish you wouldn't snap your fingers. It's very <u>annoying/worrying</u>.
f) Your friend Judith is extremely <u>attractive/striking</u>.

g) You're not <u>scared/thrilled</u> of spiders, are you?

h) If we forget to do our homework, our teacher gets <u>cross/terrifying</u>.

i) Tim completely lost his temper! He was absolutely <u>furious/upset</u>.

j) Your written work is full of <u>careless/naughty</u> mistakes.

2

Replace the word or words underlined with one of the words from the list. Use each word once only.

| confused | delightful | fascinating | irritating |
| scared | depressed | dull | glad | naughty | upset |

a) I'm afraid the children have been very <u>badly-behaved</u> today. ....

b) I felt a bit <u>frightened</u> when I went into the dark room. ....

c) Jean was very <u>unhappy</u> when her kitten was run over. ....

d) The film we saw last night was rather <u>boring</u>. ....

e) This is a <u>really interesting</u> book. You must read it. ....

f) I'm so <u>happy</u> that Helen got the job she wanted. ....

g) Sometimes when I hear the news I feel very <u>miserable</u>. ....

h) He always interrupts everyone! It's very <u>annoying</u>. ....

i) We had a <u>wonderful</u> evening with some Scottish friends. ....

j) Sorry I gave you the wrong tickets. I got a bit <u>mixed up</u>. ....

3

Complete each sentence with a suitable word or phrase from the list. Use each word or phrase once only.

| blush | grin | shake your head | scream | whisper | cry |
| nod your head | shrug your shoulders | wave | yawn |

a) When you feel embarrassed you might ....

b) When you feel tired or bored you might ....

c) When you want to talk without being heard you might ....

d) When you want to show agreement you might ....

e) When you want to show great amusement you might ....

f) When you want to show that you don't know or care you might ....

g) When you feel upset you might ....

h) When you want to show disagreement you might ....

i) When you are scared or in pain you might ....

j) When you want to attract someone's attention you might ....

4

Choose a suitable comment or reply from 1) to 10) for each sentence a) to j). Use each comment once only.

a) How do you feel about folk music? ....

b) Do you think I should order the tickets in advance? ....

c) Do you have any comment on the Prime Minister's decision? ....

d) I feel really miserable today. ....

e) Is it all right if I invite some friends round? ....

f) Shall I do the washing up? ....

g) I like this vase. Is it an antique? ....

h) Don't you think you should treat your mother better? ....

i) Is my homework all right? ....

j) Did you enjoy the concert? ....

1) You can do whatever you like, as far as I'm concerned.
2) In my opinion, the most important matter has been forgotten.
3) I didn't think much of it, actually.
4) No, it's not worth it.
5) Mind out, you might drop it!
6) I'm sorry, but it just won't do.
7) I'm not very keen on that kind of thing, to be honest.
8) No, don't bother, I'll do it.
9) Why don't you mind your own business!
10) Never mind, cheer up!

5

Match each word or phrase from the list with a suitable description.

co-operative determined helpful obedient realistic dependable embarrassed imaginative quarrelsome tolerant

a) If you are this, you can't put up with people looking at you. ....
b) If you are this, you get on well working with others. ....
c) If you this, you face up to facts. ....
d) If you are this, you might make up stories. ....
e) If you are this, you carry out instructions. ....
f) If you are this, you don't give up easily. ....
g) If you are this, you put up with other people's differences. ....
h) If you are this, people can count on you. ....
i) If you are this, you keep falling out with other people. ....
j) If you are this, you might put yourself out for someone else. ....

6

Choose the most suitable word or phrase to complete each sentence.

a) The thief returned the old lady's money, because he had a guilty ....
   A) heart   B) feeling   C) conscience   D) mind
b) I wanted to complain about my boss, but I didn't ....
   A) dare   B) risk   C) courage   D) attempt
c) I'm hungry. Do you .... going out for a pizza?
   A) like   B) want   C) desire   D) fancy
d) Let's go to a different cinema. I'm not very .... on horror films.
   A) keen   B) interested   C) enthusiastic   D) impressed
e) All my friends have big new cars. I'm becoming .... of my old Mini.
   A) embarrassed   B) ashamed   C) guilty   D) upset
f) I'm sorry I screamed. Something .... me.
   A) afraid   B) terrifying   C) scared   D) depressed
g) How do you .... about the pollution problem in this country?
   A) feel   B) think   C) believe   D) view
h) I'm sorry to .... you, but could I make a phone call?
   A) trouble   B) upset   C) worry   D) mind
i) I don't think this programme is .... for young children.
   A) wonderful   B) suitable   C) worth   D) keen
j) The African workers accused the European company of racial ....
   A) judgement   B) beliefs   C) argument   D) prejudice

7

Use the word in capitals at the end of each line to form a word that fits in the space in the same line.

Film review

'Battle for your heart' is the new film starring Hugh
Grace. I'm afraid that my first (1) .... was not
very favourable. The scenes of violence are (2) ....
and the main character, Tony, is simply (3) ....
The audience is supposed to feel great (4) .... for
Tony, an army officer, who is accused of (5) ....
because he fails to attack the village where the (6) ....
Miranda lives with her old father. Tony saves
their lives, and although the idea of marrying him
has little (7) .... for her, Miranda agrees to it out
of (8) .... However, she is still in love with Alex,
one of the enemy army, and wants to remain (9) ....
to him. The dialogue and the acting are just as bad
as the plot. At the end, I breathed a sigh of (10) ....
This is definitely one to miss!

IMPRESS
OFFEND
IRRITATE
ADMIRE
COWARD
ADORE

ATTRACT
GRATEFUL
FAITH

RELIEVE

8

Complete each sentence by putting one suitable word in each space.

a) In reply to Jack's question, Sue shook .... head.
b) You should be ashamed .... your behaviour!
c) Cheer ....! Try laughing for a change!
d) Do you like chocolate cake? I am very fond .... it.
e) Young David has got .... trouble as usual.
f) Are you laughing .... me? Do I look funny?
g) That was a terrible thing to do! I'm extremely cross .... you!
h) I don't believe .... spending a lot of money on clothes.
i) You look a bit fed .... Is anything the matter?
j) I'm very keen .... classical music, actually.

9

Decide which answer A, B, C or D best fits each space.

Noisy neighbours

Julie always thought of herself as an easy going and (1) ..... person, who put up with people's differences. She hardly ever became (2) ..... about anything, and believed that if you treated people well, they would (3) ..... with you. That is, until Alex and Harry moved in next door. At first, when their music woke her in the night, she was just a bit (4) ..... , but did not feel (5) ...... She shrugged her (6) ..... and said to herself, 'Never mind, I make a lot of noise sometimes. I'll go round and (7) ..... , in as nice a way as possible.' When she knocked at Alex and Harry's door she said,' I'm not very (8) ..... on very loud music, to be (9) ...... Do you think you could turn it down a bit?' They just (10) ..... , and then Alex said, 'You can think whatever you like, as far as we're (11) ......' Then they shut the door in Julie's face. By the end of the week, Julie felt angry, but was determined not to (12) ..... her temper. She had hardly slept, and kept (13) ..... all the time, but she kept busy. The next time she called next door, she gave Harry and Alex a present. 'It's just a cake I made for you. Please (14) ..... my apologies for last time!' And that day the noise stopped. 'What a (15) ..... ,' thought Julie. 'Now there's some peace and quiet and I can read my favourite book 'The History of Poison.....'

1) A) dull   B) glad   C) quarrelsome   D) tolerant
2) A) upset   B) helpful   C) fascinating   D) careless
3) A) scream   B) like   C) co-operate   D) mind
4) A) furious   B) irritated   C) annoying   D) thrilled
5) A) realistic   B) guilty   C) conscience   D) offended
6) A) shoulders   B) arms   C) hands   D) head
7) A) cry   B) quarrel   C) complain   D) fall out
8) A) interested   B) like   C) happy   D) keen
9) A) loud   B) honest   C) upset   D) nervous
10) A) whispered   B) cried   C) waved   D) grinned
11) A) concerned   B) determined   C) decided   D) embarrassed
12) A) have   B) lose   C) shout   D) break
13) A) blushing   B) snoring   C) yawning   D) growling
14) A) accept   B) take   C) attempt   D) invite
15) A) believe   B) naughty   C) shame   D) relief

18 Education and Learning

1

Choose the most suitable word or phrase underlined in each sentence.

a) Jack decided to take a course/lesson in hotel management.
b) Sheila always got good marks/points in algebra.
c) After leaving school, Ann studied/trained as a teacher.
d) Peter decided not to go in/enter for the examination.
e) My sister learned/taught me how to draw.
f) I can't come to the cinema. I have to read/study for a test.
g) In history we had to learn a lot of dates by hand/heart.
h) I hope your work will improve by the end of course/term.
i) Martin failed/missed his maths exam and had to sit it again.
j) If you have any questions, raise/rise your hand.

2

Complete each sentence with a word from the list. Use each word once only.

| cheat | copy | memorise | pay | revise |
| concentrate | divide | pass | punish | underline |

a) Our teachers used to .... us by making us stay behind after school.
b) The teacher saw Jerry trying to .... in the test.
c) Try to .... the most important rules.
d) It is difficult to .... attention in a noisy classroom.

e) Pauline tried her best to .... the end of year examinations.

f) Your work is the same as Harry's. Did you .... his work?

g) Your mind is wandering! You must .... more!

h) Helen decided to .... all her work at the end of every week.

i) It's a good idea to .... important parts of the book in red.

j) If you .... twenty seven by nine, the answer is three.

3

Match each person from the list with a suitable description. Use each name once only.

| classmate examiner learner principal pupil coach graduate lecturer professor tutor |

a) Someone who teaches at a university.   ....

b) Someone who has a college degree.   ....

c) The head of a school.   ....

d) Someone who studies at primary or secondary school.   ....

e) The most important teacher in a university department.   ....

f) Someone who teaches one student or a very small class.   ....

g) Someone in the same class as yourself.   ....

h) Someone who trains a sports team.   ....

i) Someone who writes the question papers of an examination.   ....

j) Someone who drives but has not yet passed a driving test.   ....

4

Complete each sentence a) to j) with one of the endings 1) to 10). Use each ending once only.

a) Joe was absent most of the time ....

b) Sue wanted to do the experiment for herself ....

c) James was a very gifted pupil ....

d) Lucy couldn't find a duster to clean the board ....

e) Dave could pick up languages very easily ....

f) Brenda wanted to leave space for corrections ....

g) Tony didn't pay attention in class ....

h) Helen was educated at home by her parents ....

i) Brian attended evening classes in photography ....

j) Cathy wanted to get into university ....

1) .... so he didn't have any problems passing his exams.

2) .... so he started talking in French after only a few days.

3) .... so she had to study for the entrance examinations.

4) .... so his name was removed from the register.

5) .... so he didn't go out with his friends much during the week.

6) .... so she wrote her answers in the corner.

7) .... so she didn't have many friends of her own age.

8) .... so she wrote everything on alternate lines.

9) .... so she went to the science laboratory.

10) .... so he could never remember what the teacher said.

5

Choose the most suitable word or phrase to complete each sentence.

a) Helen's parents were very pleased when they read her school ....
   A) report   B) papers   C) diploma   D) account
b) Martin has quite a good .... of physics.
   A) result   B) pass   C) understanding   D) head
c) In Britain, children start .... school at the age of five.
   A) kindergarten   B) secondary   C) nursery   D) primary
d) Edward has a .... in French from Leeds University.
   A) certificate   B) degree   C) mark   D) paper
e) My favourite .... at school was history.
   A) topic   B) class   C) theme   D) subject
f) It's time for break. The bell has ....
   A) gone off   B) struck   C) rung   D) sounded
g) Our English teacher .... us some difficult exercises for homework.
   A) set   B) put   C) obliged   D) made
h) Before you begin the exam paper, always read the .... carefully.
   A) orders   B) instructions   C) rules   D) answers
i) If you want to pass the examination, you must study ....
   A) hardly   B) enough   C) thoroughly   D) rather
j) Most students have quite a good sense of their own ....
   A) grasp   B) ability   C) idea   D) information

6

Use the word in capitals at the end of each line to form a word that fits in the space in the same line.

School report

Margaret started English Literature this term, and I
am afraid that her (1) .... to the subject has not been   INTRODUCE
entirely (2) .... She has not shown much enthusiasm,   SUCCESS
and does not always pay (3) .... in class. Her assignments   ATTEND
are often (4) .... , because she is so untidy, and because   READ
of her (5) .... to check her work thoroughly. She failed   FAIL
to do any (6) .... before the end of term test, and had   REVISE
poor results. She seems to have the (7) .... idea that   MISTAKE
she can succeed without studying. She has also had many
(8) .... and has frequently arrived late for class. This   ABSENT
has resulted in several severe (9) .... Although   PUNISH
Margaret is a (10) .... student in some respects, she   GIFT
has not had a satisfactory term.

7

Complete each sentence with a form of *do, make* or *take*.

a) Have you .... Exercise Three yet?
b) I can't come this afternoon. I'm .... an English exam.
c) Jack has .... very well this term.
d) I'm afraid that you haven't .... any progress.
e) Sue didn't know the answer, so she .... a guess.
f) You all look tired. Let's .... a break.
g) This is a good composition, but you have .... a lot of errors.

h) I think you should .... yourself more seriously.

i) The teacher gave a lecture, and the class .... notes.

j) Paul finds maths difficult, but he .... his best.

8

Complete each sentence with a word beginning as shown. Each space represents one letter.

a) Charles has a good k _ _ _ _ _ _ _ _ of the subject.

b) These children are badly behaved! They need more d _ _ _ _ _ _ _ _ .

c) Everyone agrees that a good e _ _ _ _ _ _ _ _ is important.

d) If you don't know a word, look it up in your d _ _ _ _ _ _ _ _ .

e) Maths is easy if you are allowed to use a c _ _ _ _ _ _ _ _ .

f) Keith spent four years studying at u _ _ _ _ _ _ _ _ .

g) Some apes seem to have as much i _ _ _ _ _ _ _ _ _ _ as humans!

h) I find listening c _ _ _ _ _ _ _ _ _ _ _ tests rather difficult.

i) At the age of eleven I went to s _ _ _ _ _ _ _ school.

j) I enjoyed doing e _ _ _ _ _ _ _ _ _ in the laboratory.

9

Complete each sentence with **one** word.

a) If you have a problem, put .... your hand.

b) Please pay attention .... what your teacher says.

c) Mary has a degree .... civil engineering.

d) David was punished .... throwing chalk at the teacher.

e) I was very good .... maths when I was at school.

f) What's the answer if you multiply 18 .... 16 ?

g) We had to write a composition .... 'Our Ideal School'.

h) Please write this .... your exercise books.

i) You might not understand things even if you learn them .... heart.

j) When Sue visited Italy, she soon picked .... the language.

10

Decide which answer A, B, C or D best fits each space.

Learning How to Learn

There is usually one important (1) ..... missing from most school (2) .... Very few students are (3) ..... how to organise their learning, and how to (4) ..... the best use of their time. Let's take some simple (5) ..... . Do you know how to (6) ..... up words in a dictionary, and do you understand all the (7) ..... the dictionary contains? Can you (8) ..... notes quickly, and can you understand them (9) ..... ? For some reason, many schools give learners no (10) ..... with these matters. Teachers ask students to (11) ..... pages from books, or tell them to write ten pages, but don't explain (12) ..... to do it. Learning by (13) ..... can be useful, but it is more important to have a genuine (14) ..... of a subject. You can (15) ..... a lot of time memorising books, without understanding anything about the subject!

1) A) theme   B) book   C) subject   D) mark

2) A) agendas   B) timetables   C) terms   D) organisations

3) A) taught   B) learnt   C) educated   D) graduated

4) A) take   B) give   C) get   D) make

5) A) sentences   B) results   C) rules   D) examples

6	A) find	B) look	C) research	D) get
7	A) information	B) advise	C) subjects	D) themes
8	A) do	B) send	C) make	D) revise
9	A) after	B) afterwards	C) lastly	D) at last
10	A) teaching	B) ability	C) instruction	D) help
11	A) concentrate	B) remind	C) forget	D) memorise
12	A) how	B) what	C) why	D) it
13	A) the way	B) heart	C) now	D) law
14	A) information	B) success	C) understanding	D) attention
15	A) pass	B) waste	C) tell	D) use

19 Word Formation 1

1
Use your dictionary to complete the word in each sentence.

a) The children never do what I tell them to! They are very dis........................ .
b) It won't rain in August, surely! That seems extremely un........................ .
c) No, I told you <u>not</u> to sell the shares! You must have mis........................ .
d) Jack gets very good marks, and is an out........................ student.
e) If you co........................ with the police you will receive a light sentence.
f) Dave was in the first sub........................ that sailed under the North Pole.
g) Just heat up the rice, it's been pre........................ .
h) Mr Jones is incredibly rich. In fact he's a multi........................ .
i) The ship hit a rock, but the lives of the passengers were not en........................ .
j) I just can't answer this question! It's im........................ .

2
Complete each sentence with a word formed from the word underlined, beginning as shown. Begin the word with a prefix from the list.

dis- in- non- over- re- trans- un- vice-

a) I'm not <u>satisfied</u> with your work. I am .... with it.
b) She doesn't have the <u>usual</u> kind of haircut. It's very ....
c) We haven't <u>decided</u> where to go yet. We are ....
d) Mary is sailing across the <u>Atlantic</u>. She is on a .... voyage.
e) Dan is the <u>president</u>'s assistant. He is the ....
f) Terry is no longer a <u>smoker</u>. Now he is a ....
g) Don't wear a <u>formal</u> suit. The dinner is quite ....
h) I don't think this rule is <u>fair</u>. It's .... to older students.
i) You haven't <u>written</u> this clearly. It'll have to be ....
j) This steak is <u>cooked</u> too much. It's ....

3

Complete each sentence with a word formed from a word given in the list, ending as shown.

| astonish fool great music thought |
| back free lead short trumpet |

a) I don't want to be a slave! I demand my ....dom.
b) How kind of you to bring flowers! That was very ....ful.
c) Martin plays the guitar, but he isn't a very good ....ian.
d) Our school has closed because there is a ....age of teachers.
e) Brian is one of the world's ....ing architects.
f) Imagine my ....ment when the cat started to speak!
g) Don't be ....ish ! There is no such thing as a ghost!
h) I prefer to begin at the end and go ....wards.
i) I always wanted to be a ....er in a jazz band.
j) A small country can still achieve ....ness.

4

Complete each sentence with a word formed from a word given in the list, using one of the prefixes or suffixes given.

| care employ home postpone satisfied |
| charged friend night pronounce skirts |

| dis- mis- out- over- -less -ment -ship -ee |

a) I travelled to Scotland on the .... train and slept all the way.
b) You're always breaking things! Why are you so .... ?
c) Jane knows a lot of French words, but she tends to .... them.
d) We all believe in .... between the people of different nations.
e) Bad weather caused the .... of nearly all the football programme.
f) George was very .... with the service at the hotel.
g) We live in a flat on the .... of London.
h) Patsy thought the shop assistant had .... her.
i) David was tired of being a/an .... so he started his own company.
j) The government is providing more money to help .... people.

5

Use the word in capitals at the end of each line to form a word that fits in the space in the same line.

Evening classes

Recently I decided to go to evening classes twice a
week. During the day I work in a (1) .... agency   SECRETARY
as a telephonist. It is not a very interesting (2) ....   OCCUPY
and I get bored. I also got tired of coming home
every evening, putting a (3) .... meal in the oven,   FREEZE
and then watching TV. So I decided to take up (4) ....   CARPENTER
as a hobby. Perhaps I should give you an (5) .... for   EXPLAIN
my choice. Learning a skill is a good (6) .... to the   SOLVE
problem of boring work. Also, I felt I was a (7) ....   FAIL
because any time I tried to put up a shelf, for example,
it always fell down! Now I am quite a (8) .... wood-   SUCCESS

worker! I am working on the (9) .... of some
furniture at the moment. And although there are only
two other girls in the class, I don't feel any (10) ....
I've turned out to be the best student in the class!

CONSTRUCT

EMBARRASS

6

Complete the
compound word
in each sentence,
using a word
given in the list.

| bow cut helmet powder storm case fire place steps writing |

a) I could hear the sound of gun................. coming from the main square.
b) We had to take shelter during a severe thunder................. .
c) Nobody can read the doctor's hand................. .
d) You look awful. Why don't you have a hair................. ?
e) I wanted to do some washing but I've run out of soap ....
f) If you ride a motorbike you have to wear a crash ....
g) There isn't room in here for another book................. .
h) After the shower, the sun came out and there was a rain................. .
i) I could hear the sound of foot................. . Someone was coming!
j) At one end of the room is a lovely old stone fire................. .

7

Choose the most
suitable word or
phrase
underlined in
each sentence.

a) Helen doesn't look well. She is extremely <u>slim/thin</u>.
b) It's really hot today, but it's nice and <u>chilly/cool</u> in here.
c) Peter <u>nodded/shook</u> his head in agreement.
d) I can't pay you anything for this old coin. It's <u>priceless/worthless</u>.
e) The house was surrounded by a <u>high/tall</u> fence.
f) The sun is shining, and it's a/an <u>attractive/lovely</u> day.
g) This chicken is good. It's very <u>tasteful/tasty</u>.
h) Be careful of the next corner. It's rather <u>dangerous/harmful</u>.
i) Graham left the film before the end because he was <u>bored/lazy</u>.
j) When I saw the child scratch my car I became very <u>angry/nervous</u>.

8

Complete each
sentence with a
word formed
from a word in
the list.

| do fall get make set draw feel give put take |

a) Those children next door are .... a lot of noise.
b) I don't really .... like going out this evening.
c) You don't have to hurry. You can .... your time.
d) Armstrong was the first person to .... foot on the moon.
e) The director .... us permission to park our motorbikes here.
f) Can you .... me a favour? I need some help with the garden.
g) I can't talk now. I'm just .... lunch.
h) When something goes wrong, people always .... the blame on me!
i) Tom has just .... in love yet again!
j) I would like to .... your attention to these instructions.

9

Rewrite each sentence so that it has the same meaning, and contains the word given in capitals. Do not change the word in any way.

a) The forest outside the town started burning last night.   CAUGHT

....

b) Suddenly Janet started crying.   TEARS

....

c) What's your occupation?   DO

....

d) We'll have to decide soon.   DECISION

....

e) Can you look after my plants while I'm away?   TAKE

....

f) You will write or phone, won't you?   TOUCH

....

g) Diane had a baby boy last week.   GAVE

....

h) Peter always remains calm in an emergency.   HEAD

....

i) Stop holding the steering wheel!   LET

....

j) He can't possibly win the race.   STANDS

....

10

Complete each sentence with **one** suitable word.

a) I've been searching high and .... for this book!

b) That man's been walking up and .... the street all day.

c) I think we've been going round and .... in circles!

d) He promised to stick by her through thick and ....

e) When we finish this, we'll be home and ....

f) Make sure you are here bright and .... in the morning.

g) It's very important! It's a matter of life and ....

h) I've been going backwards and .... to the shops all morning.

i) We cleaned the kitchen until it looked spick and ....

j) The police kept a watch on the house day and ....

20 Word Formation 2

1

Add one of the prefixes in the list to each incomplete word so that it makes sense. Use each prefix once only.

| auto- dis- ex- in- mis- non- over- semi- sub- un- |

a) Dick was very tired and suffering from ....work.
b) We couldn't see the magician! He had become ....visible.
c) I could only cross the road by going down a ....way.
d) Nobody believed what Mary wrote in her ....biography.
e) Let me introduce you to Janet, my ....-wife.
f) What he said was not clear. In fact it was rather ....leading.
g) Unfortunately our football team lost in the ....-final.
h) Mr Smith regrets that he is ....able to accept your invitation.
i) This is a good train, it goes to Manchester ....-stop.
j) Oh bother, my pencil sharpener has ....appeared again.

2

Complete each sentence with a word formed from a word given in the list, ending as shown.

| drink   equal   hand   hope   partner |
| employ   green   harm   neighbour   wide |

a) Carol and Andy have just moved into a new ....hood.
b) My new ....er is paying me a much higher salary.
c) The local council have decided to ....en the main road.
d) Jerry picked up a ....ful of the money and smiled.
e) I'm a terrible card player. I'm really ....less.
f) It's a kind of blue colour, but a bit ....ish too.
g) Bill now works in ....ship with two other architects.
h) Don't drink from the stream. You don't know if the water is ....able.
i) Most people say that they believe in the ....ity of men and women.
j) Doctors have proved that smoking is ....ful.

3

Complete each sentence with a word formed from a word given in the list, using one of the prefixes or suffixes given.

| art   cycle   friend   hope   national   circle |
| edible   ground   mountain   young |

| fore-   in-   inter-   semi-   tri-   -eer   -ful   -ist   -ly   -ster |

a) I can't eat this! It's completely ....
b) John has been interested in sailing ever since he was a/an ....
c) The teacher arranged the desks in a/an ....
d) I like it here. The people are really ....
e) There are two figures in the .... of the picture.
f) You have to have a good head for heights if you are a ....
g) It's much safer for a young child to ride a/an ....
h) Scientists are .... that a cure for the disease will be found.
i) Most countries have signed a/an .... agreement banning whaling.
j) Paintings by this .... have been sold for millions of pounds.

4

Use the word in capitals at the end of each line to form a word that fits in the space in the same line.

How to become Prime Minister

Jack had never wanted to be a (1) .... First of all, he
suffered from terrible (2) .... and blushed violently
when he had to make a speech. He also (3) .... with
people who refused to vote. After all, what difference did
it make? As a speaker, he was slow and (4) .... and
never knew what to say. He began his career as a last-minute
(5) .... for a speaker who failed to turn up. Later he
learned to (6) .... his tie, give a big smile, and read the
speech which had been prepared by his (7) .... speech-
writer. People liked him. 'He has a kind of (8) ....',
they said. They did not mind that he had no (9) .... ,
and seemed quite (10) .... in what he was saying.
They applauded him and then made him Prime Minister.

POLITICS
SHY
SYMPATHY

ORGANISE

PLACE
STRAIGHT
PERSON
INNOCENT
IMAGINE
INTEREST

5

Choose the most suitable compound word underlined.

a) The bus from Glasgow arrives at the Central <u>bus station/bus stop</u>.
b) Bob only works <u>half-time/part-time</u> at the moment.
c) Joan has lovely clothes and is always <u>well-dressed/well-worn</u>.
d) Some of Bill's ideas are rather <u>old-aged/old-fashioned</u>.
e) We left our car in the multi-storey <u>car park/car parking</u>.
f) Martin is now a <u>well-known/well-written</u> novelist.
g) Thank you. You gave me a good <u>haircut/haircutting</u>.
h) Excellent. That was a <u>first class/first course</u> lunch!
i) I prefer <u>self-made/homemade</u> jam to the jam you buy in shops.
j) I sent back the chicken because it was <u>half-baked/half cooked</u>.

6

Complete the compound word in each sentence, using a word given in the list.

| clothed | handed | hearted | looking | mouthed |
| eared | headed | legged | minded | tempered |

a) Thank you for helping me, and being so kind-.................... .
b) We searched all day, but had to return home empty-.................... .
c) Paul didn't have time to think, but jumped into the river fully-.................... .
d) It seems that long-.................... people can run faster.
e) Try to concentrate and remember! You are so absent-.................... .
f) Mary is very attractive, and her husband is good-.................... too.
g) Stop shouting! I'm tired of your loud-.................... comments!
h) Mike gets angry easily. He's a bit short-.................... .
i) Steve's book was dirty and dog-.................... .
j) Red-.................... people usually dislike being called 'Ginger'!

7
Complete each
sentence with
one suitable
word which is
the *opposite* of
the word
underlined.

a) The team expected an easy <u>victory</u>, but suffered a crushing ...defeat.....
b) The bridge is <u>dangerous</u>! It's not .....safe...... to cross it.
c) I'm sorry, I can't <u>accept</u> your invitation. I have to ...refuse..... it.
d) David thought he would <u>fail</u> the exam, but he managed to ...pass......... .
e) We had a good <u>take-off</u>, but the ...landing.. was a bit bumpy.
f) This loaf isn't <u>fresh</u>! Do you always sell ...stale...... bread?
g) The pirates <u>dug up</u> the treasure, and then ...buried...... it somewhere else.
h) These books are supposed to be <u>different</u>, but they are very ...same........ .
i) I enjoyed the <u>opening</u> of the film, but not the ...ending... .
j) The water <u>freezes</u> at night, but the ice ...melts...... during the day.

8
Complete each
sentence using
one of the words
given in the list.
Use each word
once only.

bear catch gain make think break drop lose take waste

a) Don't .... such a fuss! I'll only be gone for a week!
b) I try not to .... touch with my old friends.
c) What this paper says doesn't .... much relation to the truth.
d) Please .... me a line and tell me all your news.
e) Come on, hurry up, don't .... time.
f) I managed to .... sight of the prince through the crowd.
g) He says he's going to walk, but he'll probably .... better of it.
h) Ann was able to .... a lot of experience in her first job.
i) Please .... a seat. I'll be with you in just a moment.
j) I will .... the news to Dave of his sister's accident.

9
Rewrite each
sentence so that
it has the same
meaning, and
contains the
word given in
capitals. Do not
change the word
in any way.

a) Nothing you do will alter anything. DIFFERENCE
....
b) I hope I'm not inconveniencing you. TROUBLE
....
c) Let's measure the room. TAKE
....
d) Mark looked disappointed when I told him my name. FELL
....
e) The old car suddenly started burning. FLAMES
....
f) Susan didn't know where she was. WAY
....
g) I can't bear to look at that boy! SIGHT
....
h) Helen became responsible for the business. CHARGE
....
i) What did you do while you were waiting for the train? TIME
....
j) I now think differently about this matter. MIND
....

10

Complete each sentence with **one** suitable word.

a) The little boy who had lost his parents was .... tears.

b) I met Jack at the airport completely .... chance.

c) This wasn't an accident! You did it .... purpose.

d) We have similar tastes, and a lot of other things .... common.

e) Don't worry! Everything is .... control.

f) I'm going to study much harder .... now on.

g) Our birthday presents took him completely .... surprise.

h) This painting is now .... loan to the National Gallery.

i) Let's go to Brighton this year .... a change.

j) Go away. I want to be .... myself.

Formation Rules

1
Tenses

Present simple

I/you/we/they like.	She/he/it likes.
Do you like?	Does she like?
You don't like.	He doesn't like.

Present continuous

I am going.	You/we/they are going.
She/he/it is going.	Am I going?
Are you going?	Is she going?
I am not going.	You aren't going.
She isn't going.	

Present perfect

I/you/we/they have left.	She/he/it has left.
Have they left?	Has she left?
They haven't left.	He hasn't left.

Present perfect continuous

I/you/we/they have been waiting.	She/he/it has been waiting.
Have you been waiting?	Has she been waiting?
We haven't been waiting.	He hasn't been waiting.

Past simple

1. I/you/she/he/it/we/they started. (Regular)
   Did you start?
   You didn't start.
2. I/you/she/he/it/we/they went. (Irregular)
   Did you go?
   You didn't go.

Past continuous

I/she/he/it was going.	You/we/they were going.
Was he going?	Were you going?
She wasn't' going.	You weren't going.

Past perfect

I/you/she/he/it/we/they had left.
Had he left?
They hadn't left.

Past perfect continuous

I/you/she/he/it/we/they had been waiting.
Had they been waiting?
He hadn't been waiting.

Future perfect

I/you/she/he/it/we/they will have finished.
Will they have finished?
They won't have finished.

Future perfect continuous
I/you/she/he/it/we/they will have been waiting.
Will they have been waiting?
They won't have been waiting.
Will
See Units 3 and 19.

2
Indirect Speech

'I always drink milk.'	He said that he always drank milk.
'I'm leaving.'	She said she was leaving.
'I'll be back soon.'	He said he would be back soon.
'I've forgotten it.'	She said she had forgotten it.
'I took it.'	He said he had taken it.
'I was reading.'	She said she had been reading.
'I had left by then.'	She said she had left by then.
'I must go.'	She said she had to go/must go.
'I can help.'	He said he could help.
'I would like to help.'	She said she would like to help.
'If I had a car, I'd go.'	He said that if he had a car he would go.

3
Passive tenses

He helps.	He is helped.
He is helping.	He is being helped.
He has helped.	He has been helped.
He helped.	He has helped.
He was helping.	He was being helped.
He will help.	He will be helped.
He will have helped.	He will have been helped.

4
Infinitives

Present:	to like
Passive:	to be liked
Past:	to have liked
Past passive:	to have been liked

5
Participles (-*ing* forms)

Present:	liking
Present passive:	being liked
Past:	having liked
Past passive:	having been liked

Word List

Vocabulary
Units (1–18)

ability 18
aboard 6
abolish 14
accelerator 6
accept 17
accident 14
accommodation 1
account (n) 7, 16
accountant 2, 16
accuse 9
ace 3
ache (v) 15
act (n) 10
actor 10
add 7
adjust 6
admire 15
admit 9
adolescent 12
adore 17
adorable 12
adult 12
in advance 17
advertisement 2, 8
aerial 5, 6
afford 16
afraid 17
agent 16
aggressive 12
agony 15
agree 3, 9
agreement 9
aid (n) 14
air conditioning 13
allow 9
alternate (adj) 18
ambitious 12
ambulance 6, 15
amuse 10
ankle 15
announcer 10
annoy 17

annoying 17
anorak 4
antique 8
anxious 17
appear 4
appearance 4, 12
applaud 10
appliance 5, 13
application 2
apply 2, 7
appointment (job) 2
apron 4
architect 2
arranged 3
arrest (v) 9
ashamed 17
attempt 3
attend 18
attic 5
attract 11
attract attention 17
attractive 17
audience 3, 10
author 10
available 8
avoid 6
axe 13

bachelor 12
background 10
bad (rotten) 7
bad-tempered 12
bake 7
ban (v) 9, 14
band 10
bandage 8
bank (river) 11
bargain (n) 8, 16
bark (n) 11
basin 5
battery 13
beard 15

beat (v) 3, 7
bee 11
beetroot 8
behave 12
behaviour 12
belief 3
belt 4
best man 12
best seller 10
bet (n) 16
bill 7, 16
billiards 3
binoculars 13
biography 10
blackmailer 9
blind (n) 5
block of flats 5
blood 15
blouse 4
blunt 13
blush 17
board (n) 3
boarding school 5
body 15
boil over 7
bonnet 6
boo 10
book (v) 1, 7
bookshelves 5
boot (car) 6
boring 17
bother 17
bow tie 4
bowl 7
brain 15
brake (n) 6
brake (v) 6
branch 11
brave 12
break down 6, 13
break into 9
break the law 9

breath 15
breed (n) 11
brick 5
bride 12
briefcase 4
bring up 12
broadcast (v) 10
bruised 15
buffet 1
bulb 13
bumper 6
bungalow 5
bunk 5
burglar 9
bush 5, 11
butcher 8
button 4
buzz 11

cabin 1
call in 12
call off 10
camel 11
camp-site 1
canal 11
cancel 6, 9
cancelled 1
cap 4
capital punishment 9
caravan 6
carpenter 2
carpet 5
carriage 6
cart 6
case 9
cash 16
cashier 16
cast (n) 10
catalogue 8
catch a cold 15
catch fire 14
cattle 11
carving knife 7
cashier 2

casserole 7
castle 5
casual 4
cause trouble 9
cave 11
ceiling 5
cellar 5
central heating 5
certificate 18
chain 6
champion 3
change (n) 8, 16
channel 11
chapter 10
character 12
(in) charge 2
charge (v) 9, 16
charity 14
chat 12
chauffeur 6
cheap 16
cheat (v) 9, 18
check in 1
cheek 15
cheer up 17
cheerful 12
chef 2
chemist 8
cheque 16
chimney 5, 15
chin 15
choir 10
chop (n) 8
chop (v) 13
chorus 10
cliff 11
close down 14
close up 10
clothing 4
cloudy 11
club (golf) 3
coach (n) 6
coach (v) 18
cockpit 2, 6

cockroach 11
cod 8
coin 16
collapse (v) 14
collar 4
colleague 12
collect 14
collection 3
collide 6
collision 14
come out 10
come up 3
commit 9
commute 5
competition 3
competitor 3
complain 8
composer 10
compulsory 9
computer 13
concentrate 18
concert 10
condemn 14
condition 14
conductor (bus) 6
conductor (music) 10
confess 9
confidence 17
confused 17
congratulations 17
conscience 17
conservation 14
considerable 16
considerate 12
constable 9
control 14
cooker 5
cool 7
corn 11
corporal punishment 9
costume 3, 4, 10
cottage 5
cough (v) 15
count on 12

examine 15
examiner 18
exhaust 6
expect 3
expedition 1
expenses 2
experience 2
experiment 18
expression 15
extinct 14

facilities 14
factory 12
fail 18
faithful 17
fall ill 15
fall out 12
falsely 9
famine 14
fancy dress party 4
fare 16
fascinating 17
fashion 4
fattening 7
faulty 13
fee 16
fence 5
fever 15
fiancé 12
field 3
file 13
filling station 6
filthy 14
find guilty 9
fine 9
fire brigade 14
fire engine 6
fireman 2
fireplace 5
firm (n) 2
fishmonger 8
fist 15
fit (adj) 3, 15
fit (v) 4

fitted 5
fix 13
flat (adj) 13
flat (n) 5
flight 1
float 3, 6
flock 11
flood 11, 14
florist 8
fly 11
forecast 11
foreground 10
forest 11
forger 9
formal 4
fortnight 1
fortune 16
fountain 5, 11
fractured 15
frame 5, 10
frank 12
free 16
free of charge 8
freeze 8
fresh 7
frightened 17
frog 11
frozen 7
frying-pan 7, 8
full-time 2
fur 4
furious 17

gadget 13
gambling 3
gate 5
(change) gear 6
geese 11
generation 12
generous 12, 16
gentle 12
get away 9
get away with 9
get on well with 12

get off with 9
get over 15
gifted 18
giraffe 11
give away 12
give birth 15
glad 17
glove 3, 4
glue (v) 3
go in for 18
go off 13
go over 10
go with 4
goods 8
government 9
graduate (n) 18
grasp 18
grate (v) 7
grateful 12
greedy 12, 17
greengrocer 8
greenhouse 5
grill 7
grin 17
grind (v) 7
gripping 10
ground (adj) 7
ground (n) 3, 5,
grounded 1
group 10
grow up 12
guarantee 16
guard 6
guest-house 1
guilty 9

hairdresser 2
hammer 13
handlebars 3, 6
hang on 13
hang up 13
harbour 1
hard up 16
harm (v) 15

lip 15
list 8
litter 5
living 2
loaf 8
loan 16
lobster 11
lonely 12
look after 15
look out 13
look out (over) 1
look up 10
look up to 12
lorry 6
lose 14
lose your temper 17
loss 16
luggage 1
luxury 16

mac 4
machinery 2
mains 2
make (n) 8
make out 13, 16
mansion 16
manufacturer 13
mark (v) 18
market place 8
mashed 7
mean (adj) 12, 16
mechanic 2, 6
medal 3
melt 7
memorise 18
menu 7
microwave 13
mind (v) 17
mine (n) 2
miner 2
miser 16
miserable 17
miss (v) 14, 18
model-making 3

mosquito 11
moth 11
motorist 6
motorway 5
mouthful 15
mug 7
multiply 18
murderer 9
muscle 15
mushroom 8

nail 8
naughty 17
neck 4, 15
necklace 8
needle 3, 13
neighbourhood 5
nephew 12
nerve 15
nervous 17
nest 11
net 3
newsagent 8
niece 12
nightdress 4
nil 3
nod 17
note (n) 16
notice (n) 2
novelist 10
nuisance 17
nursery 18
nut 13

oar 6
obey 11
object 9
off (adj) 7
off-licence 8
offence 9
offend 17
offender 9
open-air 8
opera 10
operation 15

opponent 3
optician 2
orchestra 10
order (n) 9
order (v) 7, 8
out of order 13
outdoors 3
outfit 4
oven 5
overall 4
overboard 6
overcoat 4
overcrowded 14
overpopulated 14
overtake 3
overtime 2

pack (v) 1
package (tour) 1
pain 15
parachute 6
pardon 9
parking ticket 6
pass 18
pastime 3
path 5
patient (n) 12
pavement 5, 6
pay attention 18
pay back 16
pay in 16
peak 11
pedestrian 5, 6
peel (n) 11
peel (v) 7
pension 2, 16
pensioner 12, 16
perform 10
performance 3, 10
permission 9
personality 2, 12
personnel manager 2
petrol 13
photographer 2

pick 5
pick up (receive) 10, 13
pick up (learn) 18
pickpocket 9
pig 11
pile-up 14
pill 15
pillow 5
pin 13
pinch 11
pitch 3
plain 4, 11
plant (n) 11
plate 7
platform 1, 6
playwright 10
pleasant 12
plod 11
plug 13
plughole 5
plumber 2
poached 7
point (n) 18
poison (n) 15
police station 9
polite 4, 8, 12
polluted 14
(football) pools 3
porter 1, 2
portion 7
position (job) 2
poster 5
pour 7
poverty 14, 16
powdered 7
power cut 13
pram 6
preface 10
prejudice 17
prescription 15
prevent 14
priced 8
pricey 8
primary 18

principal 18
prize 3
produce (v) 10
professionally 3
professor 18
profit 2, 16
progress (n) 18
prohibited 9
promotion 2
propose 12
prospects 2
prosperity 16
protect 14
proud 12
provide 14
publish 10
puddle 11
pump 13
punch (n) 3
punch (v) 15
punctual 12
punish 18
punishment 9
puppy 11
purchase (n) 8, 16
(on) purpose 17
purse 8
put (money) aside 16
put away 4
put off 13
put on 4, 10
put up with 12

quack 11
qualifications 2
quarrel 12
quay 1, 6
queue (n) 6
queue (v) 8

rabbit 11
race 3
racket 3
radiator 5
rage 17

rail 6
raise (v) 2, 12, 18
raw 7
razor 13
receipt 2, 8, 16
receiver 13
recipe 7
reckon 16
recommend 15
recording 10
recover 15
recycle 14
reduce 8, 14, 16
reduction 8
referee 3
references 2
refuse 9
register 18
registered 2
rehearsal 10
related 12
relation 12
relationship 12
relax (v) 1
release 9
reliable 12
relieve 17
rely 12
rent (n) 5, 16
report (n) 18
rescue 6
respect (v) 12
respectable 17
resign 2
result 3
retire 2
return (ticket) 1
revenge 17
reverse 6
review 10
revise 18
reward 3
riot 14
rise 12, 18

risk 17
rival 3
roast 7
robe 4
rod 3
roll (n) 8
roof rack 6
root 11
rope 3
rotten 7
round and round 4
row (n) 12
row (v) 6
rub 11
rubbish 2, 5
rude 12
rug 5
run into 6
run out 13
runway 1, 6
rural 5

sack (v) 2
saddle 3
safe (n) 16
salary 2, 16
(for) sale 8, 16
(on) sale 8
sales representative 2
sandal 4
sane 15
saucepan 7
save 11
save up 16
saw 13
scared 17
scarf 4
scene 10
science 13
scissors 13
score (n) 3
scratch (v) 11
scream 17
screen 10

screwdriver 13
script 10
sculptor 10
sculpture 10
seasick 1
seatbelt 1, 6
secondary 18
seed 11
self-defence 9
selfish 12
semi-detached 5
sentence 9
sentimental 12
separated 12
serve 7, 8
service 7
service station 6
set 13, 18
set fire 14
settee 5
shake 17
shark 11
shed 5
shock 13
shoe-lace 4
shoplifter 9
shopper 8
shopping centre 8
show off 17
shower 5
shrug 17
shutter 5
shy 12
side by side 4
sign (v) 16
sill 5
sincere 17
single (ticket) 1
single 12
sink (n) 5
sink (v) 3, 6, 14
site 3
skate (v) 3
sketch 10

skid 3, 6
skill 3
skin 4, 11
skinny 4, 15
skyscraper 5
sleeper 6
sleeve 4
slice 7
slide (v) 3
slim 4, 15
slip 3
slither 11
slope 11
slum 14
smooth 13
smuggler 9
snake 11
snobbish 12
sociable 12
sofa 5
sole 4
solve 14
sore 15
source 11
spade 13
spanner 13
spare 13
special 13
spectator 3
spend 8, 16
spider 11
spin 11
spine 15
spinster 12
split 13
spotted 11
spread 11
sprinkle 7
square 5
squeeze 11
stage 10
stained 5
staircase 5
stale 7

vacancy 1
valley 11
valuable 16
valuables 16
value 9, 16
vandal 9
vary 8
vegetarian 7
vehicle 6
verdict 9
vet 2, 15
vicar 2
viewer 3, 10
villain 9
vintage 6
violent 12
volcano 14
volume 10
voyage 1

wag 11
wages 2
waggon 6
waist 15
waistcoat 4
wallet 8
ward 15
wardrobe 5
warm up 7
washbasin 5
wasp 11
wasted 14
waterproof 8
wave (n) 11
wave (v) 17
wealth 16
weigh 15
well off 16
whale 11
wheelbarrow 5

whisper 17
whistle 3
widow 12
wildlife 11
willing 8
windscreen 6
wing 6
wipers 6
wire 13
witness 9
work 2
work out 10
worm 11
worrying 17
worthless 16
wound 15
wrap 8
wrist 15

yawn 17

Grammar index

Grammar answers

Unit 1

1 1) a 2) c 3) d 4) f

2 a) *had forgotten*
b) was watching
c) used to live
d) was driving
e) had gone
f) had eaten
g) was doing
h) used to like
i) were you doing
j) had told
k) used to

3 a) *was trying*, stopped, offered
b) paid, had phoned
c) was not wearing, didn't notice, was driving
d) lay, were feeding
e) admitted, had hit, hadn't damaged
f) wasn't listening, was thinking
g) felt/was feeling, was finishing, fell
h) got, had disappeared
i) phoned, didn't answer, were you doing
j) didn't go, was raining

4 a) *unsuitable*
b) unsuitable
c) suitable
d) suitable
e) unsuitable
f) suitable
g) suitable
h) unsuitable
i) suitable
j) unsuitable

5 1) *invited*
2) did not hesitate
3) had discovered
4) had ever been
5) believed
6) never existed/had never existed
7) felt
8) vanished/had vanished
9) become/had become
10) had hidden
11) believed
12) were still keeping/still kept
13) set off
14) was looking forward
15) climbed
16) studied
17) were resting
18) noticed
19) was waving
20) shone/were shining

6 a) *After collecting the parcel, Norman realised it was the wrong one.*
b) Before leaving the house, Sue checked that she had her keys.
c) While parking his car, Mark noticed the wing-mirror was broken.
d) After cleaning the house, Julia fell asleep on the sofa.
e) Before buying a new television, Brian checked all the prices.
f) While skiing in Switzerland, Alan met his old friend, Ken.
g) After taking two aspirins, Kate felt a lot better.
h) Before going out for the evening, Sheila washed her hair.
i) While taking a bath, Michael heard someone at the door.
j) After reading the book, Trudy decided that she didn't like it.

7

STEM	PAST TENSE	STEM	PAST TENSE
beat	beat	mean	meant
bend	bent	pay	paid
bite	bit	rise	rose
bleed	bled	send	sent
blow	blew	shake	shook
build	built	shine	shone
catch	caught	shoot	shot
choose	chose	sink	sank
cost	cost	spring	sprang
draw	drew	steal	stole
drive	drove	stick	stuck
fall	fell	swing	swung
feel	felt	tear	tore
fly	flew	tread	trod
freeze	froze	wear	wore
hold	held	win	won
hurt	hurt	wind	wound
lay	laid	write	wrote

Unit 2

1 a) 1 b) 1 c) 1 d) 2 e) 2 f) 1

2 a) *Have you seen*
b) has been writing
c) has been asking
d) Did you give, saw
e) haven't been listening
f) have found
g) has changed
h) Did you visit
i) Have you two met
j) Did you meet

3 a) *had*, stayed
b) have/have had, saw
c) have come
d) saw, Have you sold
e) have you been doing
f) have found, went
g) has been killing, have made
h) promised, haven't finished
i) hasn't been looking/hasn't looked, went
j) have discovered, have been looking for

4 a) *for*
b) since
c) recently
d) today
e) before
f) since
g) last night
h) for ages
i) since
j) how long

5 a) *has been learning*
b) since I went to
c) Mary has become
d) been here since
e) time I have been
f) did Helen and Robert get
g) been wearing those trousers for
h) haven't spoken for a
i) already had something to
j) haven't played water-polo/have never played water-polo

281

6
a) *has eaten*
b) have you bought
c) have been singing
d) has been learning
e) have you invited
f) have been sitting
g) has been raining
h) has worn
i) have done
j) have been trying

7
1) has discovered
2) has been drilling
3) found
4) has discovered
5) lent
6) gave
7) has been
8) have already welcomed
9) has asked
10) happened
11) found
12) got
13) hasn't told
14) refused
15) have asked

8

STEM	PARTICIPLE	STEM	PARTICIPLE	STEM	PARTICIPLE
beat	beaten	feel	felt	shoot	shot
bend	bent	fly	flown	sink	sunk
bite	bitten	freeze	frozen	spring	sprung
bleed	bled	hold	held	steal	stolen
blow	blown	hurt	hurt	stick	stuck
build	built	lay	laid	swing	swung
catch	caught	mean	meant	tear	torn
choose	chosen	pay	paid	tread	trod
cost	cost	rise	risen	wear	worn
draw	drawn	send	sent	win	won
drive	driven	shake	shaken	wind	wound
fall	fallen	shine	shone	write	written

9
1) already
2) so
3) have
4) ✓
5) have
6) ✓
7) work
8) been
9) ✓
10) have
11) visiting
12) ✓
13) have
14) ✓
15) have

Unit 3

1
a) *are you going to buy*
b) I'll be studying
c) is going to fall
d) gets
e) are coming
f) arrives
g) is going to happen
h) am going to have
i) I'm leaving
j) will have gone

2
a) *am visiting*
b) won't be
c) are you going to buy
d) will have
e) Are you taking/Are you going to take
f) am going to lie down
g) are we going to spend
h) will be staying/is staying
i) does your plane leave
j) won't notice

3
a) *will have stopped*
b) will be lying
c) will be working
d) will have left
e) will have been married
f) will be living/will live
g) will be waiting
h) will/is going to land/will be landing
i) will have finished
j) will be watching

4
1) *you will be doing*
2) will soon be able
3) is holding
4) will be
5) will live/will be living
6) will be
7) will have replaced
8) will also be doing/do
9) will be directing
10) (will be) teaching

5
a) *see*, will tell
b) get, will phone
c) will go, do
d) will wait, stops/has stopped
e) will get, opens
f) take/have taken, will feel
g) finish/have finished
h) will let, hear
i) paint, will have
j) will climb, gets/has got

6
1) will
2) have
3) ✓
4) will
5) ✓
6) be
7) not
8) will
9) ✓
10) will
11) ✓
12) be
13) ✓
14) been
15) have

Unit 4

1
a) *do you do*
b) I'm cooking
c) Do you like
d) are you using it
e) do the people here do
f) you turn
g) goes
h) are you reading
i) Are you waiting
j) is building

2 a) *do we do*
   b) are you looking, Am I wearing
   c) am looking after, Do you want
   d) drives
   e) still have, is getting
   f) is Sue dancing
   g) looks, wears
   h) am writing
   i) is not growing, water
   j) do you stay, come

3 a) *future*   f) future
   b) future   g) present
   c) future   h) present
   d) present   i) future
   e) future   j) future

4 writing, beginning, swimming, studying, getting, liking, admitting, trying, annoying, deciding
   a) drop the 'e' and add 'ing'
   b) double the consonant and add 'ing'
   c) add 'ing'

5 a) *This flower smells wonderful.*
   b) I think you are being very silly.
   c) She is having a baby in the summer.
   d) Nancy is thinking of moving to Scotland.
   e) They are having a meeting.
   f) I am seeing Janet this evening actually.
   g) Good clothes are costing more and more.
   h) I am tasting the soup to see if it needs more salt.
   i) Helen is having a bath at the moment.
   j) I feel that you would be happier in another job.

6 1) *I am just writing*
   2) appreciate
   3) am getting on
   4) am really enjoying
   5) am studying
   6) am spending/spend
   7) am still staying
   8) am looking for
   9) live
   10) seem
   11) go
   12) study

13) am writing
14) think
15) costs
16) am saving
17) gets
18) know
19) have
20) am also learning

Unit 5

1 a) Mary is having a
   b) I was having
   c) been working here for
   d) are having a meeting
   e) ages since I had
   f) arrived, David had gone
   g) arrives at
   h) will have
   i) have lost my
   j) started to wear glasses

2 1) decided
   2) had spent
   3) are going to move/are moving
   4) announced
   5) have sold
   6) are going to live
   7) loaded
   8) have been trying
   9) started
   10) was mixing
   11) opened
   12) had told
   13) would be/were going to be/were
   14) spent
   15) have happened
   16) woke up
   17) was dripping
   18) have spent
   19) closed down
   20) haven't found

3 a) Jack had already
   b) you ever driven
   c) I have been to
   d) I was having/eating dinner the
   e) are you doing on
   f) been doing this job for
   g) you own this
   h) going to
   i) will have been married for
   j) last time I went to

4 1) sat
   2) read
   3) was wondering
   4) noticed
   5) began
   6) went
   7) Do you go
   8) have you been putting off
   9) was saying
   10) will hurt/is going to hurt
   11) suddenly realised
   12) had stopped
   13) was opening
   14) opened
   15) called
   16) pushed
   17) was waiting
   18) shouted
   19) Have you ever done
   20) hates

5 1) been   9) ✓
   2) by   10) have
   3) ✓   11) ✓
   4) is   12) I
   5) about   13) will
   6) have   14) at
   7) ✓   15) ✓
   8) are

6 1) B   9) A
   2) D   10) C
   3) A   11) B
   4) A   12) D
   5) C   13) C
   6) B   14) A
   7) D   15) C
   8) C

Unit 6

1 a) *Do you like*
   b) Did you do anything
   c) Does this car belong
   d) Have you seen
   e) When will you get
   f) did you go
   g) did you get
   h) is this

2 a) *'I'll see you tomorrow, Ian,' said Graham.*
   b) 'Your swimming things aren't here, children,' said Pauline.

c) 'Your letter arrived yesterday,' said David.

d) 'I'll see you this evening, Larry,' said Shirley.

e) 'I haven't been at home this morning, Stephen', said Bill.

f) 'Phone me tomorrow, John,' said Margaret.

g) 'I'm leaving this afternoon, Ron,' said Tim.

h) 'I lost my lighter last night, Michael,' said Christine.

3 a) The police officer told Jack *that he couldn't park there.*

b) Peter told Helen that he would see her in the/the next morning.

c) Janet said that she was taking the 5.30 train the next/following evening.

d) Paul told the dry-cleaners that the trousers had to be ready that afternoon.

e) Susan told them that she had left her umbrella there two days earlier/before.

f) Brian said that the parcel ought to be there by the end of the following week.

g) Diana told me that she liked the/that hotel very much.

h) William said that he thought it was going to rain that night.

4 a) I asked *Peter what time the film started.*

b) The interviewer asked Chris if he watched television every evening.

c) The sales manager asked me why I had applied for the/that job.

d) My bank manager wanted to know if I was taking much money with me to France.

e) Maria asked the examiner when she would know the results of the examination.

f) The stewardess asked me if I was enjoying my flight.

g) I asked the salesman how the photocopier worked.

h) Sue asked Paul if he had ever been to Japan.

5 a) *to tell him the time*
b) to open the window
c) to get to the cinema
d) much the bike cost
e) would help me
f) have the car for £500
g) was being a bit silly
h) wouldn't arrive until after eight.

6 a) Do you think you could tell me *what time the next boat leaves?*

b) Can you tell me where I can change some money?

c) Could you possibly tell me where the toilet is?

d) I'd like to know how much this pullover costs.

e) Can you explain how I get to/to get to Victoria station?

f) Could you tell me if this train goes to Gatwick Airport?

g) Would you mind telling me where you come from?

h) Do you think you could tell me what you think of London?

7 a) *told*
b) asked, say
c) told
d) asked, told
e) said
f) said
g) tell
h) told

8 a) *denied*
b) suggested
c) agreed
d) apologised
e) reminded
f) offered
g) admitted/confessed
h) doubted
i) advised
j) promised
k) accused
l) insisted
m) confessed
n) decided
o) refused

9 a) Paul reminded *Sue to buy some bread.*

b) I doubt if/whether it will snow tomorrow.

c) Jill apologised for not phoning me earlier.

d) William advised Chris to see a doctor.

e) Catherine refused to work on Saturday.

f) Wendy suggested going out to the pub for lunch.

g) Larry denied ever having been arrested.

h) Ann offered to help Bob do the decorating.

i) Tom promised the children that he would take them to the park on Sunday.

j) Brenda agreed to share the bill with Dave.

10 1) it
2) to
3) had
4) ✓
5) were
6) had
7) me
8) ✓
9) them
10) ✓
11) were
12) ✓
13) was
14) that
15) ✓

Unit 7

1 a) *stops, press*
b) treated, would be
c) help me, will do
d) leaves, will arrive
e) it is, will go
f) find, will get
g) take, will lose
h) I'd be, lived
i) did, would play
j) phone, will you be

2 a) *had told, would have helped*
b) hadn't stolen, wouldn't be
c) hadn't driven, wouldn't have crashed
d) smoked, wouldn't feel
e) hadn't fallen, would have won
f) had invited, would have been able
g) had come, would have noticed
h) would you feel, offered
i) lent, would pay
j) caught, would throw

3 a) *had known*, would have met
b) had come, would have met
c) had, would be able
d) hadn't helped, wouldn't have passed
e) would buy, had
f) would do, won
g) trained, would be
h) had listened, wouldn't have married
i) hadn't taken, wouldn't have had
j) bought, wouldn't look

4 a) 1
b) 3
c) 2
d) 2
e) 3

5 a) I wouldn't *have got wet if I'd had an umbrella with me.*
b) Unless you leave me alone, I'll call the police.
c) If it's snowing, we don't go to school.
d) If Jack hadn't helped me, I wouldn't have been able to move the table.
e) If you drank less coffee/didn't drink so much coffee, you would be able to sleep.
f) If you press this button, the machine stops/will stop.
g) If you make me some coffee, I'll give you one of my biscuits.
h) Unless you'd told me about Sue's hair, I wouldn't have noticed.
i) If you should see Peter, tell him to be here at 8.00.
j) If you were to ask me to marry you, I wouldn't accept.

6 a) *If I'd known, I'd have told you.*
b) Tony wouldn't have crashed if he'd been more careful.
c) If you asked me, I'd tell you.
d) If I'd had my credit card with me, I'd have bought the coat.
e) You wouldn't have got lost if you'd taken the map.
f) If you'd asked me for a loan I could have given you one.
g) If Graham hadn't lost his watch he wouldn't have missed his plane.

h) If you hadn't told me her name I would have found out from someone.
i) If I were you, I'd try getting up earlier.
j) No-one would have realised if Peter hadn't told them.

Unit 8

1 a) *didn't live*
b) had brought
c) didn't have to
d) had told
e) wouldn't make
f) could be
g) had come
h) would give
i) were
j) hadn't bought

2 a) *had gone*
b) had
c) would do
d) hadn't forgotten
e) wouldn't do
f) hadn't eaten
g) had studied
h) wouldn't leave
i) knew
j) went/could go

3 a) *paid*
b) lived
c) had
d) left
e) didn't tell
f) hadn't drunk
g) practised
h) learned
i) knew
j) stayed

4 a) *knew*
b) were
c) didn't smoke
d) saw
e) had been
f) started
g) didn't put
h) had
i) had
j) went

5 a) *could fly*
b) you didn't eat in the
c) time we
d) only we hadn't eaten
e) wish we had
f) wish you wouldn't
g) sooner you didn't
h) wish I wasn't/weren't
i) time we started
j) wish I had gone

6 1) have
2) have
3) ✓
4) the
5) have
6) to
7) ✓
8) would
9) prefer
10) ✓
11) it
12) have
13) ✓
14) been
15) ✓

Unit 9

1 a) *has being*
b) was borned
e) will been sent
i) is writing
j) are request

2 a) *hasn't been finished*
b) were arrested
c) had been born
d) will be cancelled
e) had stopped
f) were you told
g) were swimming
h) was ridden
i) had vanished
j) will be asked

3 a) *has already been sold*
b) was knocked down
c) was John given/will John be given
d) was not discovered
e) are dealt with/will be dealt with
f) has since been discovered
g) was announced
h) have been asked
i) was written
j) being invited

4
a) *not possible*
b) Most of the food at the party was eaten.
c) The poetry competition was won by Jane.
d) not possible
e) not possible
f) This cigarette lighter was lost by one of our visitors.
g) The exact time of the match hasn't been decided yet.
h) not possible
i) Some children are read to by their parents every night.
j) not possible

5
a) *marketing manager was appointed*
b) is being supplied with furniture
c) was built by
d) has been decided
e) is believed that Jenkins was
f) to get your hair
g) were being followed by the
h) has not been seen since
i) about the trip was put
j) is thought to be good

6
a) *We had our house painted last month.*
b) I am having my hair cut this afternoon.
c) I have had my motorbike stolen.
d) Ricky has had all his teeth taken out.
e) I haven't had my car washed for a long time.
f) We are having the new central heating put in on Saturday.
g) Harry had his nose broken in a fight.
h) Isn't it time you had your television fixed?
i) Helen has just had her book published.
j) Nigel had his car towed away.

7
a) *Freddie is said to have a wife in Scotland.*
b) Nothing is known about Brenda's family.
c) The fire is thought to have been started deliberately./It is thought that the fire was started deliberately.

d) You should have that cut seen to by a doctor.
e) Chris is said to have been in the army.
It is said that Chris was in the army.
f) I must have my trousers pressed before I leave.
g) This letter has not been signed.
h) Mary hasn't had her hair cut yet.
i) Norma is believed to be living in Paris./It is believed that Norma is living in Paris.
j) It has been decided that smoking is no longer allowed in the school.

8
1) it
2) to
3) it
4) were
5) ✓
6) when
7) was
8) ✓
9) and
10) to
11) ✓
12) ✓
13) is
14) ✓
15) was

Unit 10

1
a) 2
b) 1
c) 2
d) 1

2
a) rather you didn't
b) what the time/what time it
c) won't go out unless
d) wish you were
e) said (that) I couldn't
f) advise you
g) wish we had seen
h) told us his
i) me what time the next
j) accused me of

3
1) B
2) D
3) A
4) D
5) C
6) B
7) B
8) C
9) A
10) B
11) A
12) C
13) A
14) B
15) C

4
1) was walking
2) started
3) will get
4) reach
5) had remembered
6) had left
7) am always forgetting/always forget
8) Are you going
9) do you want
10) took
11) don't change
12) will fall
13) won't be able
14) have been practising
15) will wait
16) like
17) relaxed
18) have been worrying
19) worry
20) fall

5
a) are you being served
b) time we went
c) had our house painted
d) wish Charles wouldn't complain
e) will be met
f) is thought to have
g) reminded her Mum to
h) you been paid
i) get the letters finished
j) was made to study

6
1) is extracted
2) are mixed
3) dissolves
4) is also found
5) contain
6) be called
7) is made up
8) is used
9) lasts
10) eat
11) also eat
12) believe
13) is eaten
14) is said
15) has been definitely proved
16) is known
17) causes
18) damaged
19) damages
20) would be banned

7
1) ✓
2) so
3) ✓
4) up
5) like
6) that
7) ✓
8) was
9) to
10) ✓
11) been
12) me
13) us
14) ✓
15) they

Unit 11

1
a) *who*
b) none
c) none
d) that
e) which
f) none
g) which
h) none
i) who
j) that

2
a) *that I told you about*
b) not possible
c) not possible
d) that arrested her
e) that knows you
f) that have been damaged
g) not possible
h) not possible
i) that serves very good meals
j) that park outside

3
a) *defining*
b) defining
c) non-defining
d) defining
e) non-defining
f) defining
g) non-defining
h) non-defining
i) defining
j) non-defining

4
a) *whose*
b) that
c) that
d) which
e) which
f) which
g) who
h) whose
i) which
j) that

5
a) *whose, who/that*
b) which
c) blank, blank
d) which
e) blank
f) who
g) blank, blank
h) blank
i) whose
j) blank

6
a) Brenda is *the friend who I went on holiday with.*
b) This is Mr Smith, whose son Bill plays in our team.
c) Her book, which was published last year, became a best seller.
d) This is the bank from which we borrowed the money.
e) The person who I told you about is at the door.
f) Jack, whose car had broken down, had to take a bus.

7
a) The hotel, which *was miles from anywhere, was full of guests who had gone there to admire the scenery.*
b) The book I lent you was written by a friend of mine who lives in France.
c) The woman whose jewels were stolen was interviewed by a police officer who was staying in the same hotel.
d) The goal which won the match was scored by a teenager who had come on as substitute.
e) The boy I was sitting next to in the exam told me the answers.
f) My wallet, which contained over £100, was found in the street by a schoolboy who returned it/was returned by a schoolboy who found it in the street.
g) My friend Albert, whose car was stolen last week, has decided to buy a motorbike.
h) Carol, who is a vegetarian, enjoyed the meal I cooked for her last week.

8
1) *who*
2) who
3) whom
4) blank
5) who
6) which
7) whose
8) which
9) who
10) which
11) which
12) which
13) blank
14) whose
15) who

9
a) *Margaret is the girl I went on holiday with.*
b) The golf club is the only club I am a member of.
c) That's the girl we were talking about.
d) It was a wonderful present, which I was extremely grateful for.
e) This is the school I used to go to.
f) Is this the case we should put the wine-glasses in?
g) Can you move the chair you are sitting on?
h) That's the shop I got my shoes from.
i) Is that the person you usually sit next to?
j) This is Bill, who you've heard so much about.

10
a) *The train I got on didn't stop at the station I wanted to go to.*
b) The book I read was the book/one you recommended to me.
c) The ship, which had ignored the warning messages sent to it, hit an iceberg and sank.
d) The postman, who realised I was on holiday, left the parcel you (had) sent me next door.
e) The dog I used to own never barked at people who came to the door.
f) The woman I bought my car from lives in the house you can see over there.
g) The beach we went to on the first day of our holiday was covered in seaweed which smelled a lot.
h) My neighbours, whose three small children make a lot of noise, never apologise.
i) The new typewriter I bought cost me a lot of money.
j) The wallet I lost last week was found by a workman who was digging a hole in the street outside our house.

Unit 12

1
a) *to, off*
b) between, opposite
c) in, in
d) on, near
e) in, on
f) against, in
g) on, over

h) in, at
i) at, in
j) into, onto

2 a) *instead of*
b) Regardless of
c) In case of
d) in favour of
e) on behalf of
f) Apart from
g) As for
h) by means of
i) Because of
j) According to
k) in common with
l) in front of

3 a) *possible*
b) not possible
c) possible
d) possible
e) possible
f) possible
g) possible
h) possible
i) not possible
j) possible

4 a) *off*　　　f) by
b) At　　　g) without
c) in　　　h) on
d) out of　　i) to
e) under　　j) for

5 a) *in bed*
b) on time
c) in all
d) out of reach
e) by chance
f) out of doors
g) at present
h) in common
i) on the way
j) on business

6 a) *costs*　　f) strike
b) words　　g) secret
c) impression　h) stock
d) hurry　　i) return
e) fail　　　j) breath

7 a) *profit*　　f) sight
b) himself　　g) particular
c) public　　h) whole
d) practice　　i) detail
e) average　　j) force

8 a) *in two*
b) on holiday
c) without a doubt
d) out of work
e) by sight
f) in difficulties
g) by heart
h) in turn
i) in pain
j) on sale

9 a) *under orders*
b) From now on
c) out of danger
d) in person
e) out of tune
f) at any rate
g) in private
h) out of order
i) by surprise
j) by all means

10 1) the　　　9) ✓
2) by　　　10) the
3) ✓　　　11) this
4) to　　　12) ✓
5) an　　　13) the
6) ✓　　　14) in
7) as　　　15) ✓
8) with

Unit 13

1 a) *to buy*
b) to eat
c) Though
d) Although
e) so as to be
f) though
g) so windy
h) too small
i) the weather
j) so much

2 a) *went shopping to buy herself*
b) is (used) for opening
c) so (that) it would get
d) left early so as not
e) so (that) I could buy
f) in order to save
g) came here to see
h) money is for buying the
i) so that it wouldn't
j) so (that) the rabbit couldn't

3 a) Sam was *so lazy that he lost his job*.
b) The house was too expensive for me to buy.
c) It was such an interesting book that I couldn't put it down.
d) There was so much noise that we couldn't hear the speech.
e) The house wasn't large/big enough to live in comfortably.
f) William is so careful that he never makes mistakes when he reads.
William is so careful a reader that he never makes mistakes.
g) There is too little time for us to eat now.
h) I'm too busy to come to your party.
i) There were so few students that the class was cancelled.
j) It's so lovely today that I feel like taking a walk.
It's so lovely a day today that I feel like taking a walk.

4 a) *enough*　　f) so
b) such　　　g) too
c) so　　　h) so
d) not　　　i) enough
e) such　　　j) such

5 a) Although *it was cold, we all went for a walk*.
b) While John has done well in French, he has not done so well in Maths.
c) Although I tried to persuade her, I didn't succeed.
d) In spite of the rain, I went swimming.
e) Although I like fish, I don't like catching them myself.
f) Despite feeling ill, Ann insisted on going to work.
g) Although I rang the doorbell, nobody answered.
h) Although he had an early lead, Hudson lost the race.
i) While I know that I should pay, I'm not going to.
j) Even though Larry was expected to accept the job, he didn't.

6 a) *It's for painting things.*
b) They're for cutting things.
c) It's for sticking things.
d) It's for boiling water.
e) It's for keeping things cold.
f) It's for washing dishes in.
g) It's for putting rubbish in.
h) It's for cleaning your teeth with.
i) It's for opening wine bottles with.
j) It's for locking doors with.

7 1) to
2) ✓
3) even
4) the
5) so
6) ✓
7) in
8) ✓
9) so
10) ✓
11) however
12) so
13) ✓
14) too
15) so

Unit 14

1 a) *since*
b) later
c) yesterday evening
d) in
e) yet
f) in the afternoon
g) recently
h) on Thursday night
i) since
j) one day

2 a) *last*
b) in
c) already
d) soon
e) next
f) past
g) once
h) ago
i) early
j) just

3 a) *nowadays*
b) eventually
c) lately
d) yet
e) afterwards
f) soon
g) in the end
h) once
i) immediately
j) early

4 a) *at, before*
b) tonight
c) this
d) then
e) now
f) yet
g) on
h) by
i) after
j) Once

5 a) *B*
b) D
c) A
d) B
e) B
f) C
g) D
h) C
i) A
j) B

6 a) *one at a time*
b) over and over again
c) once and for all
d) in the nick of time
e) in a few moments
f) all the time
g) for hours on end
h) This time next week
i) all the year round
j) the other day
k) from time to time
l) all night long

7 a) *B*
b) A
c) A
d) C
e) A
f) B
g) A
h) C
i) A
j) C

Unit 15

1 1) which/that
2) in
3) at
4) so
5) through
6) to
7) who
8) on
9) which/that
10) of
11) although
12) until
13) later
14) by
15) who

2 a) by
b) later
c) lately/recently
d) at
e) until
f) for
g) in
h) once
i) other
j) now

3 a) about
b) whose
c) despite
d) to
e) whom
f) in
g) although
h) by
i) whom
j) on

4 a) That is the man from whom I bought my car.
b) That's the boy whose sister sits behind me at school.
c) Bill, whose typewriter had broken, had to use a pencil.
d) The girls, who were hungry, decided to have a meal.
e) I live in Croydon, which is near London.
f) Is this the book that I lent you?/ Is this the book (that) you borrowed?
g) This is Brenda, who lives upstairs.
h) The present which you gave me is very useful.
i) The car, which was in good condition, wasn't expensive. The car, which wasn't
j) The person who found the money was given a reward.

5 a) at, near/beside
b) in, on/over
c) in, case
d) under, on
e) in, on
f) by, for
g) in, in
h) on, by
i) in, by
j) out, by

6 a) this time last
b) despite having/despite his
c) was too hot to
d) so tired that she
e) so as not
f) even though I knew
g) so many people that
h) in spite of the fine
i) such a cold night that
j) wasn't deep enough to/was too shallow to

7 1) B 9) A
2) C 10) C
3) A 11) B
4) A 12) D
5) B 13) B
6) D 14) A
7) C 15) C
8) D

8 1) although 9) and
2) in 10) so
3) before 11) ✓
4) ✓ 12) in
5) so 13) ✓
6) ✓ 14) ✓
7) they 15) of
8) an

Unit 16

1 a) *must be*
b) don't have to
c) had better
d) could be
e) have to go
f) can't be
g) have to
h) should win
i) might not
j) should do

2 a) *had better give up*
b) should be/get there by
c) I have to bring
d) must be
e) have to have/use
f) you are unable to
g) can't be
h) is bound to be
i) are to report
j) ought to know

3 a) *I don't believe it*
b) She always is
c) It's the rule
d) if you don't want to
e) It's only natural
f) It isn't allowed
g) It's the rule
h) It's not a good idea
i) I expect so
j) That's my advice

4 a) *might* f) might not
b) might g) can't
c) must h) might
d) can i) must
e) can't j) mustn't

5 a) *Helen must feel really lonely.*
b) You can't/mustn't park here.
c) Harry should take a holiday.
d) Brenda can't be over thirty.
e) Do I have to have a different
driving licence for a motorbike?
f) What do you think I should do?
g) Mary can stand on her head.
h) You don't have to come with me
if you don't want to.
i) Anybody can/could break into
this house.
j) The dentist will see you soon.
He shouldn't be long.

6 a) 2 d) 1
b) 2 e) 1
c) 1 f) 2

Unit 17

1 a) *1* f) 2
b) 2 g) 1
c) 2 h) 2
d) 2 i) 2
e) 1 j) 2

2 a) *needn't have gone out*
b) was to have become
c) shouldn't have bought
d) can't have enjoyed
e) may have seen
f) must have been
g) might not have meant
h) could have left
i) shouldn't have sold your
j) had to

3 a) *We've missed the turning.*
b) That's why I liked it.
c) There is no other explanation.
d) Why didn't you?
e) There is plenty.
f) I suppose it's possible.
g) I'm sure you haven't.
h) It's the wrong kind.

4 a) *David must have taken your
books by mistake.*
b) You shouldn't have parked
outside the police station.
c) You needn't have cleaned this
floor.
d) Liz can't have met Harry before.
e) Ann might not have left yet.
f) They can't have eaten all the
food.
g) Jack should have arrived half an
hour ago.
h) Pam and Tim might have
decided not to come.
i) The cat must have taken the fish
from the table.
j) You needn't have worried after
all.

5 a) 2 d) 2
b) 2 e) 1
c) 1 f) 1

6 1) ✓ 9) ✓
2) to 10) didn't
3) gone 11) had
4) ✓ 12) ✓
5) have 13) have
6) be 14) have
7) be 15) ✓
8) been

Unit 18

1 a) *4* f) 5
b) 10 g) 9
c) 6 h) 2
d) 1 i) 7
e) 8 j) 3

2 a) 6 f) 4
b) 10 g) 5
c) 1 h) 3
d) 2 i) 7
e) 8 j) 9

3 a) *1* f) 2
b) 1 g) 2
c) 2 h) 1
d) 1 i) 1
e) 2 j) 2

4 a) *you like a lift*
b) you tell me what time
c) were you I'd sell
d) you like me to
e) this the right way for
f) wish you wouldn't make
g) you think I should
h) about going for
i) it's my
j) think you should

Unit 19

1 a) *5* f) 6
b) 8 g) 4
c) 1 h) 3
d) 10 i) 7
e) 2 j) 9

2 a) *4* f) 5
b) 8 g) 9
c) 2 h) 10
d) 7 i) 3
e) 1 j) 6

3 a) *1* f) 2
b) 2 g) 2
c) 2 h) 1
d) 1 i) 1
e) 1 j) 2

4 a) you think of
b) am grateful
c) all right if I
d) don't we go
e) rather go sailing than
f) you think you could open
g) you mind taking
h) should go
i) are in my
j) Ron on passing his

5 1) a 9) to
2) are 10) it
3) ✓ 11) ✓
4) an 12) ever
5) ✓ 13) to
6) with 14) ✓
7) ✓ 15) it
8) to

Unit 20

1 1) had 9) should
2) should 10) should
3) miss 11) have
4) on 12) couldn't
5) must 13) could
6) can/could 14) gave
7) is 15) able
8) ought

2 a) apologise for breaking
b) me how to get to
c) would you like some
d) think you should buy a
e) can't have left
f) must be
g) might/could have been
h) needn't have
i) should have been
j) could be

3 1) ✓ 9) ✓
2) have 10) not
3) be 11) ✓
4) ✓ 12) or
5) ✓ 13) been
6) if 14) done
7) am 15) be
8) can

4 a) 2 f) 3
b) 1 g) 1
c) 3 h) 3
d) 1 i) 1
e) 2 j) 2

5 1) C 9) D
2) D 10) C
3) B 11) D
4) A 12) A
5) C 13) A
6) C 14) C
7) B 15) B
8) A

Unit 21

1 a) *weather*
b) hairs
c) chicken
d) businesses
e) works
f) baggage
g) thunder and lightning
h) papers
i) toast
j) accommodation

2 a) blank
b) some/blank
c) blank
d) blank/some
e) an
f) an
g) a
h) some
i) some
j) a

3 a) *journey* f) car park
b) paper g) cold
c) timetable h) licence
d) luggage i) beach
e) loaf j) friends

4 a) *accommodation*
b) advice
c) education
d) paper
e) information/advice
f) job
g) fruit
h) hair
i) help
j) scissors

5 a) *B* f) B
b) A g) A
c) C h) C
d) D i) D
e) A j) B

6 a) 2 f) 2
b) 1 g) 1
c) 2 h) 2
d) 2 i) 1
e) 1 j) 2

7 a) *are a lot of people*
   b) these your
   c) had good weather
   d) was a lot of/lots of traffic
   e) has great strength
   f) is litter
   g) have definitely made
   h) parking allowed
   i) this machinery is
   j) a loaf

8 a) *piece*   f) head
   b) item   g) slice
   c) flight   h) set
   d) sheet   i) blade
   e) lump   j) clap

9 a) *bread*
   b) spelling
   c) parking
   d) cash
   e) information
   f) lightning
   g) advice
   h) luggage
   i) cookery
   j) accommodation

10 1) B   9) D
   2) A   10) A
   3) C   11) B
   4) C   12) D
   5) B   13) B
   6) D   14) A
   7) A   15) D
   8) C

Unit 22

1 a) *blank, the*
   b) the, the, the
   c) the, blank, blank
   d) blank, the, the
   e) the/blank, the, blank
   f) the, blank
   g) blank, blank
   h) the, blank
   i) the, the, a
   j) the, blank

2 a) *the person*
   b) the only cinema
   c) a Thames barge
   d) the thousand pounds
   e) church

f) a milk jug
g) The Prime Minister
h) The computer
i) an open-air theatre
j) the British Museum

3 a) C   f) D
   b) B   g) C
   c) A   h) B
   d) B   i) C
   e) D   j) A

4 (Suggested) a) *9*
              b) 1
              c) 4
              d) 3
              e) 7
              f) 6
              g) 2
              h) 10
              i) 5
              j) 8

5 a) *the, the*
   b) an, the, the
   c) blank, the
   d) the, blank, blank
   e) blank, blank, blank
   f) the, blank, the
   g) the, blank, blank
   h) blank, a, blank
   i) the, blank, the, a
   j) a, a

6 a) *only problem here is*
   b) good on at the cinema
   c) that the fastest you
   d) the first time I have
   e) French drink
   f) faster you drive the more
   g) truth is difficult to
   h) play the piano
   i) one at a
   j) film of Hamlet on

7 a) *under the impression*
   b) in a hurry
   c) at a profit
   d) on the whole
   e) on average
   f) in pain
   g) out of danger
   h) in the way
   i) the cross-channel ferry
   j) the back of my neck

8 a) *the, blank, a*
   b) the, the, the, the
   c) a, blank, the, blank
   d) blank, blank, a
   e) blank, blank
   f) a, blank
   g) a, blank
   h) the, blank, a, blank
   i) the, a/the, blank, the
   j) a, the, the

Unit 23

1 a) *This is all the money I have left.*
   b) There were no people at the meeting.
   c) Neither singer/of the singers had a good voice.
   d) None of the cups is clean.
   e) All the people were cheering loudly.
   f) Each of you deserves promotion/You each deserve promotion.
   g) I read both books but I didn't like either of them.
   h) Every time I cross the Channel by boat I feel seasick.
   i) All I had/ate for lunch was a sandwich.
   j) There are parking meters on either side of the street.

2 a) Each *person in the office was given a personal parking space.*
   b) There are no good hotels in this town.
   c) All you need is love.
   d) Neither of these pens writes properly.
   e) Each of us is responsible for our own actions.
   f) We all feel lonely sometimes.
   g) None of the shops is open.
   h) Neither job was suitable for Helen.
   i) The cakes have all been eaten.
   j) Unfortunately the meal was no different from/than usual.

3 a) C   f) B
   b) D   g) A
   c) A   h) B
   d) A   i) C
   e) D   j) B

4 a) *either*　　f) all
   b) no　　　　　g) either
   c) each　　　　h) each
   d) every　　　 i) none
   e) no　　　　　j) every

5 a) *every Thursday*
   b) none of your
   c) all (of) the seats
   d) no lorries are allowed
   e) day it gets
   f) couldn't understand either
   g) want to do is listen
   h) fewer than 20,000 people
   i) children were given
   j) is not time to

6 1) the　　　　9) ✓
   2) the　　　 10) a
   3) ✓　　　　11) ✓
   4) one　　　 12) ✓
   5) a　　　　 13) the
   6) ✓　　　　14) ✓
   7) any　　　 15) the
   8) of

Unit 24

1 a) *than*　　f) as
   b) as　　　　g) little
   c) as　　　　h) harder
   d) much　　　i) does
   e) less　　　j) did

2 a) Peter *can't run as fast as Jill (can)*.
   b) This journey didn't last as long as I thought it would.
   c) I arrived later than I expected.
   d) You'll have to work harder/faster.
   e) I have an elder/older brother.
   f) Martin didn't think the first part of the film was as interesting.
   g) Paul has been working less carefully than before.
   h) This is the earliest train.
   i) This pub is the nearest.
   j) Can't you offer a better price?

3 a) C　　　　f) C
   b) B　　　　g) B
   c) A　　　　h) A
   d) D　　　　i) C
   e) D　　　　j) B

4 a) *better*　　f) hottest
   b) most　　　 g) better
   c) latest　　 h) further
   d) happier　　i) best
   e) deeper　　 j) worst

5 a) I've never eaten a *better meal*.
   b) Fish costs just as much as meat in some countries.
   c) I've never had such a good time.
   d) The more you run, the fitter you will get.
   e) Wednesday is the earliest the doctor can see you, I'm afraid.
   f) I must have a rest, I can't go (on) any further.
   g) Home computers aren't as expensive as they used to be.
   h) Sue knows more Italian than I do.
   i) Learning to drive isn't as difficult as I thought it would be./is easier than I thought it would be.
   j) John isn't a better skater than Barbara.

6 a) *cost less than mine*
   b) are better at maths than
   c) is a little taller than
   d) was growing angrier and
   e) did her
   f) isn't/wasn't as good as
   g) driven along such a bumpy
   h) more you eat, the fatter
   i) was the best he could
   j) was just as difficult as

7 1) ✓　　　　9) ✓
   2) so　　　 10) it
   3) more　　 11) and
   4) the　　　12) the
   5) the　　　13) ✓
   6) ✓　　　　14) ✓
   7) than　　 15) that
   8) of

Unit 25

1 1) every　　　9) most
   2) the　　　 10) the
   3) come　　　11) the
   4) the　　　 12) some
   5) that　　　13) none
   6) the　　　 14) a
   7) neither　 15) more
   8) which

2 a) never seen a worse
   b) all the sandwiches have been
   c) latest novel is not as
   d) talk to either of
   e) can't swim as well
   f) slowly you walk, the longer
   g) no good calling
   h) was the last person I
   i) never been to such a
   j) cost less than I (had)

3 a) slice　　　f) lumps
   b) flight　　 g) glass
   c) head　　　 h) helping
   d) sheet　　　i) clap
   e) item　　　 j) pair

4 a) Parking is not allowed here/There is no parking here.
   b) There is no/There isn't any furniture in the house.
   c) There seem to be a lot of people in this city.
   d) Can you give me any information about guided tours of the city?
   e) The audience was enthusiastic.
   f) Maths is my favourite subject.
   g) There is a lot of traffic on this road today.
   h) Sue has gone to the theatre.
   i) I'm looking for accommodation.
   j) Jim doesn't have a job at the moment.

5 a) works as a French
   b) was the first man
   c) that the best you can
   d) first lobster I have ever
   e) play the violin
   f) all you need is
   g) of the lifts was
   h) [that] every Friday he goes
   i) couldn't lift either
   j) earns £15,000 a

6 a) them　　　f) is
   b) some　　　g) a
   c) some　　　h) the
   d) it　　　　i) the
   e) some　　　j) the

7 1) here
   2) more
   3) ✓
   4) the
   5) were
   6) ✓
   7) one
   8) of
   9) both
   10) ✓
   11) ✓
   12) than
   13) a
   14) ✓
   15) such

Unit 26

1 a) *Sorry, but I haven't got round to fixing your bike yet.*
   b) Oh bother, we have run out of milk.
   c) It took me a long time to get over my illness.
   d) Peter takes after his father.
   e) I think we've come up with an answer to the problem.
   f) I don't think I feel up to playing football today.
   g) Ann is someone I really look up to.
   h) I must see about having the kitchen painted.
   i) Please help me, I'm counting on you.
   j) Julie must have grown out of biting her nails.

2 a) *ran into Philip*
   b) have to face up to
   c) women stood up for their
   d) put up with so much
   e) got away with
   f) called on a few friends
   g) are you getting
   h) and get my teeth seen
   i) get on with your
   j) have come into all

3 a) *for*
   b) up
   c) against
   d) on
   e) in
   f) across
   g) round
   h) with
   i) into
   j) to

4 a) C
   b) D
   c) B
   d) A
   e) C
   f) D
   g) A
   h) B
   i) D
   j) C

5 a) *B*
   b) B
   c) C
   d) B
   e) A
   f) C
   g) C
   h) A
   i) C
   j) C

Unit 27

1 a) *Jack always turns up late for work.*
   b) Look up their number in the phone directory.
   c) I'm putting money aside to buy a new bike.
   d) A large black limousine drew up outside the house.
   e) I'm afraid the match has been called off.
   f) The government refused to give in to the demands of the terrorists.
   g) We offered them £100,000 for the house but they turned down our offer/turned it down.
   h) We can put you up if you come to Cambridge.
   i) I can't work out how much the whole trip will cost.
   j) After a few days the pain in Dave's leg wore off.

2 a) *round/around*
   b) up
   c) out
   d) off
   e) up
   f) out
   g) up
   h) out
   i) off
   j) out

3 a) *rain has set in for*
   b) how to fill in
   c) took over this job
   d) have made up this
   e) thinking it over
   f) you held up
   g) broke down
   h) to give up (drinking)
   i) has been put off until
   j) has just been taken over

4 a) *carried*
   b) take
   c) give
   d) try
   e) clear
   f) worn
   g) falls
   h) went
   i) come
   j) fill

5 a) *C*
   b) A
   c) D
   d) C
   e) C
   f) A
   g) B
   h) D
   i) C
   j) A

6 a) *made up*
   b) come out
   c) clearing up
   d) work out
   e) look out
   f) give up
   g) take over
   h) take off
   i) fallen out
   j) show off

7 a) *B*
   b) C
   c) A
   d) B
   e) A
   f) C
   g) B
   h) C
   i) A
   j) C

Unit 28

1 a) *playing*
   b) to write
   c) meeting
   d) to pay
   e) buying
   f) working
   g) to feed
   h) to meet
   i) taking
   j) not having

2 a) *denied cheating*
   b) couldn't help laughing
   c) regret to tell you that
   d) to drink some/to get a drink of
   e) avoided paying
   f) suggest taking
   g) to turn off the lights
   h) can hear someone talking
   i) appears to have forgotten
   j) threatened to call

3 a) *to eat*
   b) not to sell
   c) seeing/having seen
   d) not to notice/not to have noticed
   e) starting/having started
   f) to buy
   g) living
   h) moving/having moved
   i) waiting
   j) to finish/to have finished

4 a) *demanded* f) refused
b) fancy g) risk
c) bear h) expect
d) mind i) intend
e) happen j) keep

Unit 29

1 a) *in* f) with
b) of g) at
c) of/like h) to
d) at/by i) about
e) on j) to

2 a) The old lady was *robbed of her handbag*.
b) John is interested in photography.
c) Helen knows a lot about car engines.
d) France is famous for its food.
e) I am very grateful to your brother for his help.
f) Can you share this book with Stephen?
g) I'm not used to studying all night.
h) Harry is afraid of snakes.
i) Please forgive me for breaking your camera.
j) Peter is good at drawing.

3 a) *ashamed*
b) keen
c) talking/boasting
d) late
e) full
f) trust
g) accused
h) succeeded
i) pleased
j) begins/began

4 a) *is capable of*
b) belongs to
c) applied for
d) died of
e) congratulated Tony on passing
f) lent Jean her
g) not certain
h) was bored by
i) felt sorry for
j) should be kind to

5 a) *angry* f) reminds
b) agree g) jealous
c) approve h) surprised
d) argued i) add
e) look j) ask

6 a) *B* f) B
b) A g) A
c) D h) C
d) C i) D
e) A j) B

7 1) with 9) them
2) to 10) ✓
3) about 11) us
4) ✓ 12) ✓
5) and 13) and
6) for 14) ✓
7) ✓ 15) last
8) up

Unit 30

1 1) grew
2) put
3) join
4) wore
5) getting
6) deal
7) take
8) spent
9) showing
10) getting
11) got
12) grown
13) taken
14) talking/thinking
15) face

2 a) get round to
b) get on
c) getting at
d) got over
e) got away

3 a) come out
b) come up with
c) came across
d) came into
e) come up against

4 a) miss working
b) will mean moving to
c) regrets having sold his
d) forget to post
e) to learn how to

f) denied stealing
g) you like to go to
h) mind looking after the
i) promised (that) she would be there
j) our first meeting in

5 a) keep
b) stand
c) relying/counting/depending
d) looking
e) seen
f) clear
g) knocked
h) turned
i) wore
j) breaking

6 1) B 9) B
2) D 10) D
3) C 11) A
4) C 12) C
5) A 13) B
6) D 14) C
7) B 15) A
8) A

7 a) capable of
b) fond of
c) ashamed of
d) good of
e) jealous of

8 a) certain about
b) unhappy about
c) right about
d) anxious about
e) upset about

9 a) washing
b) looking
c) bringing
d) taking
e) doing/going

10 a) taking f) takes
b) got g) turned
c) put h) think
d) made i) clear/clean
e) getting j) keep/catch

11 a) to look into
b) we have run out of
c) fill in
d) broke out
e) getting at

f) won't stand for
g) leave out
h) come across
i) take over
j) got round to it

Unit 31

1 a) *shall we*   f) will you
   b) should you   g) can he
   c) has he   h) haven't you
   d) will you   i) didn't they
   e) are you   j) is he

2 a) *will you*   f) do you
   b) isn't he   g) does it
   c) won't you   h) shall we
   d) wasn't he   i) are you
   e) do they   j) doesn't she

3 a) Not only *was Tony late, but he had left all his books behind.*
   b) No sooner had I gone to bed than someone rang my doorbell.
   c) Seldom have I stayed in a worse hotel.
   d) Never have I heard such nonsense.
   e) Only then did I realise that I had lost my keys.
   f) Rarely has the economic situation been worse.
   g) Not once did the manager offer us an apology.
   h) Under no circumstances should you send money to us by post.
   i) Only after seeing 'Hamlet' on the stage did I understand it.
   j) Little did the embassy staff realise that Ted was a secret agent.

4 a) *Now is the best time to buy a house.*
   b) Round the corner came the bus.
   c) Up went the price of petrol.
   d) On the top of the Acropolis stands the Parthenon.
   e) Round and round went the wheels of the engine.
   f) In this house lived Winston Churchill.
   g) Down went the flag.
   h) Now comes the best part of the story.

5 1) C   9) C
   2) A   10) A
   3) D   11) A
   4) A   12) B
   5) B   13) C
   6) C   14) D
   7) D   15) D
   8) B

Unit 32

1 a) *However*
   b) as
   c) First of all, In addition to this, As a result
   d) moreover, In contrast, Personally
   e) Owing to, Consequently

2 a) *In*
   b) As/Since
   c) as
   d) on
   e) of
   f) well
   g) For
   h) view/opinion

3 1) A   6) C
   2) D   7) D
   3) C   8) B
   4) A   9) D
   5) B   10) B

Unit 33

1 a) Whatever *you do, don't tell Jane I was here.*
   b) Whoever stole the painting must have been tall.
   c) Whatever is the time?
   d) Why ever did you tell me a lie?
   e) Whenever I go on goliday, the weather gets worse.
   f) Wherever have you been?
   g) However did you know I was going to be here?
   h) Wherever I hang my hat I call home.
   i) Whatever you say, I won't believe you.
   j) Whatever you're going to do, do it now!

2 a) *gave me a pat on*
   b) pick a rabbit up by
   c) Tanya in the face
   d) grabbed the thief by the
   e) took the baby by the
   f) stung me on the
   g) punched me in the
   h) patted the dog on the
   i) wounded in the arm
   j) pat me on the

3 a) There *is a good film on at the local cinema* at the moment.
   b) It's impossible for me to drink coffee so late at night.
   c) It doesn't matter if you can't answer all the questions.
   d) There is a storm coming, I think.
   e) There is nothing in the fridge.
   f) It has been a tiring journey.
   g) There won't be any beer left if you don't hurry.
   h) It is a long way to the station.
   i) It's time for a break now.
   j) It was good to see you.

4 a) Did you *enjoy yourself at the beach, Joe*?
   b) What we really need is a new fridge.
   c) It's very foggy today.
   d) Anyone who believes in ghosts is a bit crazy!
   e) Whenever you need me, just call me.
   f) It was interesting to talk to you.
   g) John has hurt himself
   h) Whatever did you do that for?
   i) It doesn't matter.
   j) I made these bookshelves myself.

5 a) C   f) A
   b) D   g) D
   c) B   h) D
   d) A   i) A
   e) C   j) B

Unit 34

1 a) *studying*, receipt
   b) destroying, wonderful
   c) donkeys, swimming
   d) flies, regretted
   e) niece, hopefully
   f) hurried, applying

g) furniture, heard
h) enough, insurance
i) welcome, happily
j) hotter, advertisement

2 a) *search*   f) come
   b) wait   g) cow
   c) stuff   h) white
   d) go   i) plumber
   e) home   j) store

3 a) *supplying*   f) cries
   b) destroyed   g) silliness
   c) applied   h) annoys
   d) loneliness   i) beautiful
   e) employs   j) prettiness

4 a) *cold*   f) iced
   b) treat   g) gone
   c) blouse   h) heart
   d) ought   i) two
   e) lost   j) refer

5 a) *sincerely*, dictionary
   b) different, interesting
   c) lovely, necessary
   d) writing, uninteresting
   e) pullover, definitely
   f) friend, responsible
   g) holiday, quantity
   h) likelihood, luggage
   i) impatient, student
   j) finally, pavement

6 a) *tomorrow*, glasses
   b) conversation, magazine
   c) atmosphere, patient
   d) sandwich, bicycle
   e) guard, running
   f) recommend, skilful
   g) tobacco, acquaintance
   h) receive, attach
   i) chimney, cupboard
   j) electricity, expensive

Unit 35

1 1) all   9) There
   2) Whoever   10) what
   3) there   11) As
   4) myself   12) After
   5) myself   13) Someone
   6) which   14) whoever
   7) Not   15) result
   8) no-one

2 a) You should not press both buttons at once under any circumstances.
   b) As it was cold, I decided to wear two pullovers.
   c) Did you enjoy yourself at the party?
   d) Outside the cinema I was grabbed by the arm.
   e) The army was defeated owing to/because of poor organisation.
   f) Not once did Jean offer her boss a word of apology.
   g) There's nothing to eat in the house, I'm afraid.
   h) There's no point (in) going on any further tonight.
   i) What Sally saw is difficult to describe.
   j) Seldom have I had a more relaxing holiday.

3 a) D   f) B
   b) B   g) C
   c) A   h) C
   d) C   i) D
   e) D   j) B

4 1) that   9) was
   2) whether   10) ✓
   3) ✓   11) in
   4) they   12) they
   5) herself   13) ✓
   6) so   14) although
   7) them   15) ✓
   8) ✓

Unit 36

1 a) have been waiting, have you been doing
   b) was walking, had left
   c) had known, would have come
   d) am phoning, are doing
   e) became, had won
   f) haven't seen, have you been doing
   g) thought, would be
   h) were, wouldn't spend
   i) arrives, will meet/are going to meet
   j) get, will let

2 a) rather you didn't
   b) unless we take
   c) advised Tom not to go
   d) despite twisting
   e) as much as Mike
   f) wish I hadn't sold
   g) hasn't been cut
   h) can't have meant to
   i) this the smallest size
   j) feel like going

3 1) the   9) visited
   2) had   10) the
   3) of   11) As
   4) ✓   12) ✓
   5) ✓   13) having
   6) have   14) a
   7) up   15) ✓
   8) ✓

4 a) play tennis better than I
   b) ought to be
   c) two years since I went
   d) such a funny film
   e) the first time I've
   f) accused Joe of stealing
   g) must be posted
   h) know whether the train was
   i) you'd better
   j) is believed to have

5 1) C   9) A
   2) A   10) D
   3) D   11) B
   4) D   12) C
   5) B   13) D
   6) C   14) A
   7) A   15) B
   8) C

6 a) time last year we hadn't
   b) hadn't been for you/your help,
   c) is known about
   d) was made to work
   e) apologised to Carol for breaking
   f) leave the door open
   g) time you had your hair
   h) these two fields belong to
   i) has business
   j) price you offer me for

Vocabulary answers

Unit 1 Travel and holidays

1
a) deck
b) platform
c) departure-lounge
d) coach-station
e) harbour
f) buffet
g) cabin
h) destination
i) quay
j) runway

2
a) delayed
b) crew
c) landed
d) flight
e) diverted
f) suitcase
g) seat belt
h) check in
i) declared
j) stewardess
k) took off
l) single

3
a) cancel
b) platform
c) took off
d) destination
e) passengers
f) buffet
g) cabin
h) single
i) declare
j) harbour
k) luggage
l) delay

4
a) cruise
b) flight
c) itinerary
d) trip
e) expedition
f) package tour
g) travel
h) voyage
i) tour
j) crossing

5
a) itinerary
b) tour
c) crossing
d) cruise
e) package tour
f) expedition
g) flight
h) voyage
i) travel
j) trip

6
a) a fortnight
b) accommodation
c) hitch-hike
d) double
e) guest-house
f) book
g) camp-site
h) vacancy
i) hostel
j) porter

7
a) seaside
b) seafood
c) seaweed
d) sea level
e) sea front
f) seagulls
g) seasick
h) seashore

8
a) C
b) D
c) A
d) D
e) B
f) C
g) B
h) A
i) D
j) B

9 (suggested)
a) I sunbathed for a while and then had a swim.
b) I had a good time on my holiday last year.
c) David had a car-crash while he was driving to Spain.
d) 'Goodbye,' said Maria, 'and have a safe journey.'
e) Most of the people on the beach had very little on.
f) We couldn't decide about our holiday, until Sue had an idea.
g) Martin had a party at his house last night.
h) Brenda couldn't go away for the weekend because she had work to do.
i) Ian didn't know how to water-ski but he had a go.
j) Laura had a suspicion that the hotel food was going to be bad.

10
1) B
2) A
3) C
4) B
5) D
6) A
7) D
8) D
9) B
10) A
11) C
12) A
13) C
14) B
15) D

Unit 2 Work and Employment

1 *cashier-bank* cook-restaurant/kitchen dentist-surgery farmer-field hairdresser-salon librarian-library mechanic-garage miner-coal-mine musician-concert hall/studio photographer-studio pilot-cockpit porter-hotel typist-office vicar-church waiter-restaurant

2
a) *vet*
b) refuse-collector
c) estate agent
d) carpenter
e) chef
f) plumber
g) accountant
h) firefighter
i) electrician
j) architect
k) postman/postwoman
l) optician

3
a) plumber
b) optician
c) porter
d) dentist
e) hairdresser
f) carpenter

g) vet
h) waiter
i) electrician
j) mechanic

4 a) living   f) business
   b) work   g) job
   c) business   h) work
   d) work   i) work
   e) living   j) work

5 a) go   f) turn
   b) come   g) face
   c) fall   h) draw
   d) fill   i) take
   e) get   j) call

6 a) 4   f) 10
   b) 9   g) 5
   c) 2   h) 3
   d) 7   i) 8
   e) 1   j) 6

7 1) advertising
   2) resignation
   3) economic
   4) unemployed
   5) applications
   6) qualified
   7) profitable
   8) employee
   9) earnings
   10) retirement

8 a) wages
   b) temporary
   c) pension
   d) earns
   e) in charge
   f) off
   g) sacked
   h) notice
   i) make
   j) expenses

9 (suggested)
   a) Terry has a different job now.
   b) A good employer looks after everyone in the company.
   c) I am sure you will gain/get a lot of experience in this job.
   d) This job is a living, but that's all.
   e) The firm raised my salary after I had worked there a year.
   f) The company made a profit last year.

g) I had to attend an interview at the head office.
h) I earn/make £12,000 a year.
i) Jack works for a firm of accountants.
j) We put an advertisement for the job in the paper.

10 1) B   9) C
   2) D   10) A
   3) A   11) C
   4) D   12) A
   5) B   13) D
   6) C   14) B
   7) D   15) C
   8) A

Unit 3 Sport and Leisure

1 a) costume
   b) saddle
   c) club
   d) net
   e) handlebars
   f) rope
   g) ice
   h) gloves
   i) whistle
   j) glasses
   k) racket
   l) rod

2 a) cards
   b) embroidery
   c) crossword
   d) model-making
   e) draughts
   f) hiking
   g) billiards
   h) gambling
   i) jigsaw
   j) do-it-yourself
   k) camping
   l) gardening

3 a) race
   b) ground
   c) fit
   d) won
   e) spectators
   f) interesting
   g) pastime
   h) prize
   i) competitors
   j) draw

4 a) professionally
   b) postponed
   c) champion
   d) score
   e) arranged
   f) spare
   g) second
   h) captain
   i) record
   j) referee
   k) outdoors
   l) side

5 1) photography
   2) skilful
   3) failure
   4) imaginative
   5) successful
   6) unexpected
   7) valuable
   8) misunderstanding
   9) unbelievable
   10) disagreement

6 a) jacket
   b) repairs
   c) making
   d) collection
   e) court
   f) hooligan
   g) field
   h) pools
   i) course
   j) track
   k) board
   l) site

7 a) B   f) C
   b) D   g) D
   c) C   h) B
   d) A   i) D
   e) A   j) B

8 a) better
   b) stuck
   c) ready
   d) lost
   e) anywhere
   f) dinner
   g) back
   h) right
   i) off
   j) through
   k) together
   l) used

9 a) After Paul's leg was injured, it took him a long time to recover.
  b) Unfortunately Sally rode her bike into the mud and became stuck.
  c) An hour before the race I went to the stadium and started to prepare.
  d) Some of the competitors lost their way because of the thick fog.
  e) I tried learning to do embroidery but I didn't succeed.
  f) Jean worked on her stamp collection while Barry was cooking.
  g) I didn't arrive home from the match till late because of the crowds.
  h) David practised hitting the ball until he perfected it.
  i) Kate enjoyed riding the horse but found it hard to dismount.
  j) I tried to phone the tennis club but there was no answer.
  k) We have a great time whenever our rugby team meets.
  l) I find playing football on plastic grass strange.

10 1) C
   2) A
   3) A
   4) D
   5) C
   6) B
   7) C
   8) D
   9) A
   10) C
   11) D
   12) B
   13) C
   14) A
   15) C

Unit 4 Clothes and Appearance

1 1) earrings
  2) blouse
  3) shoulder bag
  4) skirt
  5) sandals
  6) shoes
  7) trousers
  8) briefcase
  9) belt
  10) waistcoat
  11) shirt
  12) tie
  13) glasses
  14) jacket
  15) suit
  16) socks

2 a) uniform
  b) formal
  c) suit
  d) sleeves
  e) dressing gown
  f) overalls
  g) mac
  h) scarf
  i) shoelaces
  j) pockets
  k) fashion
  l) fur
  m) hats
  n) aprons
  o) bow

3 1) appearance
  2) parting
  3) striped
  4) unsuitable
  5) undresses
  6) cleaner's
  7) worn
  8) unbuttoned
  9) fashionable
  10) informal

4 a) This shirt is too small, it's not my size.
  b) You have so many clothes. Why did you buy these clothes as well?
  c) correct
  d) correct
  e) I like your new trousers. How much were they?
  f) Excuse me for a moment. I have to put on/change into some different clothes.
  g) As far as I can see, the man in this photograph is wearing a suit.
  h) The blouse is a good fit, but it doesn't suit you.
  i) correct
  j) You're soaked! Take off your clothes immediately!

5 a) B   f) B
  b) D   g) A
  c) A   h) B
  d) C   i) C
  e) D   j) B

6 a) sweater
  b) shawls
  c) jacket
  d) belt
  e) shorts
  f) sleeves
  g) tight
  h) silk
  i) wardrobe
  j) underwear

7 a) C   f) B
  b) A   g) C
  c) C   h) B
  d) B   i) D
  e) D   j) C

8 1) B   9) B
  2) C   10) A
  3) A   11) D
  4) C   12) C
  5) D   13) C
  6) B   14) A
  7) D   15) B
  8) A

Unit 5 Towns and Buildings

1 a) gates, path
  b) entrance, side
  c) fitted
  d) cupboards, bookshelves
  e) fireplace, washbasins
  f) stairs, stained
  g) shower, taps
  h) attic, greenhouse, shed
  i) fence, hedge
  j) detached, neighbourhood

2 a) letter box
  b) cooker/stove
  c) shelf
  d) drive
  e) door knocker
  f) dishwasher
  g) central heating
  h) rug
  i) settee/sofa
  j) aerial
  k) landing
  l) doormat
  m) curtains
  n) stool
  o) washing machine

3 a) 6   f) 5
    b) 3   g) 2
    c) 8   h) 9
    d) 1   i) 4
    e) 10   j) 7

4 a) home
    b) housework
    c) house
    d) homeless
    e) housekeeper
    f) home
    g) house
    h) home
    i) housing
    j) home

5 a) D   f) A
    b) B   g) B
    c) D   h) A
    d) C   i) A
    e) B   j) D

6 1) neighbourhood
    2) shortage
    3) upstairs
    4) sale
    5) loan
    6) rebuilt
    7) undamaged
    8) furnished
    9) length
    10) cooker

7 a) armchair
    b) lane
    c) wallpaper
    d) oven
    e) picking
    f) lawn
    g) cellar
    h) car park
    i) floor
    j) radiator
    k) motorway
    l) is
    m) frame
    n) sill
    o) at

8 a) eiderdown
    b) cushion
    c) urban
    d) shutters
    e) litter
    f) ceiling
    g) bunk
    h) rural
    i) roof
    j) pillow
    k) blind
    l) rubbish
    m) kennel
    n) kerb
    o) chimney

9 1) A   9) C
    2) C   10) B
    3) B   11) A
    4) D   12) A
    5) B   13) D
    6) C   14) B
    7) A   15) D
    8) D

Unit 6   Vehicles and Transport

1 a) pram
    b) coach
    c) tandem
    d) tractor
    e) vintage
    f) ambulance
    g) vehicles
    h) fire engine
    i) caravan
    j) deckers

2 a) chauffeur
    b) motorist
    c) driver
    d) captain
    e) guard
    f) traffic warden
    g) steward
    h) crew
    i) conductor
    j) cyclist
    k) pedestrian
    l) mechanic

3 1) roof rack
    2) aerial
    3) boot
    4) exhaust
    5) tyre
    6) mirror
    7) wing
    8) wheel
    9) bumper
    10) headlight
    11) engine
    12) bonnet
    13) steering wheel
    14) windscreen
    15) wiper

4 a) B   f) D
    b) A   g) B
    c) D   h) B
    d) B   i) A
    e) A   j) D

5 1) cancellation
    2) Unfortunately
    3) collision
    4) unexpectedly
    5) unsuitable
    6) unavoidable
    7) injuries
    8) widening
    9) adjustable
    10) payment

6 a) sailor
    b) shipped
    c) sail
    d) shipment
    e) sail
    f) sailed
    g) ship
    h) sailing
    i) shipping
    j) sails

7 a) wings
    b) gear
    c) handlebars
    d) parachute
    e) oars
    f) chain
    g) brakes
    h) bonnet
    i) deck
    j) cockpit
    k) accelerator
    l) reverse

8 a) looking
    b) take/use
    c) pick
    d) made/headed
    e) put
    f) keep/catch
    g) showing
    h) put
    i) trying
    j) dealing

9
1) B
2) D
3) A
4) C
5) C
6) D
7) A
8) C
9) B
10) D
11) B
12) A
13) B
14) D
15) A

Unit 7 Food, Restaurants and Cooking

1
a) bill
b) book
c) portion
d) help
e) menu
f) ordered
g) dish
h) raw
i) vegetarian
j) course

2
a) 6
b) 2
c) 10
d) 8
e) 1
f) 5
g) 7
h) 4
i) 3
j) 9

3
a) saucers
b) chips
c) forks
d) butter
e) bacon
f) pepper
g) bread
h) wine
i) beer
j) chocolate
k) instant coffee
l) grapes

4
1) jar
2) jug
3) frying pan
4) food mixer
5) kettle
6) tin opener
7) mug
8) saucepan
9) bowl
10) casserole

5
a) on
b) off
c) around/round
d) out
e) to
f) off
g) round
h) up
i) up
j) out

6
a) C
b) A
c) B
d) D
e) C
f) A
g) D
h) A
i) B
j) C

7
a) cooks
b) cookery
c) cooker
d) cooked
e) cooking
f) uncooked

8
a) peel, slice
b) beat, add
c) melt, heat
d) pour, cool
e) grate, sprinkle

9
a) *teaspoon*
b) tablecloth
c) bottle-opener
d) teapot
e) toaster
f) a coffee cup
g) a mushroom omelette
h) a food mixer
i) a paper napkin
j) a tablespoonful
k) a dishwasher

10
1) B
2) A
3) D
4) B
5) C
6) C
7) A
8) B
9) D
10) A
11) D
12) C
13) D
14) C
15) B

Unit 8 Shops and Shopping

1
a) bargains
b) shoppers
c) change
d) pricey
e) receipt
f) on sale
g) purchase
h) discount
i) pay
j) prices

2 (suggested)
a) I can't make out (what) the price (is). Let's ask inside.
b) Can I try it on?
c) Two masked men held up the supermarket yesterday.
d) You have grown out of your old one.
e) I feel worn out.
f) I'll come and pick up the goods on Thursday.
g) Sorry, we have run out of bread.
h) Are you calling (in) at the chemist's?
i) I can't put up with the queues.
j) I'll think it over. (suggested answers)

3
a) queue
b) deliver
c) change
d) serve
e) wrap
f) fit
g) help
h) order
i) pay
j) try
k) find
l) go

4
a) 5
b) 8
c) 2
d) 10
e) 1
f) 6
g) 4
h) 9
i) 3
j) 7

5
a) C
b) A
c) C
d) B
e) D
f) C
g) D
h) B
i) D
j) B

6
a) toothpaste
b) flowers
c) jam
d) baked beans
e) paper tissues
f) chocolates

g) breakfast cereal
h) soap
i) orange juice
j) margarine

7 a) trolley
b) receipt
c) advertisement
d) wallet
e) manager
f) list
g) deposit
h) bargain
i) purse
j) catalogue

8 1) variety
2) shortages
3) likelihood
4) frozen
5) successful
6) expensive
7) reduction
8) complaints
9) impolite
10) willingness

9 1) D   9) B
2) B   10) D
3) A   11) A
4) A   12) C
5) C   13) A
6) D   14) D
7) B   15) C
8) C

Unit 9 Crime and the Law

1 a) broken
b) banned
c) licence
d) order
e) let
f) illegally
g) rules
h) commit
i) court
j) prohibited

2 a) hijacker
b) witness
c) smuggler
d) shoplifter
e) murderer
f) kidnapper

g) forger
h) vandal
i) pickpocket
j) burglar
k) blackmailer
l) hooligan

3 a) 5   f) 9
b) 3   g) 7
c) 6   h) 10
d) 2   i) 4
e) 1   j) 8

4 a) charged
b) evidence
c) fine
d) guilty
e) jury
f) lawyer
g) statement
h) suspect
i) accused
j) sentence

5 a) D   f) C
b) A   g) D
c) C   h) B
d) B   i) A
e) A   j) A

6 a) They accused John of stealing the money.
b) Ian denied punching/having punched anybody.
c) The detective gave Andy permission to go.
d) The judge sentenced James Frogget to ten years in prison.
e) Mary admitted forging/having forged the signature.
f) Harry was arrested for stealing £30,000.
g) The witness stated that they had seen the accused break into the car.
h) Graham refused to go to the police station.
i) Norman confessed to murdering Alan/having murdered Alan/Alan's murder.
j) The detective asked Helen to go with him/her.

7 1) innocence
2) theft
3) offences

4) stolen
5) defence
6) accidentally
7) worthless
8) criminal
9) punishment
10) imprisonment

8 a) against   g) from
b) of   h) in
c) for   i) off
d) under   j) by
e) in   k) on
f) in   l) in

9 1) B   9) A
2) A   10) D
3) D   11) B
4) A   12) C
5) B   13) A
6) C   14) D
7) C   15) B
8) D

Unit 10 Entertainment and the Arts

1 a) chapters
b) sketch
c) intervals
d) screen
e) orchestra
f) seller
g) frame
h) published
i) costumes
j) scene

2 a) conductor
b) author
c) director
d) announcer
e) playwright
f) sculptor
g) composer
h) critic
i) novelist
j) editor

3 a) at   g) out of
b) out of   h) on
c) in   i) at
d) in   j) in
e) on   k) out of
f) in   l) on

4
a) live
b) humorous
c) gripping
d) modern
e) current
f) popular
g) special
h) public
i) dull
j) still
k) readable
l) electric

5
a) A f) D
b) C g) A
c) D h) D
d) B i) B
e) A j) B

6
1) production
2) advertising
3) imaginative
4) artistic
5) scenery
6) amusing
7) accompanied
8) entertaining
9) applause
10) performance

7
a) piece
b) operas
c) biography
d) rehearsal
e) back
f) circle
g) ground
h) scripts
i) book
j) fair

8
a) My radio doesn't pick up the BBC World Service very easily.
b) Our school is going to put on *The Tempest* next month.
c) The management called off the performance an hour before the opening.
d) I looked up the reference in the index.
e) I can't hear the radio. Can you turn it up?
f) Colin's new book comes out/is coming out next week.

g) The conductor went over the music carefully before the concert.
h) The publishing company was taken over by a Japanese firm.
i) I like detective stories where I can't work out who did the murder.
j) Jim has taken up painting as a hobby.

9
1) C   9) C
2) B   10) D
3) A   11) B
4) A   12) C
5) C   13) C
6) B   14) A
7) D   15) C
8) A

Unit 11 The Natural World

1
a) banks
b) puddles
c) cave
d) stream
e) waves
f) top
g) desert
h) fountain
i) cloudy
j) lightning

2
a) roots
b) forest
c) stone
d) leaves
e) lawn
f) plant
g) trunk
h) seeds
i) twig
j) peel

3
a) 5   f) 6
b) 8   g) 9
c) 3   h) 2
d) 10   i) 7
e) 1   j) 4

4
a) rabbit
b) moth
c) bee
d) giraffe
e) shark
f) worm

g) leopard
h) whale
i) camel
j) pig
k) dolphin
l) fly

5
a) B   f) A
b) D   g) B
c) A   h) D
d) C   i) A
e) D   j) D

6
1) childhood
2) unsuitable
3) destruction
4) protection
5) loneliness
6) hunters
7) wooden
8) disobedient
9) discovery
10) savings

7
a) trap
b) mower
c) fountain
d) forecast
e) side
f) top
g) house
h) hive
i) hole
j) skin

8
a) off
b) out
c) off
d) around/round
e) off
f) to
g) out
h) up
i) up
j) to

9
1) C   9) B
2) A   10) B
3) D   11) A
4) C   12) D
5) B   13) C
6) D   14) A
7) A   15) D
8) C

Unit 12 People and Behaviour

1. a) rude
   b) mean
   c) strict
   d) lazy
   e) shy
   f) jealous
   g) aggressive
   h) thoughtful
   i) patient
   j) generous

2. a) punctual
   b) cheerful
   c) reliable
   d) frank
   e) selfish
   f) determined
   g) mean
   h) bad-tempered
   i) considerate
   j) honest
   k) sympathetic
   l) lazy

3. a) sociable
   b) ambitious
   c) polite
   d) imaginative
   e) kind
   f) stubborn
   g) brave
   h) snobbish
   i) greedy
   j) grateful
   k) proud
   l) tolerant

4. 1) annoying
   2) disobedient
   3) talkative
   4) impolite
   5) unfriendly
   6) dishonest
   7) pride
   8) conscientious
   9) violence
   10) bravery

5. a) B   f) A
   b) A   g) B
   c) D   h) D
   d) C   i) A
   e) B   j) D

6. a) nephew
   b) bride
   c) toddler
   d) fiancé
   e) twin
   f) neighbour
   g) niece
   h) adult
   i) widow
   j) best man
   k) sister-in-law
   l) colleague

7. a) in   g) up
   b) out   h) of
   c) if   i) with
   d) up   j) with
   e) to   k) out
   f) like/as l) in

8. a) turn up
   b) look up to
   c) put up with
   d) get on well with
   e) call in
   f) count on
   g) give away
   h) fall out
   i) turn down
   j) take after

9. 1) A   9) A
   2) C   10) D
   3) A   11) B
   4) D   12) C
   5) B   13) B
   6) D   14) D
   7) C   15) A
   8) B

Unit 13 Technology and Machines

1. a) engine
   b) electric
   c) switch
   d) typewriter
   e) order
   f) go
   g) work
   h) cut
   i) factory
   j) invented

2. 1) spanner
   2) razor
   3) needle
   4) file
   5) pin
   6) axe
   7) screwdriver
   8) spade
   9) scissors
   10) hammer
   11) corkscrew
   12) saw

3. a) saw
   b) corkscrew
   c) needle
   d) screwdriver
   e) file
   f) razor
   g) axe
   h) pin
   i) spade
   j) hammer
   k) scissors
   l) spanner

4. a) 5   f) 7
   b) 9   g) 10
   c) 3   h) 2
   d) 8   i) 6
   e) 4   j) 1

5. a) D   f) C
   b) B   g) D
   c) B   h) D
   d) A   i) A
   e) C   j) B

6. 1) scientist
   2) engineering
   3) product
   4) equipment
   5) electricity
   6) powerful
   7) useless
   8) specialised
   9) embarrassment
   10) difficulty/difficulties

7. a) off
   b) in
   c) up
   d) by
   e) out
   f) together
   g) of

h) of
i) for
j) together

8 a) keep up with
b) run out
c) pick up
d) break down
e) put off
f) hang up
g) look out!
h) do without
i) stand for
j) go off

9 1) C
2) D
3) A
4) C
5) B
6) A
7) D
8) B
9) C
10) D
11) A
12) B
13) A
14) D
15) C

Unit 14 Problems

1 a) collapsed
b) difficulties
c) poor
d) made
e) environment
f) increase
g) unemployed
h) collision
i) high
j) demonstration

2 a) famine
b) slums
c) living
d) earthquake
e) hooliganism
f) invasion
g) disaster
h) floods
i) injuries
j) rubbish
k) disease
l) emergency

3 a) B
b) D
c) C
d) D
e) B
f) A
g) D
h) A
i) A
j) C

4 a) banned
b) solved
c) protected
d) improved
e) polluted
f) ignored
g) unemployed
h) flooded
i) overpopulated
j) increased

5 a) C
b) A
c) C
d) B
e) D
f) A
g) A
h) C
i) B
j) C

6 1) collision
2) unexpectedly
3) overboard
4) exhausted
5) freezing
6) solution
7) improvement
8) unhealthy
9) loneliness
10) destruction

7 a) charity
b) drought
c) conservation
d) demonstration
e) pile-up
f) famine
g) emergency
h) strike
i) aid
j) riot

8 a) at
b) on
c) under
d) by
e) of/from
f) with
g) at
h) in
i) on
j) in

9 1) B
2) D
3) A
4) D
5) C
6) A
7) D
8) D
9) B
10) C
11) A
12) C
13) B
14) D
15) A

Unit 15 Health and the Body

1 a) surgery
b) fell
c) heal
d) ankle
e) slim
f) aches
g) sick
h) examines
i) temperature
j) caught

2 a) spine
b) agony
c) body
d) brains
e) heart
f) tongue
g) breath
h) stomachache
i) look
j) beard

3 a) throat
b) knees
c) cheek
d) nose
e) lips
f) wrist
g) chin
h) thumb
i) waist
j) neck

4 a) 3
b) 8
c) 1
d) 6
e) 10
f) 2
g) 5
h) 9
i) 7
j) 4

5 a) B
b) D
c) B
d) A
e) D
f) B
g) C
h) B
i) A
j) D

6 1) muscular
2) weight
3) painful
4) poisonous
5) infectious
6) expression
7) heartened
8) incurable
9) treatment
10) recovery

7	a) 4	f) 2
	b) 6	g) 7
	c) 1	h) 8
	d) 5	i) 3
	e) 10	j) 9

8	a) from	f) came
	b) in	g) on
	c) on	h) down
	d) off	i) for
	e) on	j) of

9	1) A	9) A
	2) C	10) C
	3) B	11) B
	4) D	12) D
	5) D	13) B
	6) C	14) D
	7) A	15) C
	8) B	

Unit 16 Money

1
a) lend
b) fees
c) afford
d) bill
e) let
f) earn
g) charge
h) reduced
i) fortune
j) reckon

2
a) generous
b) well off
c) profit
d) take out
e) expensive
f) poverty
g) cash
h) save
i) purchase
j) worthless

3
a) pension
b) wealth
c) credit card
d) loan
e) receipt
f) tip
g) rent
h) guarantee
i) safe
j) coin

4	a) 6	f) 7
	b) 3	g) 5
	c) 10	h) 9
	d) 1	i) 8
	e) 4	j) 2

5	a) C	f) B
	b) A	g) D
	c) B	h) B
	d) A	i) A
	e) D	j) D

6
1) wealthy
2) luxurious
3) generosity
4) savings
5) insurance
6) profitable
7) cashier
8) loan
9) worthless
10) signature

7
a) payments
b) pay you/it back
c) pay for
d) paid out
e) pay up
f) pay day
g) unpaid
h) payable
i) pay it into
j) well paid

8
a) miser
b) heir
c) manager
d) pensioner
e) accountant
f) customer
g) cashier
h) agent
i) investor
j) swindler

9	1) B	9) D
	2) A	10) B
	3) D	11) C
	4) B	12) A
	5) C	13) D
	6) A	14) B
	7) D	15) C
	8) C	

Unit 17 Feelings and Opinions

1
a) angry
b) interested
c) afraid
d) sincere
e) annoying
f) attractive
g) scared
h) cross
i) furious
j) careless

2
a) naughty
b) scared
c) upset
d) dull
e) fascinating
f) glad
g) depressed
h) irritating
i) delightful
j) confused

3
a) blush
b) yawn
c) whisper
d) nod your head
e) grin
f) shrug your shoulders
g) cry
h) shake your head
i) scream
j) wave

4	a) 7	f) 8
	b) 4	g) 5
	c) 2	h) 9
	d) 10	i) 6
	e) 1	j) 3

5
a) embarrassed
b) co-operative
c) realistic
d) imaginative
e) obedient
f) determined
g) tolerant
h) dependable
i) quarrelsome
j) helpful

6
a) C   f) C
b) A   g) A
c) D   h) A
d) A   i) B
e) B   j) D

7
1) impression
2) offensive
3) irritating
4) admiration
5) cowardice
6) adorable
7) attraction
8) gratitude
9) faithful
10) relief

8
a) her   f) at
b) of   g) with
c) up   h) in
d) of   i) up
e) into   j) on

9
1) D   9) B
2) A   10) D
3) C   11) A
4) B   12) B
5) D   13) C
6) A   14) A
7) C   15) D
8) D

Unit 18 Education and Learning

1
a) course
b) marks
c) trained
d) enter
e) taught
f) study
g) heart
h) term
i) failed
j) raise

2
a) punish
b) cheat
c) memorise
d) pay
e) pass
f) copy
g) concentrate
h) revise
i) underline
j) divide

3
a) lecturer
b) graduate
c) principal
d) pupil
e) professor
f) tutor
g) classmate
h) coach
i) examiner
j) learner

4
a) 4   f) 8
b) 9   g) 10
c) 1   h) 7
d) 6   i) 5
e) 2   j) 3

5
a) A   f) C
b) C   g) A
c) D   h) B
d) B   i) C
e) D   j) B

6
1) introduction
2) successful
3) attention
4) unreadable
5) failure
6) revision
7) mistaken
8) absences
9) punishments
10) gifted

7
a) done
b) taking
c) done
d) made
e) made
f) take
g) made
h) take
i) took/made
j) does

8
a) knowledge
b) discipline
c) education
d) dictionary
e) calculator
f) university
g) intelligence
h) comprehension
i) secondary
j) experiments

9
a) up   f) by
b) to   g) about/on
c) in   h) in
d) for   i) by
e) at   j) up

10
1) C   9) B
2) B   10) D
3) A   11) D
4) D   12) A
5) D   13) B
6) B   14) C
7) A   15) B
8) C

19 Word Formation 1

1
a) disobedient
b) unlikely
c) misunderstood
d) outstanding
e) cooperate
f) submarine
g) pre-cooked
h) multi-millionaire
i) endangered
j) impossible

2
a) dissatisfied
b) unusual
c) undecided
d) trans-Atlantic
e) vice-president
f) non-smoker
g) informal
h) unfair
i) rewritten
j) overcooked

3
a) freedom
b) thoughtful
c) musician
d) shortage
e) leading
f) astonishment
g) foolish
h) backwards
i) trumpeter
j) greatness

4 a) overnight
   b) careless
   c) mispronounce
   d) friendship
   e) postponement
   f) dissatisfied
   g) outskirts
   h) overcharged
   i) employee
   j) homeless

5 1) secretarial
   2) occupation
   3) frozen
   4) carpentry
   5) explanation
   6) solution
   7) failure
   8) successful
   9) construction
   10) embarrassment

6 a) gunfire
   b) thunderstorm
   c) handwriting
   d) haircut
   e) soap powder
   f) crash helmet
   g) bookcase
   h) rainbow
   i) footsteps
   j) fireplace

7 a) thin
   b) cool
   c) nodded
   d) worthless
   e) high
   f) lovely
   g) tasty
   h) dangerous
   i) bored
   j) angry

8 a) making
   b) feel
   c) take
   d) set
   e) gave
   f) do
   g) getting
   h) put
   i) fallen
   j) draw

9 (suggested)
   a) The forest outside the town
      caught fire last night.
   b) Suddenly Janet burst into tears.
   c) What do you do (for a living)?

   d) We'll have to make/take a
      decision soon.
   e) Can you take care of my plants
      while I'm away?
   f) You will keep in touch, won't
      you?
   g) Diane gave birth to a baby boy
      last week.
   h) Peter always keeps his head in
      an emergency.
   i) Let go of the steering wheel!
   j) He stands no chance of winning
      the race.

10 a) low
   b) down
   c) round
   d) thin
   e) dry
   f) early
   g) death
   h) forwards
   i) span
   j) night

20 Word Formation 2

1 a) overwork
   b) invisible
   c) subway
   d) autobiography
   e) ex-wife
   f) misleading
   g) semi-final
   h) unable
   i) non-stop
   j) disappeared

2 a) neighbourhood
   b) employer
   c) widen
   d) handful
   e) hopeless
   f) greenish
   g) partnership
   h) drinkable
   i) equality
   j) harmful

3 a) inedible
   b) youngster
   c) semi-circle
   d) friendly
   e) foreground
   f) mountaineer

   g) tricycle
   h) hopeful
   i) international
   j) artist

4 1) politician
   2) shyness
   3) sympathised
   4) disorganised
   5) replacement
   6) straighten
   7) personal
   8) innocence
   9) imagination
   10) uninterested

5 a) bus-station
   b) part-time
   c) well-dressed
   d) old-fashioned
   e) car park
   f) well-known
   g) haircut
   h) first-class
   i) home-made
   j) half-cooked

6 a) kind-hearted
   b) empty-handed
   c) fully-clothed
   d) long-legged
   e) absent-minded
   f) good-looking
   g) loud-mouthed
   h) short-tempered
   i) dog-eared
   j) red-headed

7 a) defeat
   b) safe
   c) decline/refuse
   d) pass
   e) landing
   f) stale
   g) buried
   h) similar
   i) ending
   j) melts

8 a) make
   b) lose
   c) bear
   d) drop
   e) waste
   f) catch
   g) think
   h) gain
   i) take
   j) break

9 (suggested)
   a) Nothing you do will make any difference.
   b) I hope it's not too much trouble/I hope I'm not putting you to any trouble.
   c) Let's take measurements of the room.
   d) Mark's face fell when I told him my name.
   e) The old car suddenly burst into flames.
   f) Susan had lost her way.
   g) I can't stand/bear the sight of that boy!
   h) Helen was put in charge of/took charge of the business.
   i) How did you pass the time while you were waiting for the train?
   j) I have changed my mind about this matter.

10 a) in
   b) by
   c) on
   d) in
   e) under
   f) from
   g) by
   h) on
   i) for
   j) by